KITES
to make and fly

KITES
to make and fly

Jim Rowlands

B. T. Batsford Ltd, London

First published in 1989

ISBN 0 8521 9801 9

Set in Plantin light
Typeset by Servis Filmsetting Ltd., Manchester
and printed in Great Britain by
Redwood Burn Limited, Trowbridge, Wiltshire
for the Publishers
Dryad Press Ltd.
4 Fitzhardinge Street
London W1H 0AH

A CIP record for this book is available from the
British Library.

contents

preface

Without doubt, kiteflying has become one of the fastest growing leisure activities not only in Britain but also throughout Europe and North America, as more and more people discover this simple, yet fascinating, delight. Kites are no longer just novelties seen occasionally at the beach or park, but are being enjoyed by everyone, young and old alike, flying high amongst the clouds, creating rich and captivating patterns as their colours contrast against and combine with the backcloth of sky.

Along with this renewed enthusiasm for flying kites has grown an interest in the kitemaking craft, and an eagerness to learn the techniques of design and construction. My own interest in kitemaking in fact grew from using kites in a general craft workshop with children. But unlike many enthusiasts, who have moved on to the larger, more sophisticated designs, my joy remains with the simple paper and string workshop kite.

In *Kites to Make and Fly* I have tried to produce a range of kites for you to enjoy, with designs suitable for both novice kitemakers and teachers, as well as youth leaders and community arts workers.

All the kites featured can be made from easily available materials, dowel, paper, polythene and plastic tube – most of which can be bought from stationery and hardware stores. They have all been made and tested, some of them perhaps hundreds of times over, in the kitemaking workshops I have presented over the past six years.

My thanks to those friends and colleagues who have offered their assistance and support over the past years, particularly Fred Waterhouse, Derek Kuhn, Bill Souten and Don Eccleston. Thanks too to John Crooks for producing such quality drawings from my appalling sketches; to Tony Cartwright and Martin Lester for allowing me to reproduce their designs; and finally to those many workshop participants who through these past years have allowed me to share their successes and been prepared to tolerate my failures.

Jim Rowlands

February 1989

CHAPTER ONE

introduction: kitemaking materials and techniques

Kiteflying is one of those pastimes which you either love or have yet to appreciate: you cannot actually dislike it. Out on the hills on a spring afternoon, there's nothing quite like a kite and a good breeze to blow away the cobwebs spun during the sedentary winter months. While at the beach on a lazy summer's day, a kite can add to the fun and fond memories of an enjoyable family outing.

What brings that very special magic to the joy of kiteflying is to make a kite for yourself and to see it riding high on the winds. But because of limited success or lack of understanding many people seem to think that making a kite is somehow very difficult or expensive, or demands special tools or materials. This is of course not the case. Kites can be as simple or as complicated as you wish to make them; as cheap or as expensive; as large or indeed as small.

Let's look at what you need to make a start.

TOOLS

Most of the kites featured in later chapters can be made using a relatively small tool-kit: a soft pencil (B or 2B); ballpoint or felt-tipped pen; a craft knife; scissors; a wooden rule; compasses; set squares; a junior hacksaw and, if you can obtain one cheaply, a hole punch.

MATERIALS

Sails

The sail, also sometimes called the canopy or cover, can be made from almost any material which will hold the wind, from scrap paper to specialist plastic films and fabrics. You should have little difficulty finding something suitable. Ideally, the sail material should be light, no more than perhaps 120 g per square metre (0.35 oz per square yard); it should have a low porosity – will it hold the wind or let it all blow through?; it should have a high tensile strength – is it going to stretch out of shape in the wind?; it should have a high shear strength – will it tear?; and it should also retain its strength when wet. Kitemakers are, however, constantly seeking new and better materials and even those used on commercially-made kites are a compromise between 'ideal' and 'acceptable' qualities.

Kraft or Manilla papers (brown wrapping papers), available from most stationers, are reasonably good materials from which to make your first kites. Both are quite strong, cheap, and available in large sheets, but of course neither is waterproof, and whatever type of decoration you use your kites can never really be made to look attractive.

To add a quick dash of colour to the sail you might like to try using some of the patterned wrapping papers now available. They are not quite as strong as brown paper, and will tear, but they do have a waterproof coating and their bright colours overcome some of the early frustrations of having to create your own decoration.

You can also make some attractive kites from tissue paper, available from stationers in a wide range of colours. It is quite cheap to buy, although not too strong, nor is it waterproof. Kitchen wrapping papers, greaseproof or silicon-coated papers are also widely available and, besides being quite strong and waterproof, will accept a range of colours and adhesives.

If you are really stuck to find a cheap sail material, don't, of course, forget newspaper. Okay, it's messy, it tears easily and newspaper kites look pretty tacky, but at least give it a thought. Also, if you want to experiment with a new design, or are uncertain how various elements fit together, newspaper is cheap enough to throw away if things don't quite work out in the way anticipated.

Polythene is another reliable and very popular material used in kitemaking. Two forms of polythene are available, described as low density and high density. The difference is mainly in the chemical structure but, in simple terms, low density tends to stretch, whereas high density will tear more easily. Also, its surface does not feel as waxy. Most of the polythene you come across, as garden waste bags, bin-liner bags and supermarket shopping bags, for example, is low density. Plastics wholesalers occasionally hold stocks of large bags, or layflat tube, in both high and low density, which may be worthwhile buying if you are making a large number of kites. In terms of thickness, 300 gauge (75 micron) low density is about right for kitemaking: more than 500 gauge is too heavy, while less than 100 gauge is perhaps not strong enough. If you can buy it, 100–150 gauge (25–40 micron) high density polythene is particularly good!

One of the most specialist materials you may like to try is *Tyvek*, available from some paper merchants and specialist kite shops. It is sold in two forms and in a variety of weights. Type 14 is soft, perforated and both feels and handles like a fabric. In contrast, Type 10 is non-porous, stiffer, and more like a lightweight card. Both are very strong, and have the great advantage that they will accept most adhesives and colours.

Polyester films, used extensively for commercial kitemaking, are also very popular for homemade kites. They are light and very strong, but unfortunately tend to tear if punctured. Of the two main trademarked products available today, *Melinex*, in silver, clear or white, is probably easier to obtain from plastics suppliers, whereas *Mylar* is usually only available from specialist kite stores. You can also buy small sheets of *Mylar* sold in stationers as beautifully-coloured parcel wrapping film, which, used effectively, can enhance the decoration of your kite without any real additional effort.

Finally, schools in particular may be able to obtain some of the newer synthetic papers from educational suppliers. These have similar qualities to polyester films but have the advantage that they will accept a range of non water-based adhesives and colours, and are just as strong. *Synteape*, from Wiggins Teape Ltd, is most widely available in Britain and sold in standard paper sized (A2, A3, etc) sheets or by the roll. Other imported (Japanese) synthetic papers are also sometimes available from specialist paper merchants.

Although many of the kites featured can also be made from fabrics such as rip-stop nylon, cotton or polyester, the construction techniques involved are of course very different and will not be dealt with in detail here. Those wishing to learn about fabric techniques are instead referred to the many books listed in the section on *Further reading*.

Spars

To make the frame of the kite you do of course need to buy a range of spars or 'sticks'. Generally, the spars need to be light in weight, of fairly even section, strong and rigid enough to withstand the pressure of the wind, yet flexible enough to survive the occasional crash.

As bamboo is widely used in oriental kite construction, the temptation here might be to rush out to buy bamboo canes from the local garden centre, but don't be quite so eager. Garden canes are certainly cheap, but are not really suitable for general kitemaking, at least not if they are in the form found in garden centres. Split canes are marginally better, but usually only available in short lengths and invariably coated with messy green preservative.

Many of the softwoods – pine, birch and spruce – can be used quite successfully in kitemaking, but it is likely that you will only find birch ready cut in small enough sections.

Instead, most commercial, and indeed homemade, kites have spars made from Ramin, a lightweight hardwood. Also, any good lumber yard or hardware store should be able to offer dowels in 5 mm ($\frac{3}{16}$ inch), 6.4 mm ($\frac{1}{4}$ inch) and 8 mm ($\frac{5}{16}$ inch) diameters and in various standard lengths. If you are given a choice, try to select the pieces with a good straight grain, free from weaknesses shown by knots or surface deformities.

For very small kites, less than say 30 cm (12 inch) span, however, it is more usual to use very light bamboos – kebab skewers, for example, or plastic drinking straws, both of which may be obtained from the catering sections of department stores, or from catering suppliers.

Although most kites do have a rigid framework, this is certainly not true of them all and there is a small range of designs in which the spars are required to flex in the wind, where dowel would of course be totally unsuitable. Traditionally, such spars would be made by trimming and tapering split bamboo cane but nowadays, with a wider variety of materials available, it is much easier to use a narrow fibreglass with diameters of 1.5–3 mm ($\frac{1}{16}$–$\frac{1}{8}$ inches). Fibreglass, however, is not so easily available and unless you are able to buy a large quantity direct from the manufacturer the only reliable source is likely to be a specialist kite shop.

Adhesives

Although we refer to the 'sail' as though it was a single piece of material, the sails on most kites are in fact made from several pieces joined to make up the final shape. And as our materials have different qualities and surface finishes, it is inevitable that each will demand a different adhesive.

Papers and *Tyvek* can be fixed using water-soluble glues – a glue stick, cellulose wallpaper adhesive, or a general purpose adhesive such as *Gloy, Uhu, Bostik* or *Copydex*, widely available from stationers and hardware stores. In addition to the number of trade named products, it is also possible to buy PVA (Polyvinyl-acetate) adhesive in bulk, in anything from 100 cc to 5 litre (8 oz to 5 quart) pots, from craft and some hardware shops. PVA is a very popular adhesive with kitemakers working in paper and *Tyvek*, and if you are making a lot of kites, either for yourself or in a group project, it will certainly work out as the best value.

Polyester films and the polythenes, on the other hand, do not accept adhesives quite as easily, and the only way to construct the kite is to use an adhesive tape, such as celluloid tape (Sellotape), polyester or PVC (electrical) tape, all of which can be purchased from stationers or hardware stores.

As well as light tapes used for construction, you will need a range of tapes specifically for reinforcing. PVC (electrical) tape, carpet (fabric) tape or fibreglass strapping tape are ideal, even if a little expensive. Good strong tapes can also be made from wide double-sided (carpet) tape on some fabric scraps or scrap pieces of sail material.

PVC tube

As with the sails, the frame of the kite is rarely a single stick, and we must use other materials to create joints and connections.

The more traditional method of joining spars is to lash them together with twine and glue, but for novice kitemakers this technique is not easy and, with modern materials, somewhat unnecessary. On smaller kites the connections are instead made from PVC tube in 8 mm ($\frac{5}{16}$ inch), 6.4 mm ($\frac{1}{4}$ inch) and 5 mm ($\frac{3}{16}$ inch) internal diameters. Plastics merchants, model shops and of course kite stores are usually able to supply a range of tubes, by the metre or standard reel, and you should have little difficulty obtaining something suitable.

Bits and pieces

It is inevitable that a craft like kitemaking also demands a selection of odd bits and pieces.

Punched aluminium rings, 10–15 mm ($\frac{3}{8}$–$\frac{5}{8}$ inch) diameters, have many uses in kitemaking, principally in relation to the bridle, by providing a good strong connection for the flying line. Kite or camping shops are usually able to supply a good selection of such rings at very little cost.

Although the line can be tied directly to the kite or towing ring, many kite fliers prefer to include a snap connection and swivel. Fishing tackle shops can often provide a wide selection of such connections in various sizes and designs. 'American' snap swivels, either painted or nickel plated steel, are perhaps the easiest to use and sizes 0–6 are about the right strength for the kites featured in later chapters.

Kite line

Kite line is of course the final and most important requirement in the construction of any kite, and most shops stocking kites will be able to offer a small range of reasonably priced lines wound on either cardboard or plastic handles.

Polyester button thread makes a good kite line, especially for the lighter kites, and is available from haberdashery (notions) stores in bobbins of anything from 50 metres upwards. Specialist kite shops may also be able to supply large bobbins of polyester or nylon industrial sewing thread, which can work out to be quite economical for a group project.

Medium and large sized kites do, however, call for something much stronger, such as nylon or polyester braids which may be purchased by the metre or standard cop from some hardware stores, or if you live near a port, a ship's chandlers or yacht suppliers. Kite stores also generally have a good range available.

CONSTRUCTION TECHNIQUES

Cutting out the sail

To begin, prepare a clear section on your desk or workbench and cover it with some chipboard, hardboard or thick card to make a strong, flat working surface.

In a group project, to mark out the design, it may be easier to prepare a cardboard template for each sail piece and just draw or cut around it as required. When making a large number of kites templates do save a considerable amount of time, and also mean that all the sails are cut with some degree of accuracy. But for single kites, there is no real advantage and you should instead draw directly on the material.

Most sail sections have at least one axis of symmetry and the easiest method of ensuring that both sides are evenly matched is to fold the sail material along the line of symmetry and mark out the shape as a half (Fig 1.1). Mark out the pattern as carefully and as accurately as you can, take your time and, above all, check your measurements before cutting.

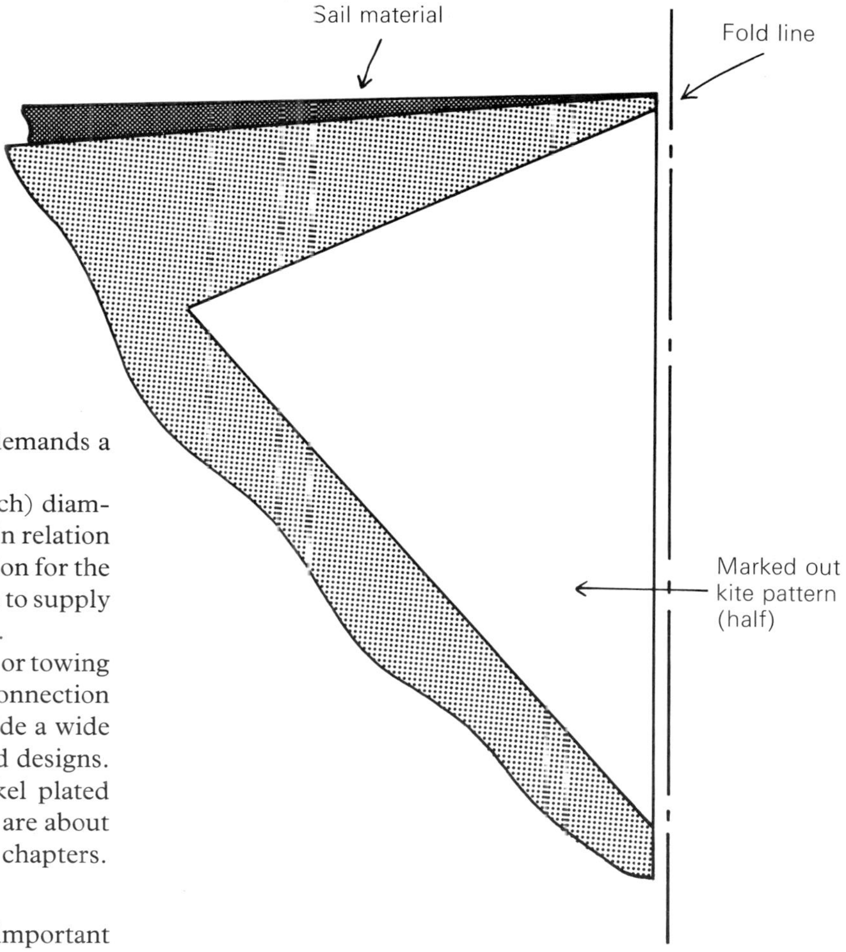

Fig 1.1 Axis of symetry – cutting half shape

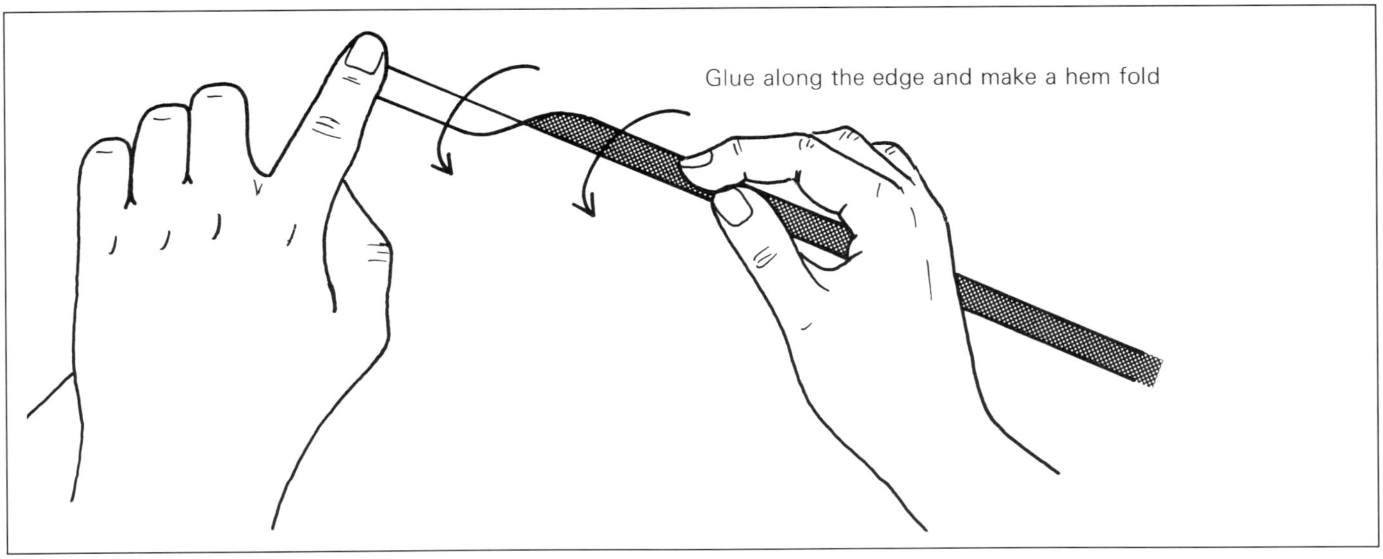

Fig 1.2 Hem fold

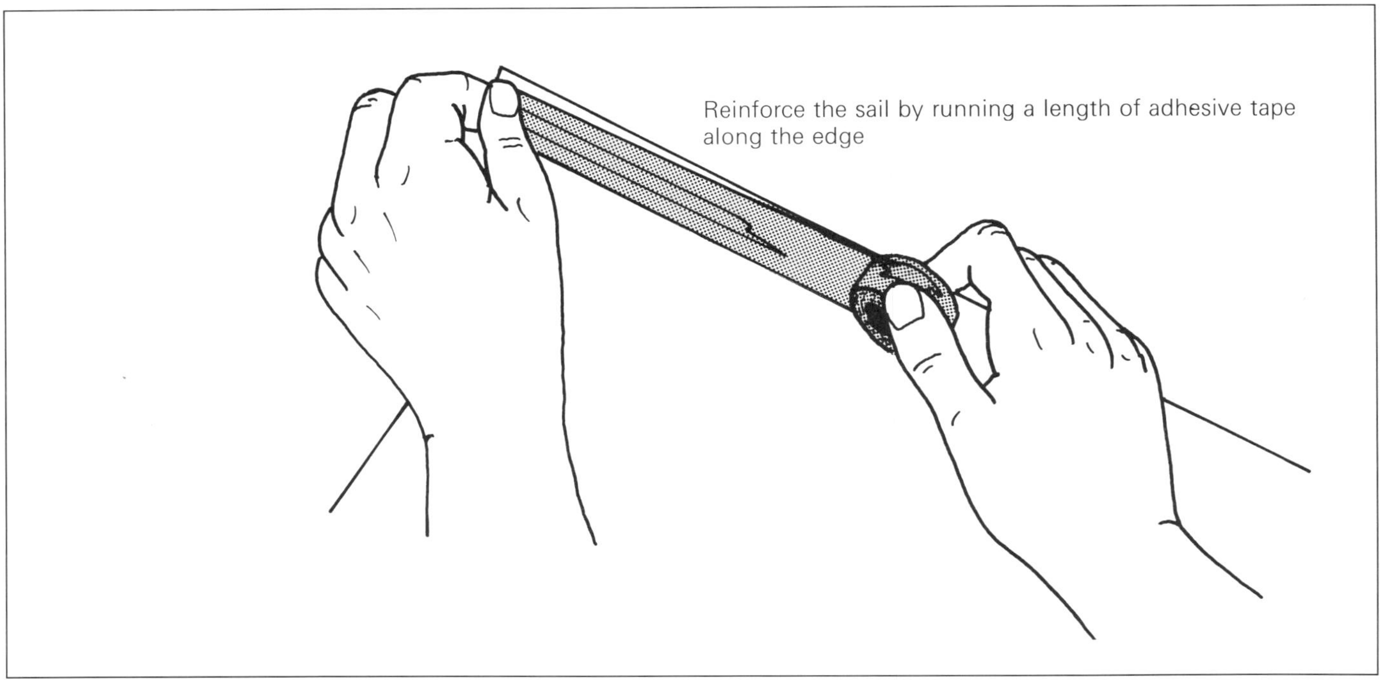

Fig 1.3 Reinforcing edges

Once the sail has been marked out, it can be cut with a sharp knife using a wood or metal rule as a guide, or with scissors if you prefer.

Reinforcing

Even if you only fly your kites in light winds, the sails are still going to be subjected to some pretty strong forces, so to reduce stretching, fraying and tearing, it is always good practice to reinforce them with either a single, glued 'hem' fold (Fig 1.2) or by running a length of tape along the edges (Fig 1.3).

Papers and *Tyvek* are possibly better hemmed, while plastics need to be reinforced.

Joining

With materials such as *Tyvek*, papers and plastics there are really only two methods of joining sail sections: using either glues or adhesive tapes. To glue two flat sections, overlap by perhaps 6 mm ($\frac{1}{4}$ inch) (Fig 1.4a) with a layer of glue on one or both surfaces, according to the instructions. Where two or more pieces are to be joined at an angle, include an extra 'glue' flap (Fig 1.4b).

Those materials which do not accept adhesives, such as polythene and polyester, may be joined using strong adhesive tape in a simple butt joint (Fig 1.4c, d). If you feel the joint warrants extra reinforcement for strength, tape on both sides.

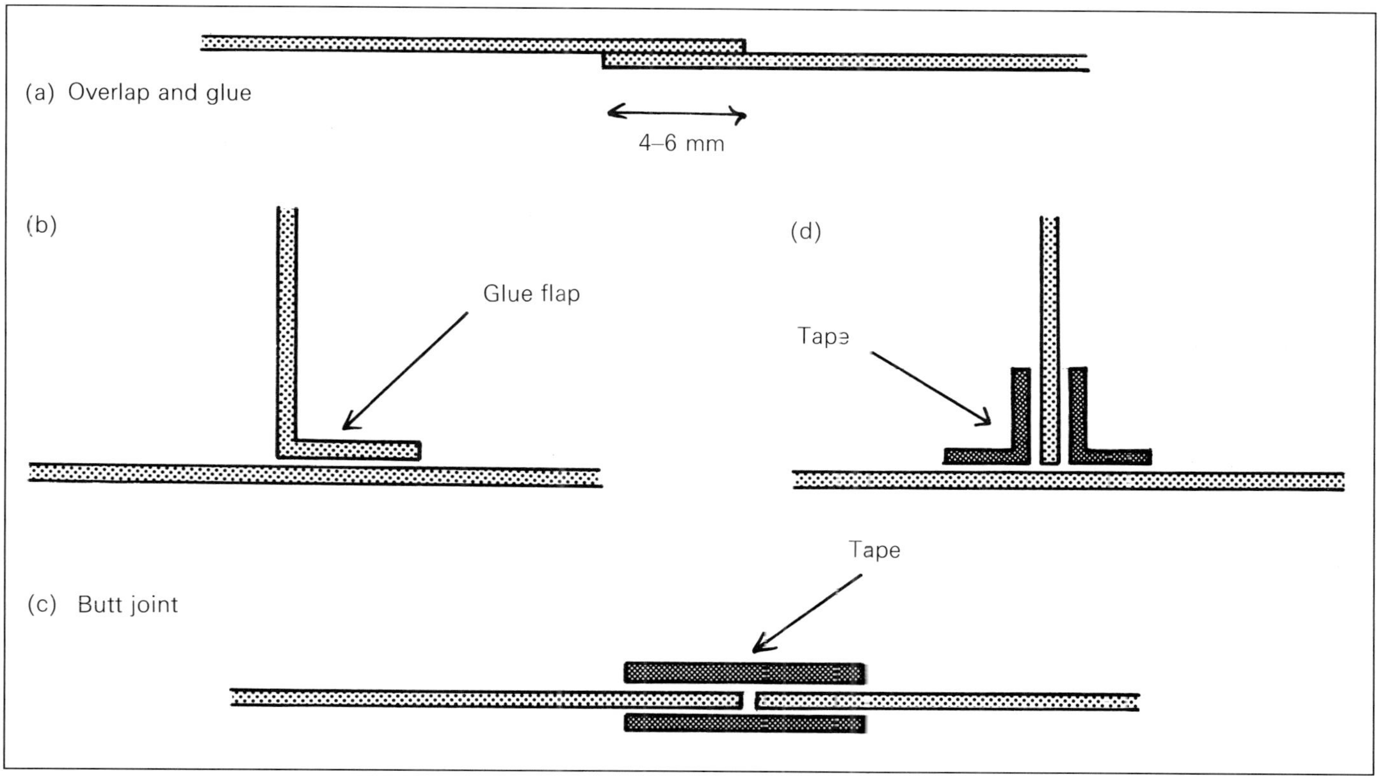

Fig 1.4 Glue flap and tape joint

Spars

With the right technique, spars can be cut both easily and accurately. To cut a length of dowel, mark the size required with a pencil and roll it under the blade of the craft knife two or three times. If the blade has not cut through, break the dowel at the cut then trim and sand the end, or give it a few turns in a pencil sharpener, to take off any splinters or sharp edges (Fig 1.5).

Narrow diameter fibreglass, 1.5–2 mm ($\frac{1}{16}$ inch), can be snipped easily enough with pincers or wire cutters, but larger diameters (3 mm and above) should be sawn using a fine hacksaw blade.

Method of cutting wooden spars

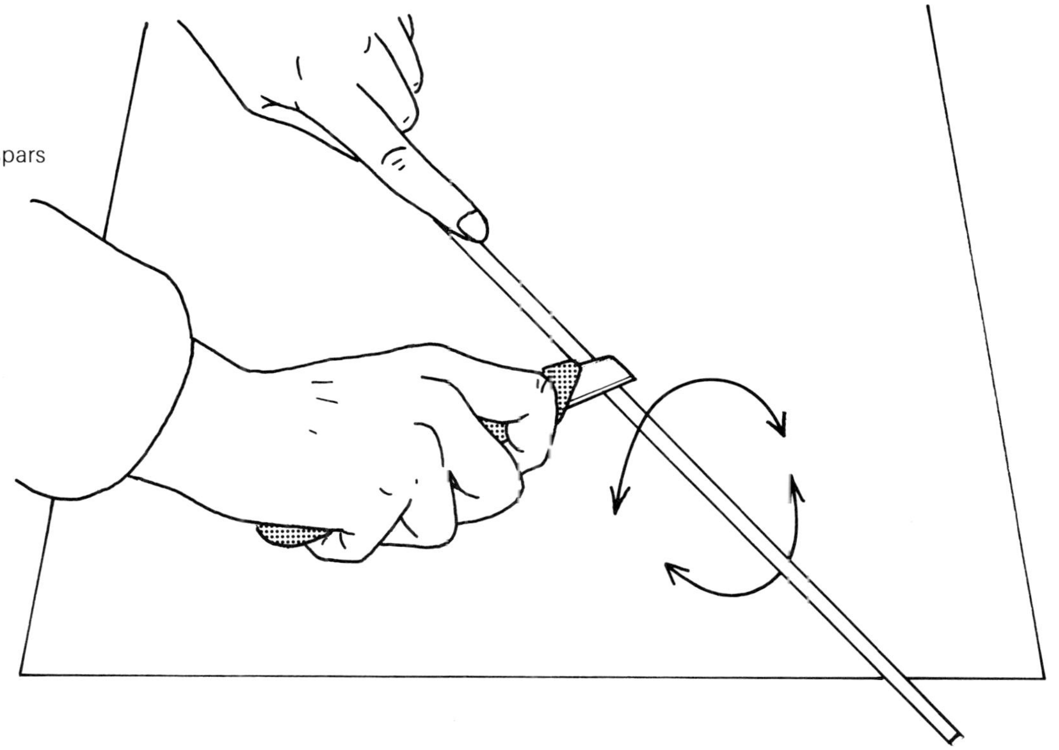

Fig 1.5 Rolling to cut kite spar

Knots

There are perhaps hundreds of different knots which could be used in kite construction, but that does not mean that you have to learn them all. The best approach is to learn how to tie about half a dozen, and the types of situation to which they are best suited.

The simplest knot is an 'overhand loop', used most often to create a fixed towing point at the centre of the bridle line. Fold the end of the line back along itself to the depth of about 7 cm ($2\frac{1}{2}$ inches), make a loop (around your finger if it helps), then finally bring the folded end of the line through the loop and pull tight (Fig 1.6).

Where it is necessary to move the towing point up and down the bridle to take account of different wind conditions, it is more usual to tie a 'Lark's head hitch'. Thread the bridle through the ring (Fig 1.7a) and lay it flat. Now pull the ring along and under the loop (Fig 1.7b).

Two other basic knots are used to tie lines to each other, or more usually to tie the bridle to the kite spars. The 'half-blood' knot is quite easy. Loop the line around the spar and twist the loose end around the other three or four times (Fig 1.8a). Now thread the loose end underneath the twists and pull tight (Fig 1.8b).

To tie the 'bowline', make a loop of line and tie a single slip knot (Fig 1.9a). Next bring the loose end of line around the other, thread it through the loop so created, and pull tight (Fig 1.9b,c).

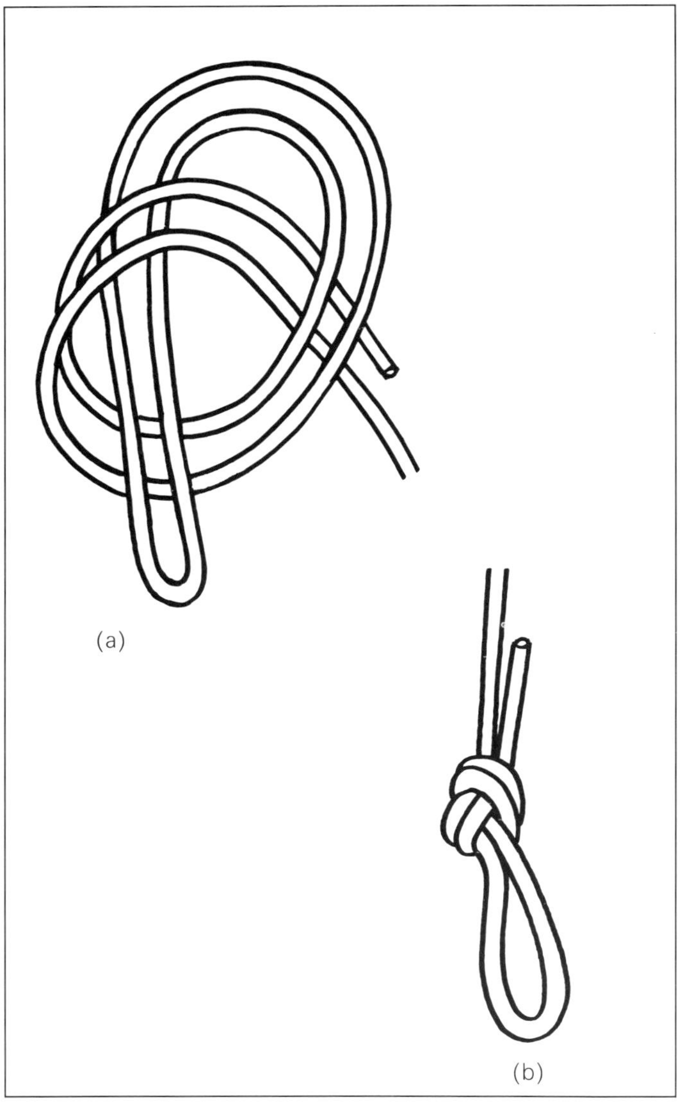

Fig 1.6 Overhand loop

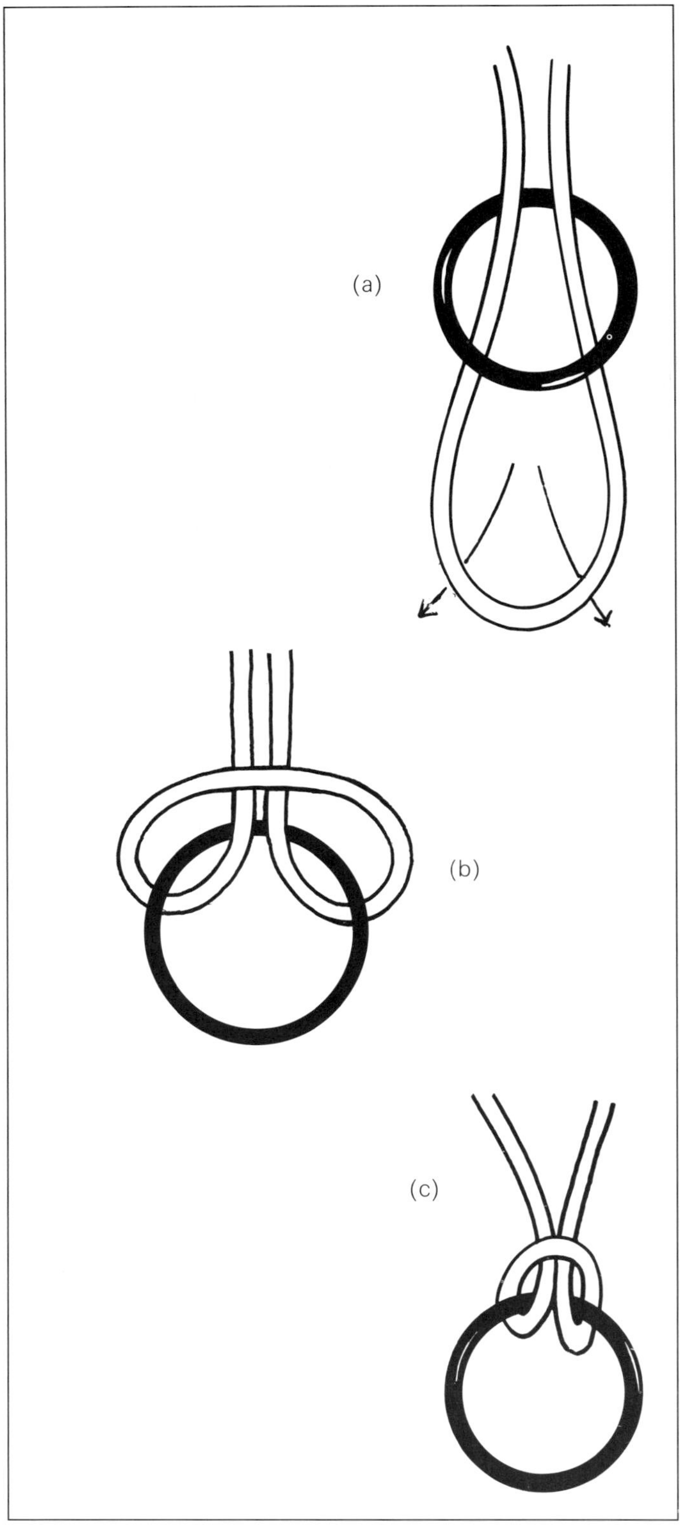

Fig 1.7 Lark's head hitch

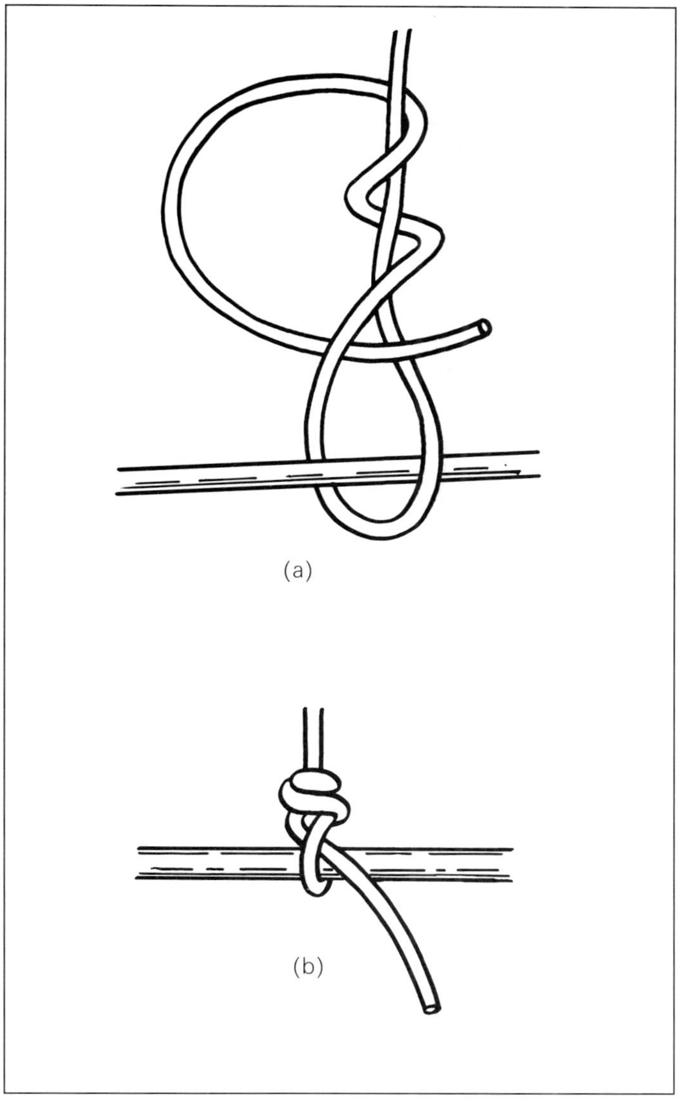

Fig 1.8 Half blood knot

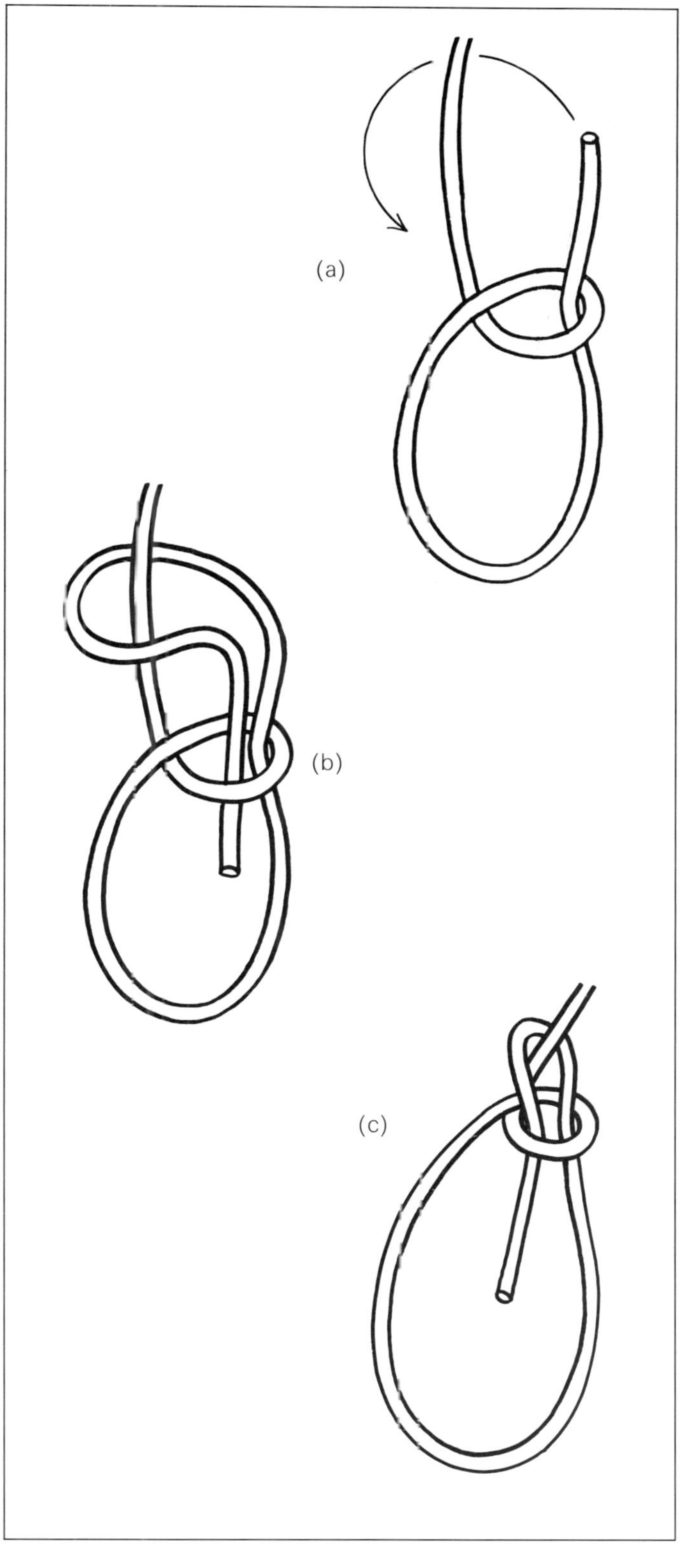

Fig 1.9 Bowline

REELS AND HANDLES

The purpose of the reel or handle is to provide a simple and convenient way of both storing the line and holding on to your kite during flight.

Simple reel

The simplest type of reel is of course a length of dowel, perhaps 8 mm–20 mm ($\frac{5}{16}$–$\frac{3}{4}$ inch) diameter, around which the line is wound in a criss-cross fashion (Fig 1.10a).

You can of course make the 'stick' from a cardboard tube such as the former from a toilet roll or kitchen towel (Fig 1.10b). Or from a piece of cardboard folded into a triangular section (Fig 1.10c).

Two-handed reels

These can be constructed by gluing lengths of semi-circular Ramin moulding each side of shaped pieces of stiff card, plywood or hardboard (Fig 1.11 a,b).

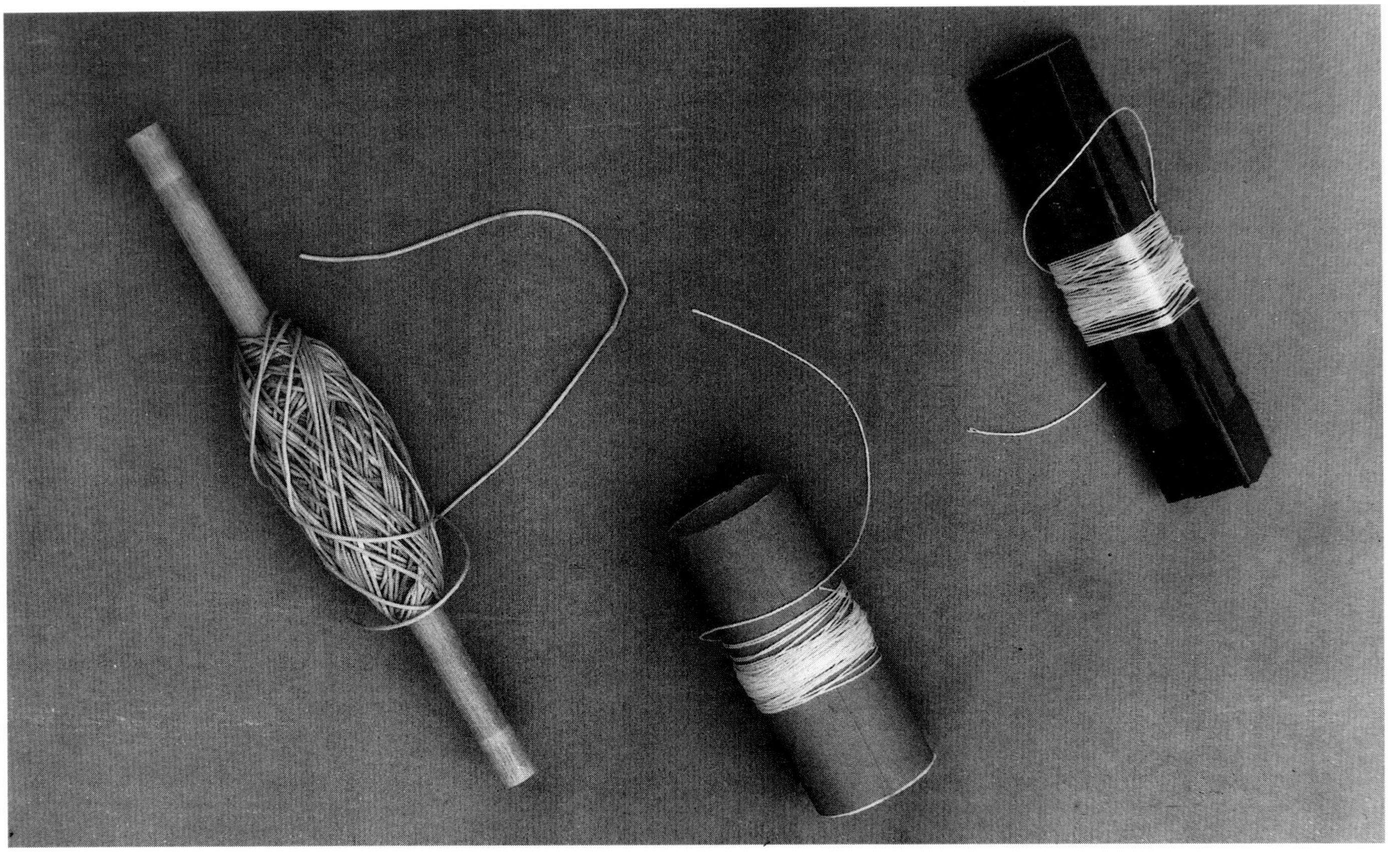

Fig 1.10 Stick, tri and round section

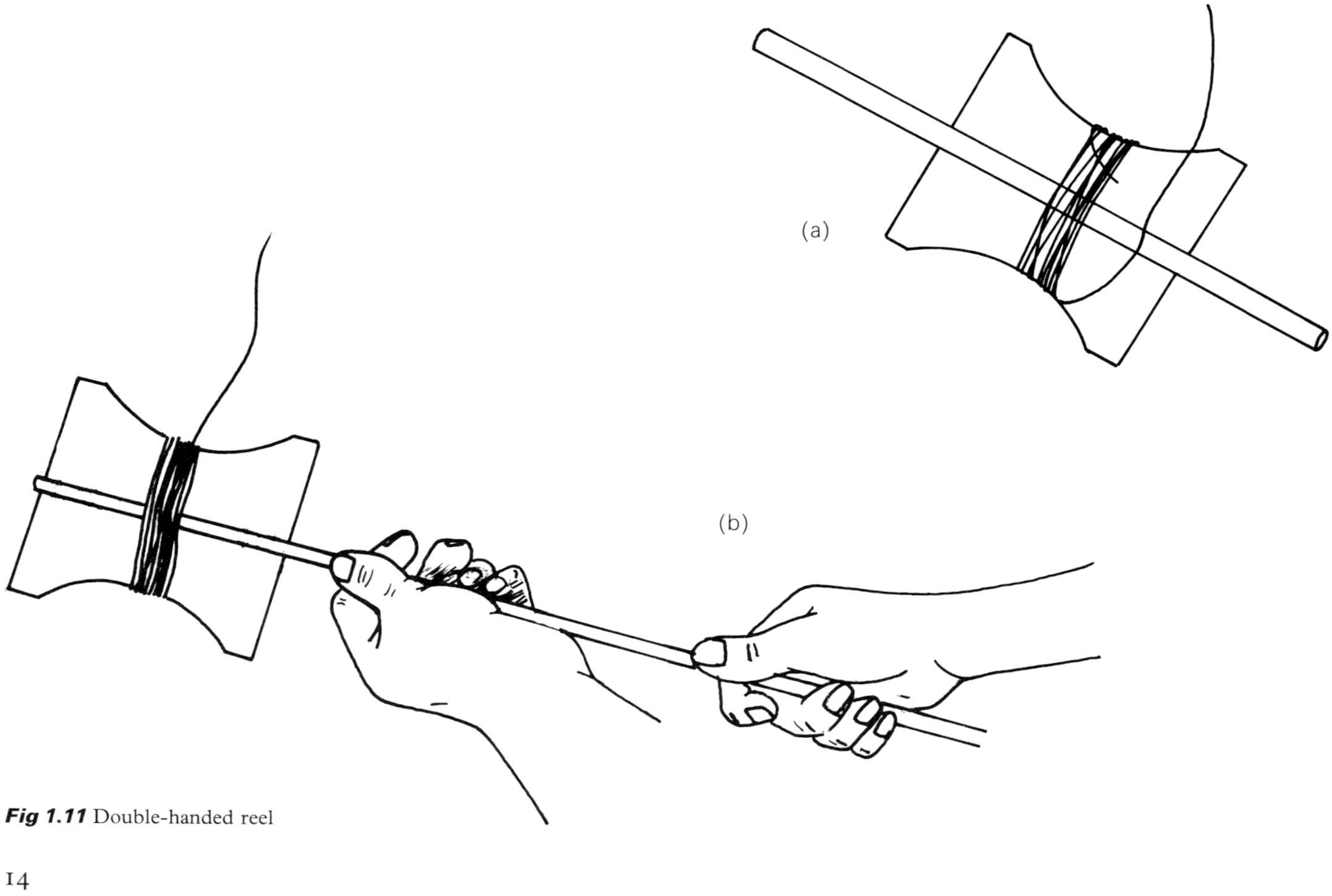

Fig 1.11 Double-handed reel

If you have access to a workshop, similar designs can be constructed by fitting dowels into solid pieces of timber or box sections (Fig 1.12a,b).

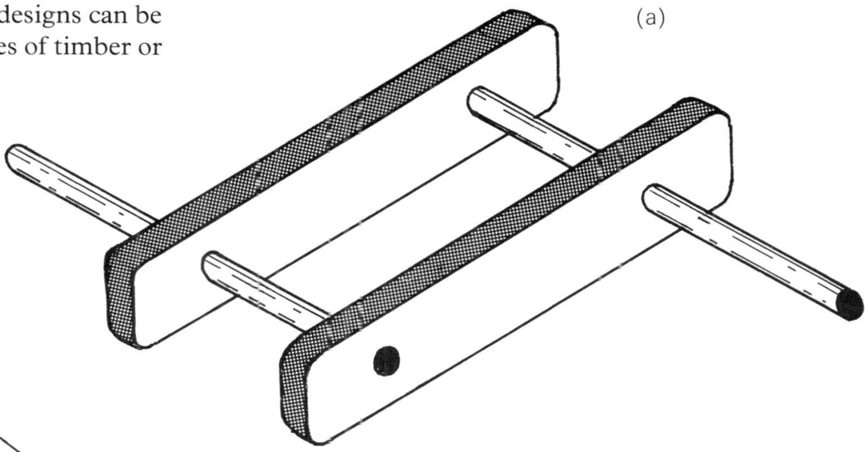

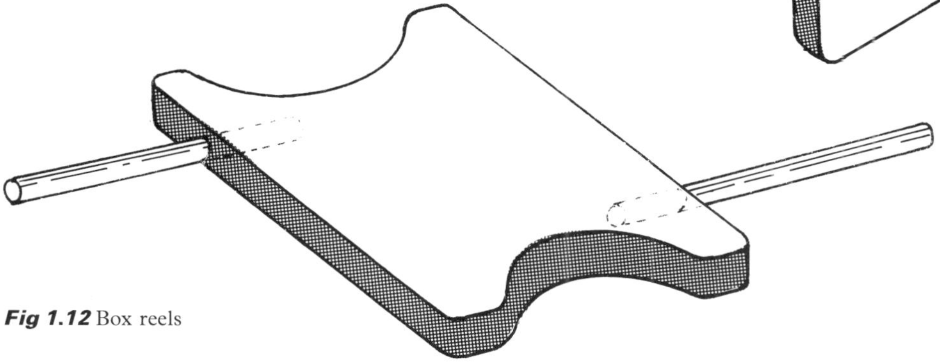

Fig 1.12 Box reels

Handles

Most shops selling kites will also be able to supply moulded plastic handles at reasonable prices. These are quite adequate for all the designs featured in the book (Fig 1.13).

Alternatively, similar handles to these can be cut from hardboard or light 5 mm ($\frac{3}{16}$ inch) plywood (Fig 1.14).

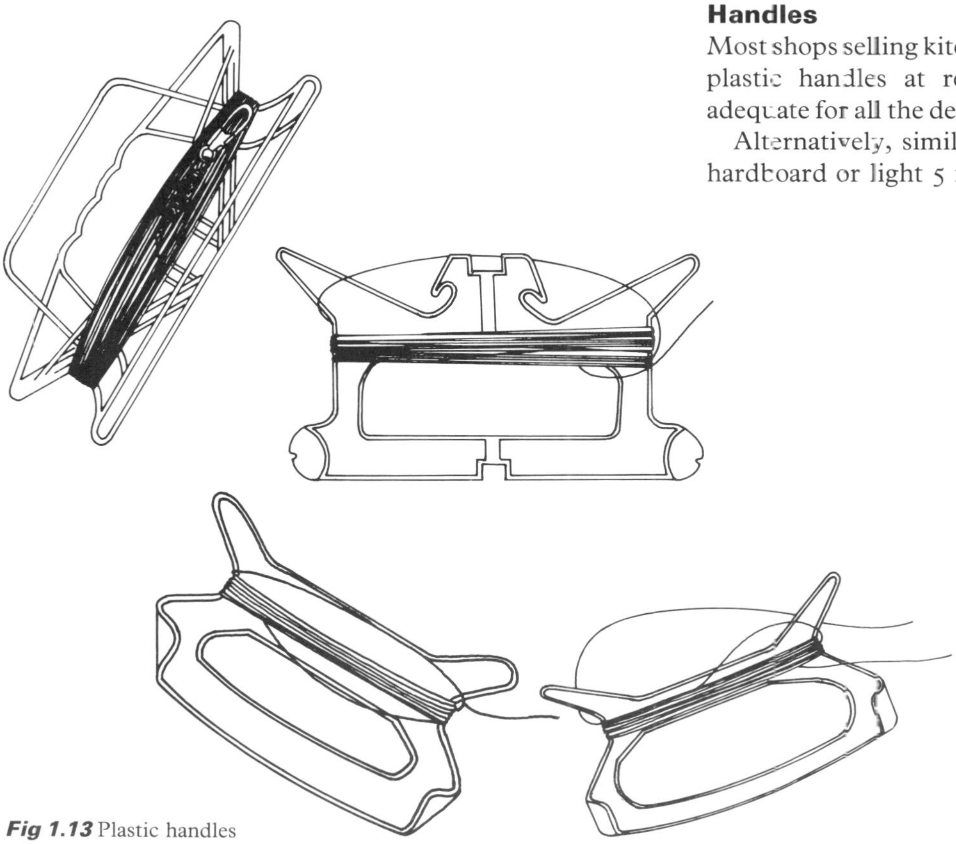

Fig 1.13 Plastic handles

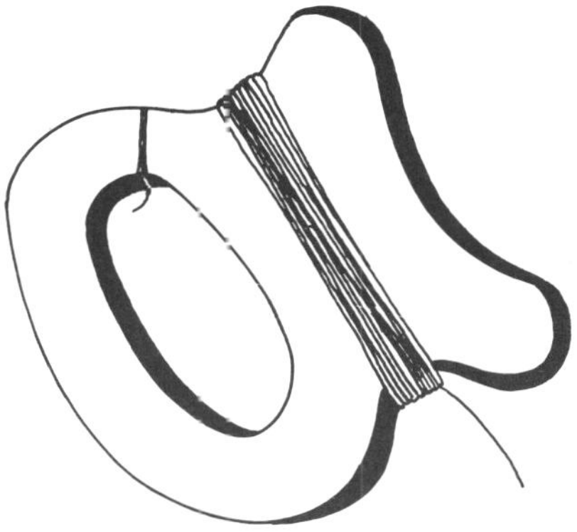

Fig 1.14 Wooden handles

CHAPTER TWO

decoration techniques

Decorating your kite is the most interesting part of its construction, when you can add your own individual ideas, patterns and colours, anything from geometric patterns to character pictures, or to slogans to promote your own particular cause.

COLOURING

The simplest way of creating a design on your kite is of course to colour the sail material, using inks, paints or dyes. The only basic advice to offer is to choose bold shapes rather than finely detailed ones, since such detail cannot be appreciated, or indeed even seen, when the kite is flying some distance away.

Whether you use painting, stencilling or marbling, you should take some care to select the correct colouring medium to match the sail material. Firstly, choose a colour which dries quickly to a waterproof finish. There is nothing more heartbreaking than to spend hours creating an attractive design on a kite only to have it destroyed in seconds by carelessly brushing it against wet grass.

As well as differing in qualities such as weight, strength and porosity, sail materials also have varying surface finishes which determine the types of colour they will accept. Papers will, of course, accept a wide range of both spirit and water colours, and you should have little difficulty obtaining a good range at reasonable prices. Waterproof poster paints, for example, are now available in bold colours. Acrylics and vinyls also dry quickly to a hard waterproof finish, but are more expensive.

Although *Tyvek* is described as a 'paper', you have to be a little more careful in your choice of colour. It will accept water colours, poster paints and acrylics without difficulty, but avoid spirit colours, such as household gloss paints and modeller's enamels, since these will soften the base and weaken it, or, more likely, take hours (and hours and hours . . .) to dry.

Unless you treat the surface, polythene will not accept any type of colour, either water or spirit. Those colours which do adhere to the surface when wet can usually be guaranteed, with the flexing of the sail when dry, to flake off on to your hands and your clothes, and leaving you wishing you had never started. If you are making a large number, of polythene kites, it may be worthwhile buying a spray surface coating to improve the adhesion of colours, but such coatings are very expensive and should only be used with extreme care. For small designs, polythene can of course be coloured with a spirit-based felt-tip marker, although they can get tedious where larger areas are involved.

Polyester film is another material which only accepts a small range of colours. Spirit-based felt-tip pens provide the easiest means of creating a design, but, as with polythene, can be hard work. Modeller's enamels, either water or spirit, are adequate and give only limited flaking, but perhaps the best advice for those wishing to colour plastics is to seek the help of your local art dealer who may be able to recommend a suitable industrial colouring medium.

Synteape and other synthetic papers are fortunately a little more tolerant. Although water colours can be used, they sometimes take a long time to dry, usually overnight; spirit colours are marginally better but still need care in their application since as with *Tyvek* they can damage the base. The old standby, the spirit felt-tip pen, will dry to a good hard finish, but is no less tedious to apply.

1. Painting

By far the easiest way of creating a design on your kite is, of course, to paint it on. Except for repeating the general advice to choose large shapes in bold colours, there is little to add.

2. Stencilling

When you want to make the same pattern on more than one kite, or where the design is made up of a number of similar shapes, painting each one becomes bit laborious, so stencilling is the answer. To be effective, though, the design should be limited to two or three colours, since with any more the process gets a little complicated.

Any thin, durable, waterproof card should prove reasonably satisfactory for stencils making up to five or so prints. If you are in any doubt, or if you want to colour a larger number of kites, your local art dealer may be able to supply a much stronger oiled manilla card or a translucent stencil board. Both are on the expensive side, however.

Draw the design on the stencil material, leaving a gap of at least 3 mm ($\frac{1}{8}$ inch) between any two adjacent colours, and cut out the pattern with a sharp craft knife or scissors.

Lay the sail on a flat surface and tape it firmly at the corners. Since the colours are added one at a time, it is safest, to prevent confusion, to mask out the cut parts of the stencil not requiring colour this time before positioning it on the sail.

Position the stencil carefully on the sail. Mix the colour to a fairly thick paste and work it on to the sail using a broad, medium-soft paint brush or sponge pad in a vertical dabbing motion, from the edges of the stencil shape inwards (Fig 2.1). Work gently trying to create an even shade and when you have finished remove the stencil and leave the sail to dry before adding the next colour.

Fig 2.1 Stencilling

3. Marbling

Marbling is a very interesting and indeed fun way of decorating a kite sail, though even if a bit messy.

To start, you need a small ball – an old tennis ball, golf ball, ping-pong ball, ball of plasticine or a ball of paper and some broad 2–3 mm diameter ($\frac{1}{8}$ inch) string. Wrap the string around the ball, making about two dozen turns in criss-cross fashion. Mix the colour into a paste on a plate or saucer, and roll the ball so that the colour is taken into the string.

With the sail material on a flat surface, transfer the

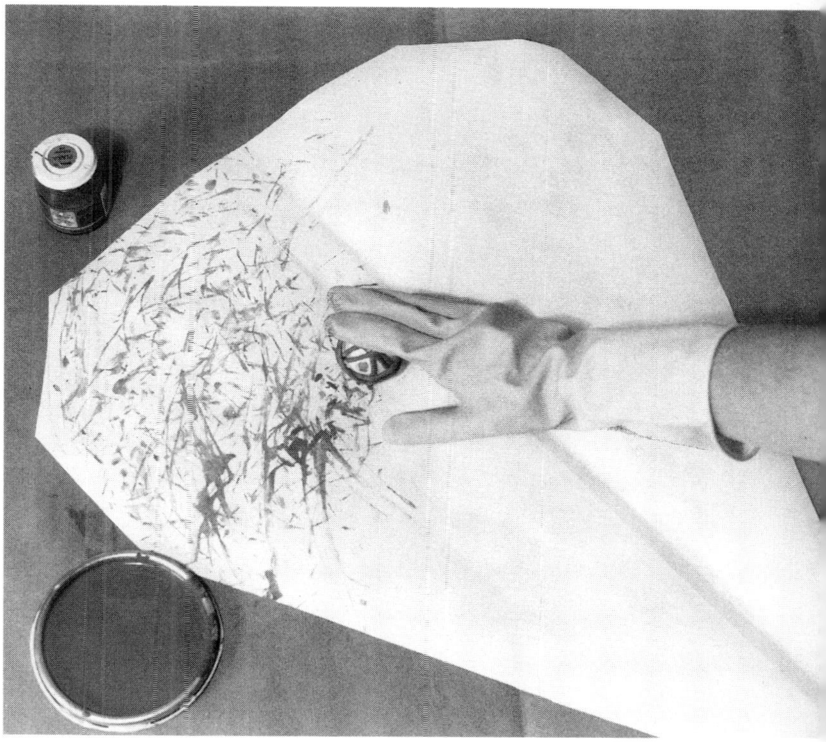

Fig 2.2 Marbling

colour, again by rolling the ball (Fig 2.2). You can combine several colours this way to create most interesting effect.

GEOMETRIC PATTERNS

A slightly more complex way to add some colour to your kite is to cut individual sail pieces from different coloured materials, or to make the sail from a combination of coloured units, in some simple geometric pattern. This method works particularly well with materials available in a range of colours, such as tissue and polythene.

If you are new to this technique, keep your design simple and give all your shapes straight edges. Also, with both papers and taped, low density polythenes, since the join or seam produced tends to be stronger than the body of the sail, it is very important that the pattern must show the same symmetry as the wing shape. Looking at the patterns in Fig 2.3: after a few hours' flying, both sails will stretch and as a result become a little distorted. For the top sail, because the pattern is symmetrical, such distortions will be balanced on both sides and stability unaffected. This is not, of course, true for the bottom sail, which would probably not survive more than a few outings.

APPLIQUÉ

Appliqué is more usually associated with quilts, bedcovers, sweaters, and fabric kites, although it can be easily adapted to other materials. In essence, it involves making the pattern from coloured shapes of material and sticking them to the sail surface. But because the shapes are fixed to the

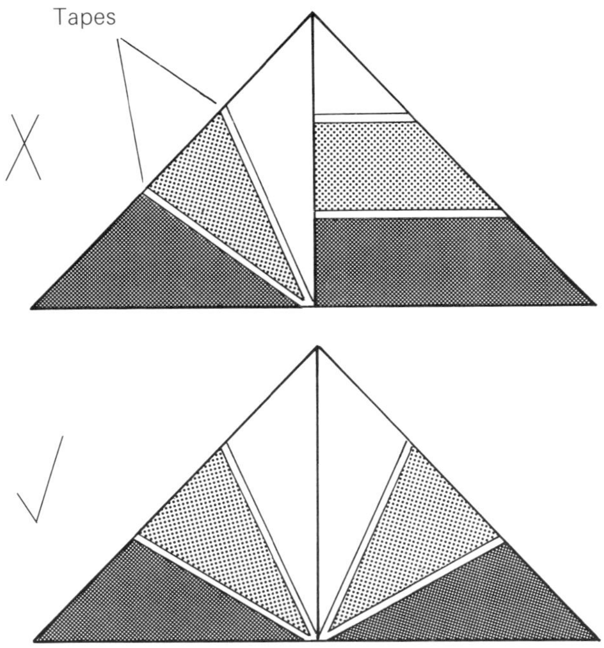

Fig 2.3 Keep the patterns of pieced sails symmetrical

surface only, you can make any type of pattern you wish, without having to worry about symmetry – clowns, faces, birds, fish, clouds, or your favourite cartoon character.

Paper, particularly tissue, works best as it is quite light and available in a wide range of colours; polythene, on the other hand, starts to get very heavy with additional appliquéd layers, which must also be welded; whereas *Tyvek*, since it is available in so few colours, is better painted.

To start, draw your outline design on a sheet of paper at least the same size as the kite sail. Try to create a pattern or design which can be enclosed within a dark outline colour, separating individual colour shapes, such as the wing pattern on the butterfly shown in the photographs (Fig 2.4a). As with other decoration techniques, choose bold shapes rather than finely detailed ones.

Cut out the outline pattern then, using it as a template, lightly draw the shape on the kite sail. Cut out the internal colour shapes, and, again using them as templates, transfer the whole design to the sail (Fig 2.4b).

Using the templates again, cut out coloured pieces of material and glue them in position on the sail. Start with the lighter colours, gradually working towards the darker ones to build up the pattern, then add the outline colour to complete the design (Fig 2.4c,d). In the design illustrated, the butterfly body is my darkest colour, actually black, and was added last (see jacket photograph).

Fig 2.4 (a–d) Appliqué

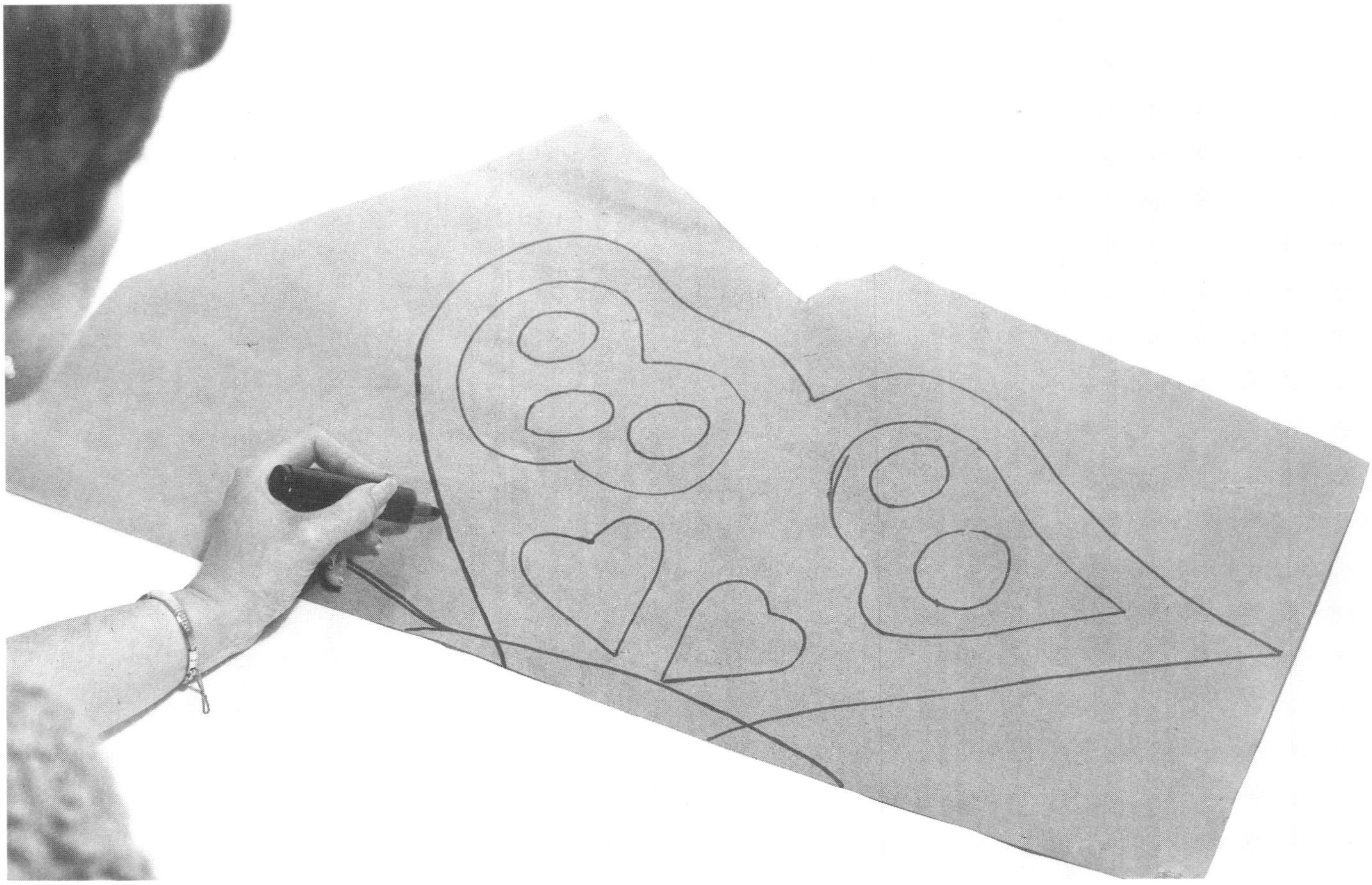

(a)

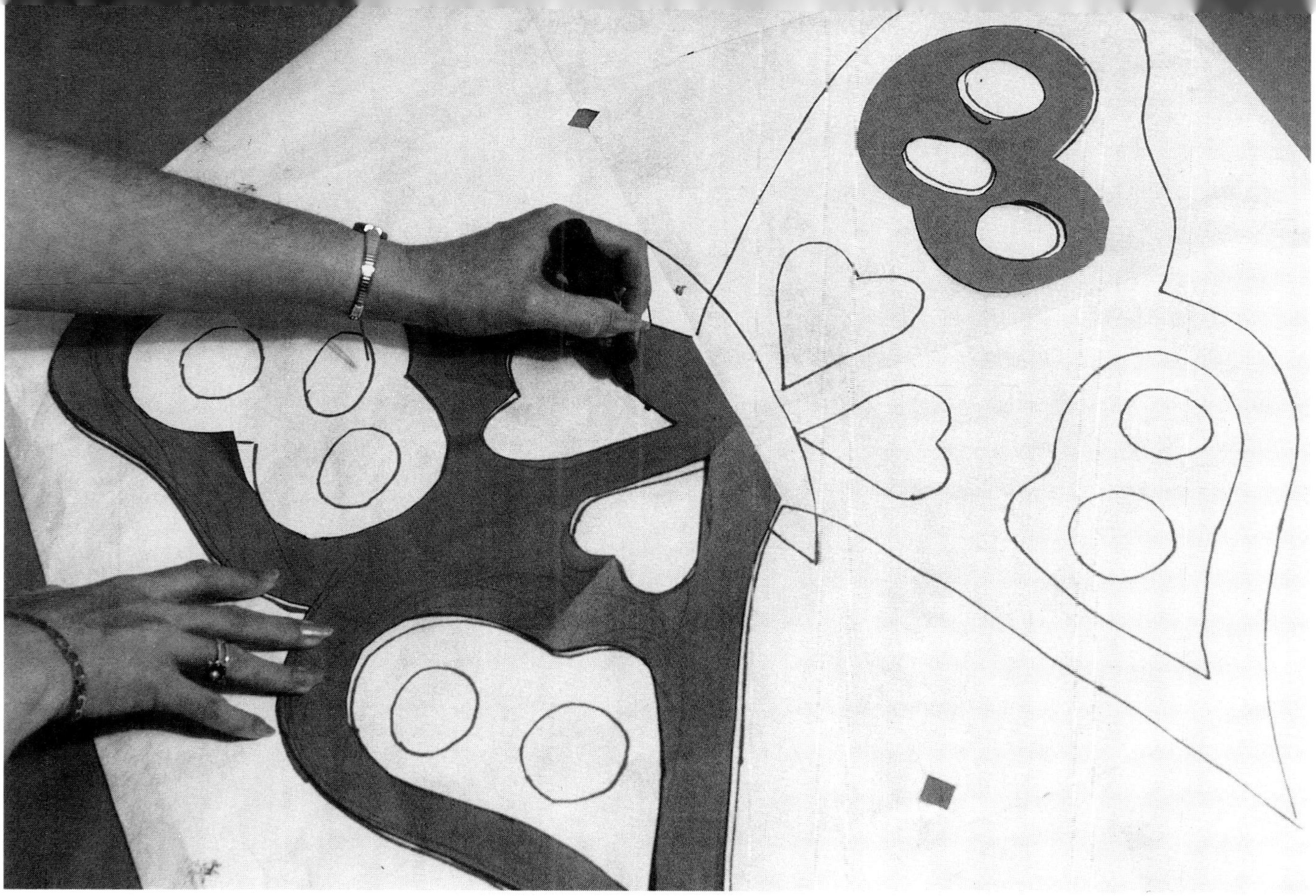
(b)

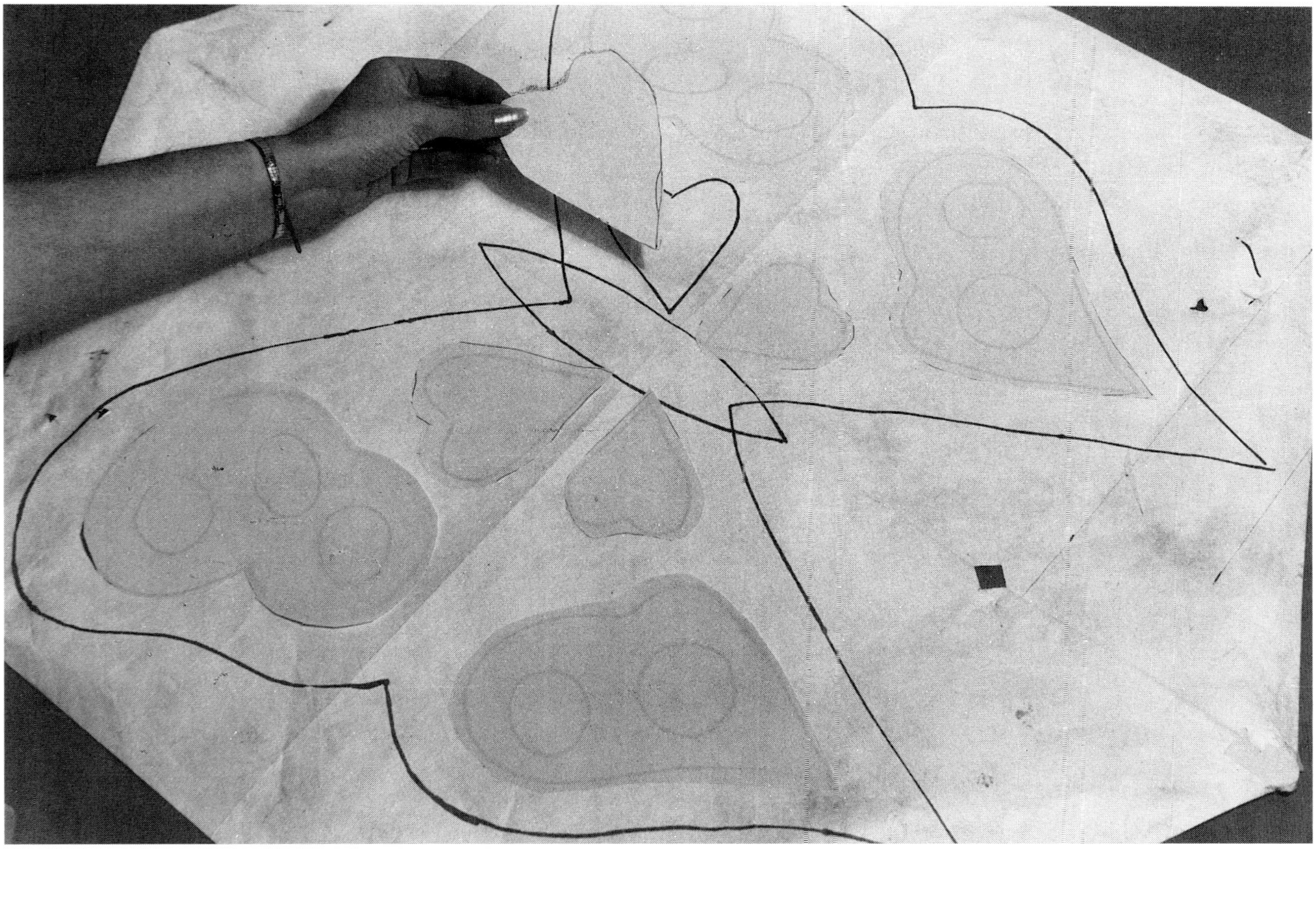
(c)

(d)

TAILS AND WINDSOCKS

Tails and windsocks are usually added to the kite to assist stability, and prevent it swaying too much in changing air currents, but they can also become part of the overall form, adding both colour and interest to the display.

Ribbon tail

This is made from a length of ribbon, polythene, *Tyvek* or polyester 2–5 cm (1–2 inches) wide, attached at the mid point of the lower edge of the kite (Fig 2.5).

Serrated tails

To create an even more efficient stabilising device, but without increasing the total weight, the edges of a wide ribbon tail can be serrated. On this type of tail, however, the unserrated edge must be reinforced to prevent it from ripping (Fig 2.6).

Tassle tails

These can be made from short lengths of material, all attached to a single point (Fig 2.7).

Streamer tails

Streamer tails are great fun to make, especially if you can

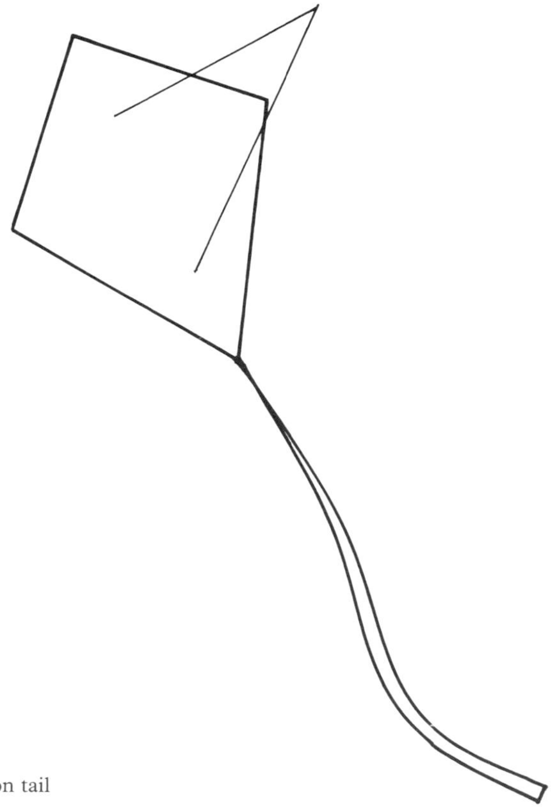

Fig 2.5 Ribbon tail

find materials in lots of different colours. Add individual streamers to the lower edge of the kite symmetrically about the centre line (Fig 2.8).

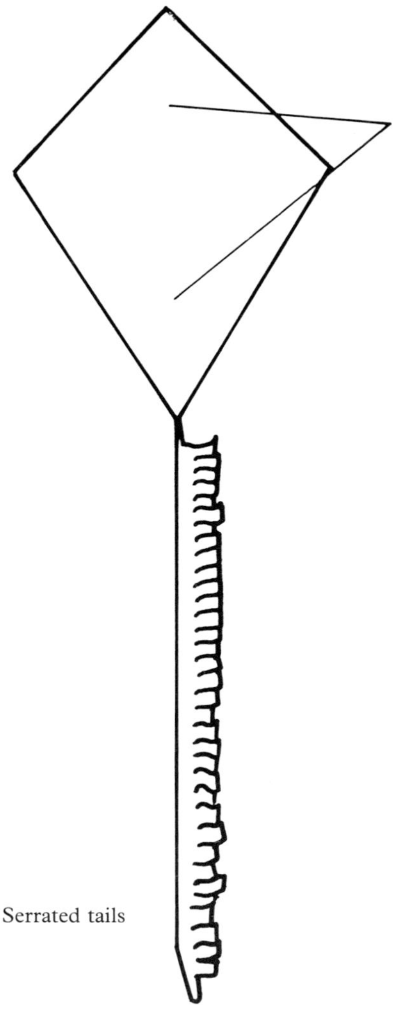

Fig 2.6 Serrated tails

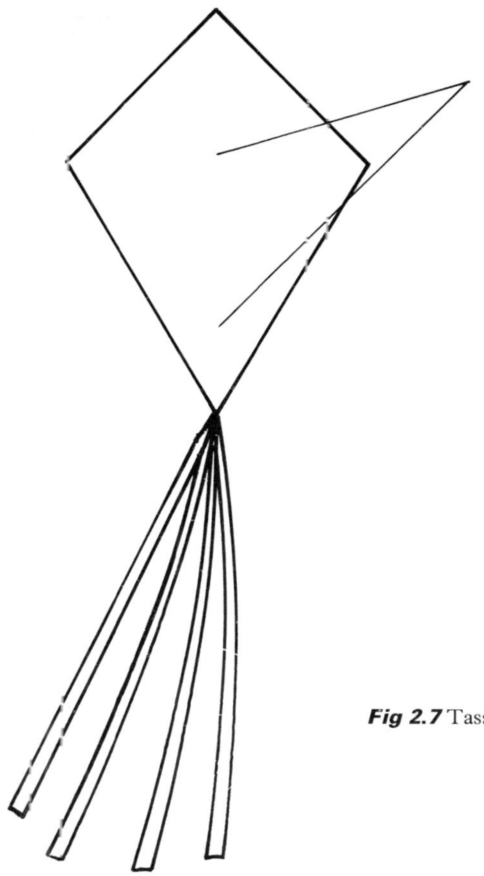

Fig 2.7 Tassle tail

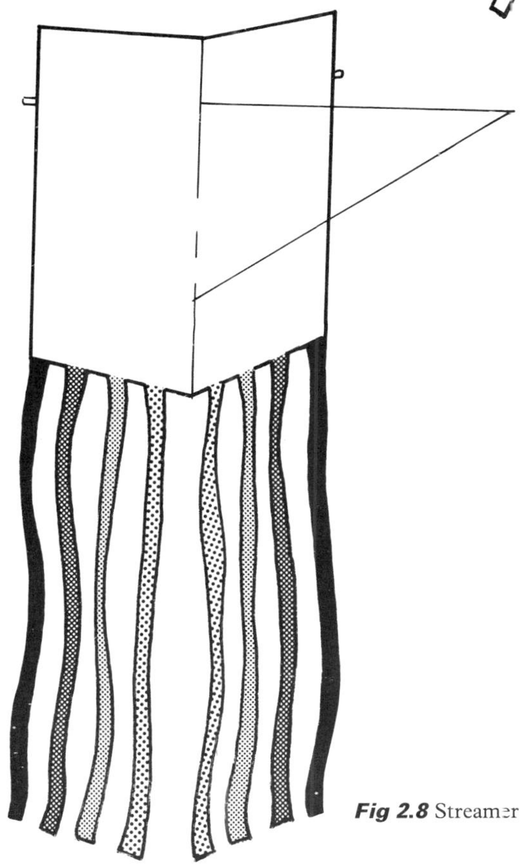

Fig 2.8 Streamer tails

Flat tails

These are the big daddies of them all and if you take care to make them properly, they can be really beautiful (Fig 2.9). Flat tails are best decorated in a similar fashion to the kites themselves.

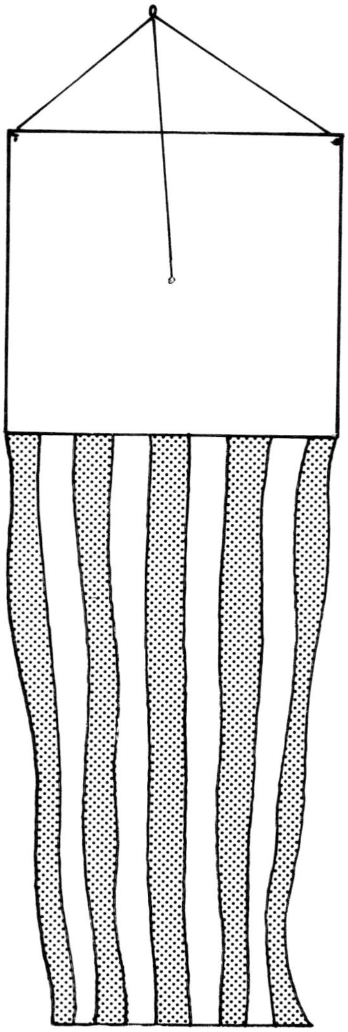

Fig 2.9 Flat tail

Helix tail

The helix is a most interesting variation of the flat tail. To start, you will need a flat sheet of light card about 30 cm (12 inches) square and on it draw a number of concentric circles, say 2 cm ($\frac{3}{4}$ inch) apart.

Using the circles as a guide, draw and cut out a helix (Fig 2.10). Reinforce the central point and attach it to the edge of your kite via a couple of light swivels (Fig 2.11).

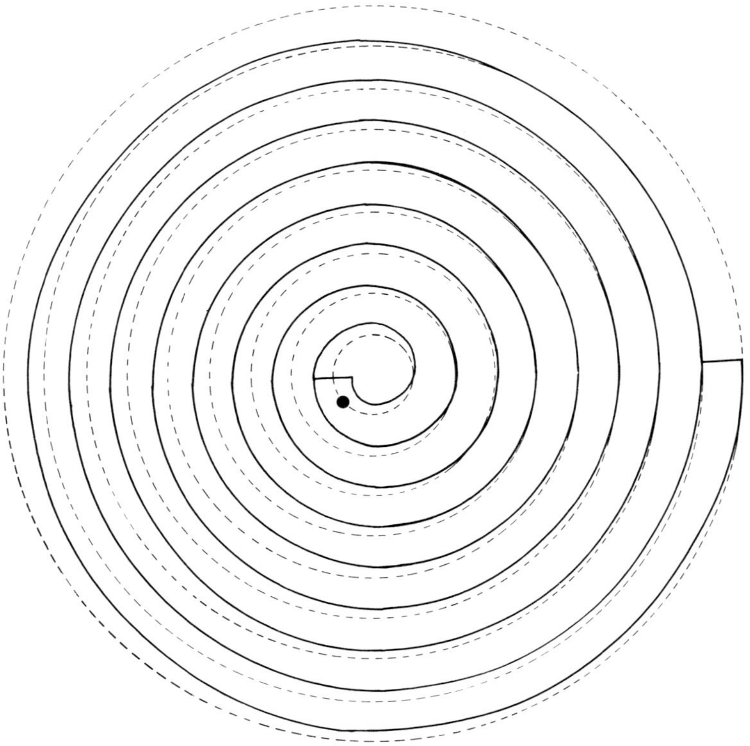

Mark out concentric circles 2 cm apart on a square of material, then using these as a guide draw and cut out the helix

Fig 2.10 Helix tail – pattern

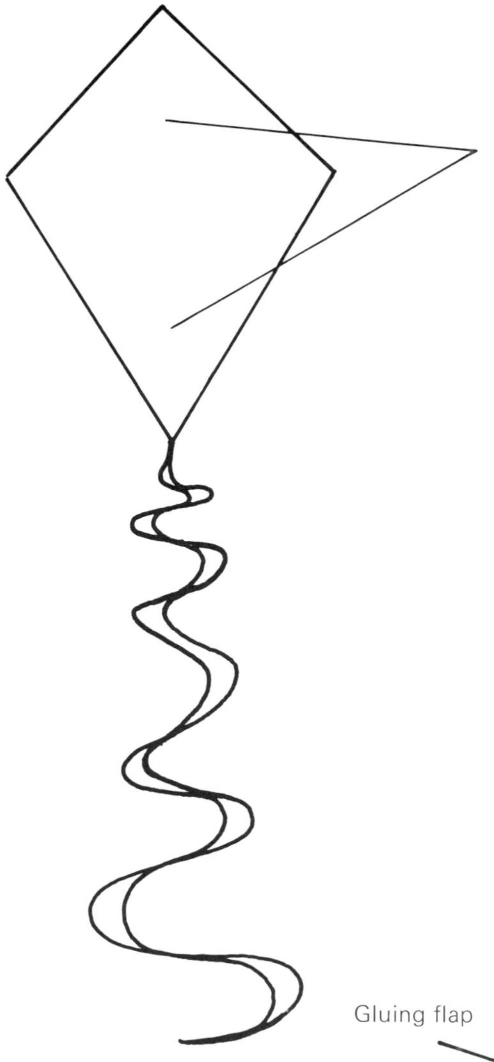

Fig 2.11 Helix tail on kite

Drogues and windsocks

Windsocks are devices in the shape of a long cone which capture the wind, causing them to inflate.

To make a simple windsock cut out a long rectangle of material, trimming one side so that it is slightly shorter than the other (Fig 2.12). Join the two long sides AC/BD to create the cone. You can choose your own dimensions: either short and fat, or long and narrow – providing, of course, that you don't go to extremes!

Run a length of reinforcing tape round the larger end and punch four or six holes evenly around the edge. Now cut lengths of line and tie one end of each through the holes. Join the lines in a loop, evenly supporting the windsock, with each about 1–2 times the diameter in length (Fig 2.13).

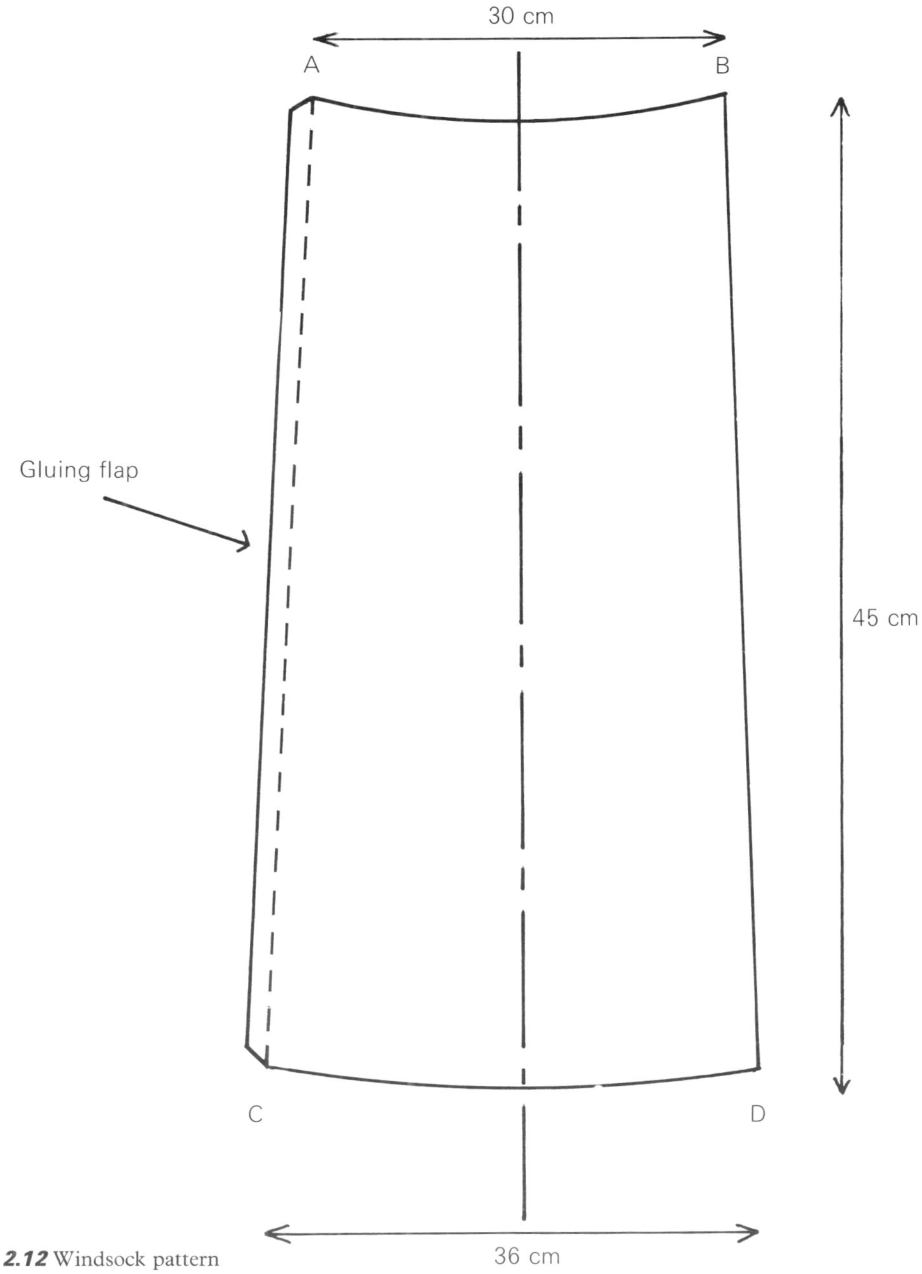

Fig 2.12 Windsock pattern

Fig 2.13 Fit the lines round the perimeter, evenly supporting the windsock

To decorate the windsock, you can paint coloured rings, add streamers, write your name or any other message (Fig 2.14).

Spinning drogue

Drogues are, in their simplest form, just miniature windsocks, though their purpose is less for decoration and more for stability. The spinning drogue is the exception, however, and can be a fun toy – with or without a kite.

Draw the pattern (Fig 2.15) on a square of material using compasses and a protractor. These dimensions are not absolute and can be regarded as ratios. Cut out the shape and join the edges of the triangles with short lengths of tape (Fig 2.16).

When the ring is complete, add another strip of tape as reinforcement and punch holes evenly around the perimeter, at the centre or junction of the triangles. Thread and tie lines through each hole, then gather them together with an overhand loop so that the spinner is evenly supported, each line about the same diameter as the original large circle. Finally tie the loop to the kite using two or three swivels in series (Fig 2.17).

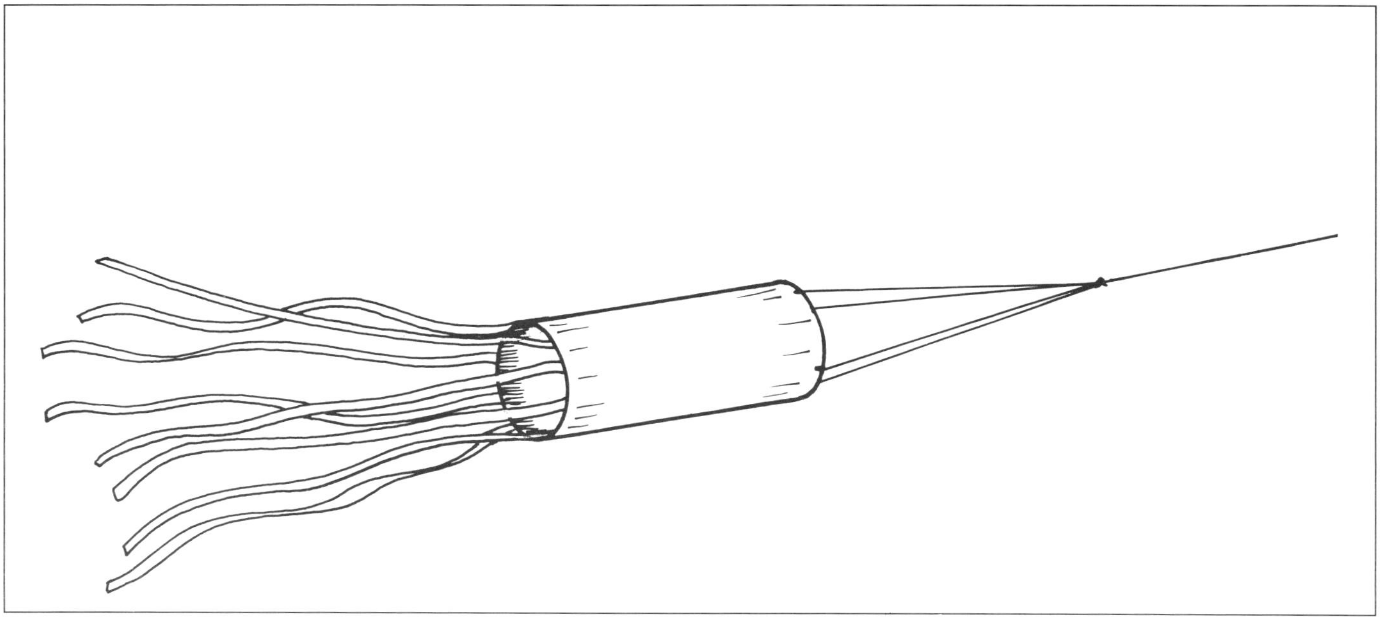

Fig 2.14 Windsock and streamers

Fig 2.15 Spinning drogue pattern

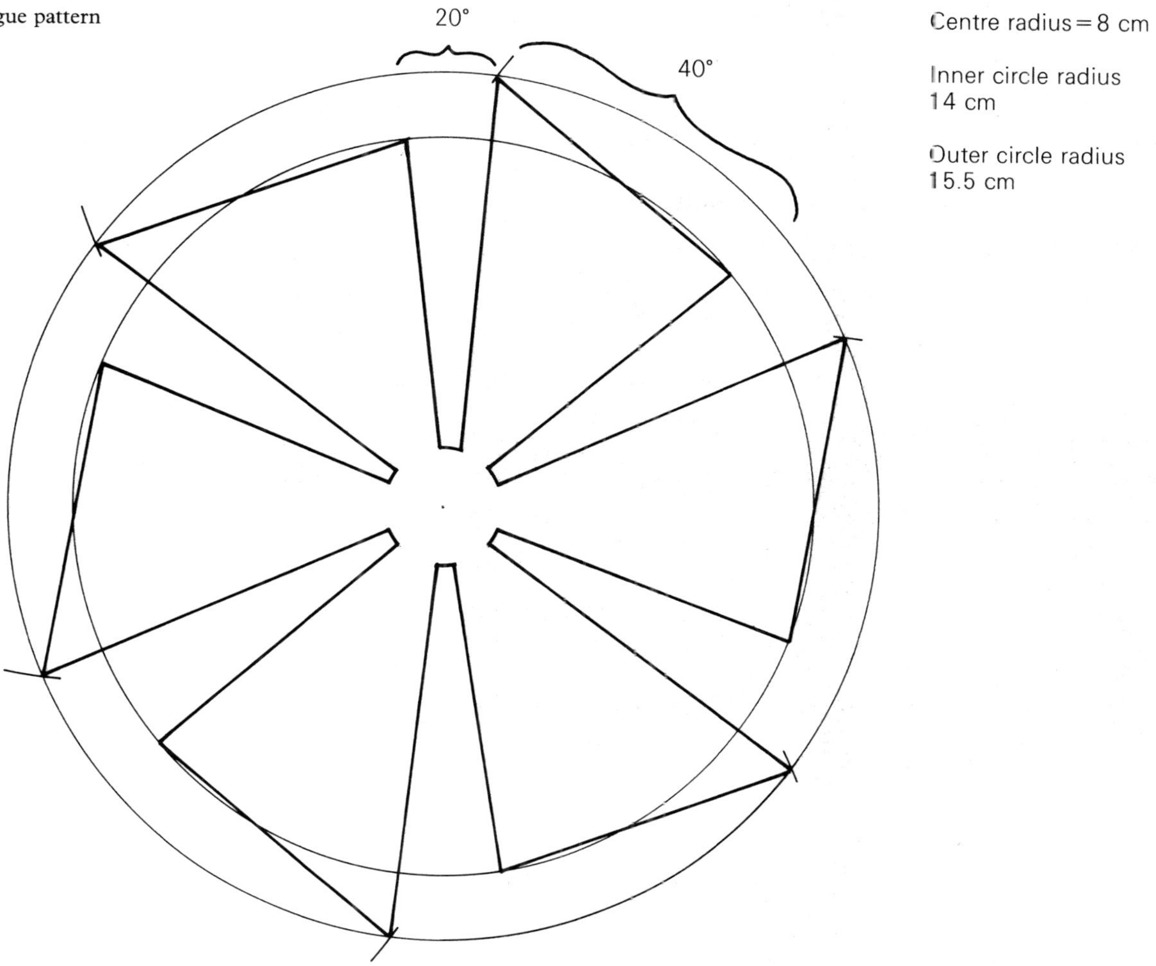

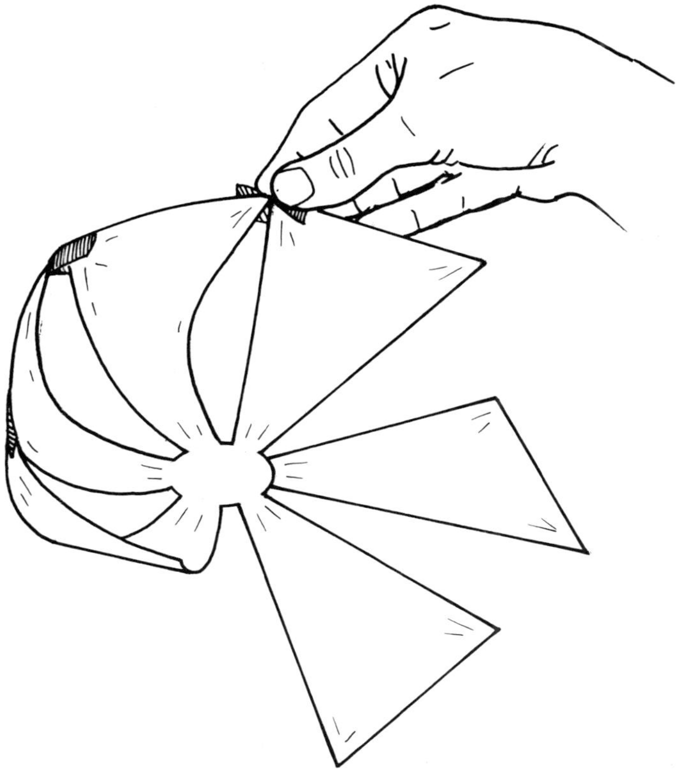

Fig 2.16 Join each section with a short length of tape

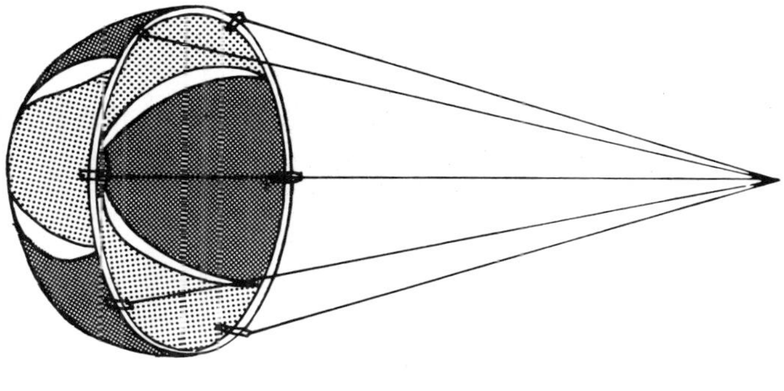

Fig 2.17 Spinning drogue

CHAPTER THREE

fly your kite

Although you can both build and fly a kite without knowing anything whatever about aerodynamics, to get the best out of it, to control and adjust the kite for different conditions, to make simple repairs, and to correct faults, it does help to have at least some elementary understanding of the concepts involved.

Using a very simple model, the kite can be thought of as a flat plate inclined to the oncoming wind (Fig 3.1). In this position it presents an obstacle to the air flow, causing it to change direction and speed; that flowing across the upper surface moves faster over the kite, while the flow across the lower surface starts to move more slowly. These changes in speed also result in a change of air pressure, lower on the upper surface and higher on the lower surface, the effect of which is to produce a net force upwards, described as 'lift'. And if this force is greater than the weight of the kite, it will of course be lifted upwards – that is, it will 'fly'.

Lift, however, is only half the story. As the angle of attack (inclination) increases, the airflow is not only split, directed along the upper and lower surfaces, it is also some distance before the two air flows meet up again, resulting in a lower air pressure immediately behind the kite. It is consequently pushed or sucked into this area of low pressure – the force described as 'drag'.

The values of lift and drag are both related to the surface area of the kite, its shape, the angle of attack and wind speed, but not, fortunately, in exactly the same way. At lower angles of attack, lift increases at the greater rate, but as the angle becomes larger, drag becomes more significant until lift eventually begins to fall. In terms of the performance, there are consequently two important angles of attack; $\alpha 1$ when the ratio of lift/drag is maximum at which the kite will also fly at its maximum elevation: and $\alpha 2$ when the lift is maximum, described as the stalling angle, (Fig 3.2).

Although lift and drag of course act over the whole surface of the kite, for convenience it is more usual to regard them as acting at a single point, described as the 'Centre of Pressure'.

When the kite is flying in equilibrium, stationary in the sky, the forces maintaining it there (lift and drag) must be equal and opposite to the force pulling it down – the line tension (Fig 3.3). (For simplicity the effects of the weight of the kite and of the flying line have been ignored). All three forces must consequently pass through the same point – the

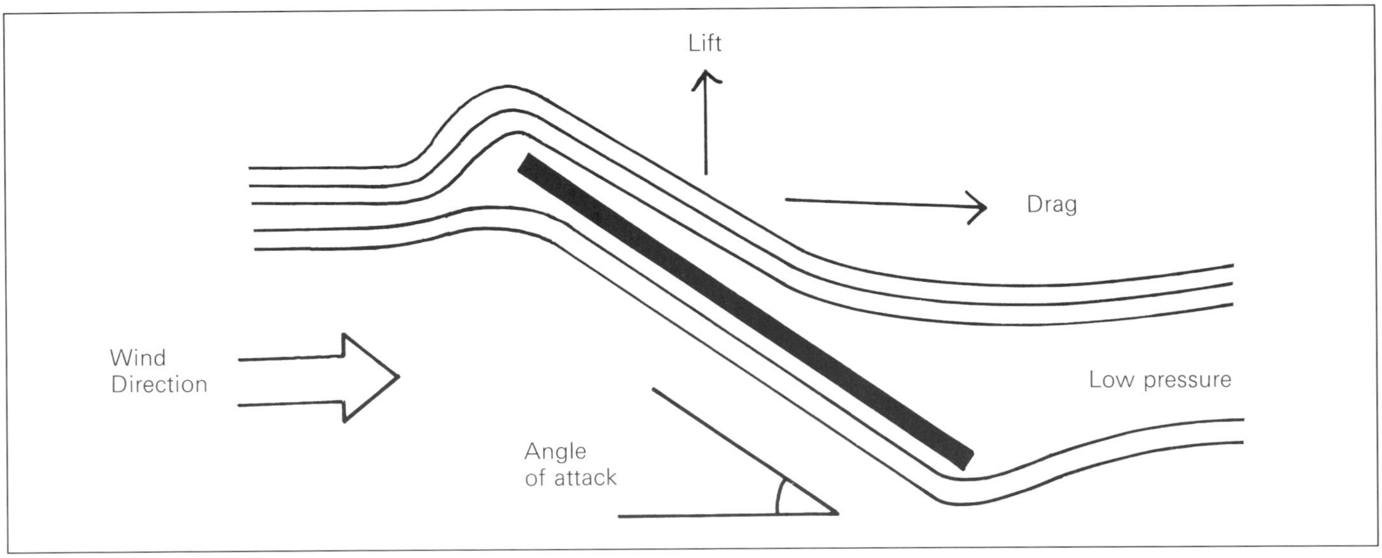

Fig 3.1 Flat plate inclined to the wind

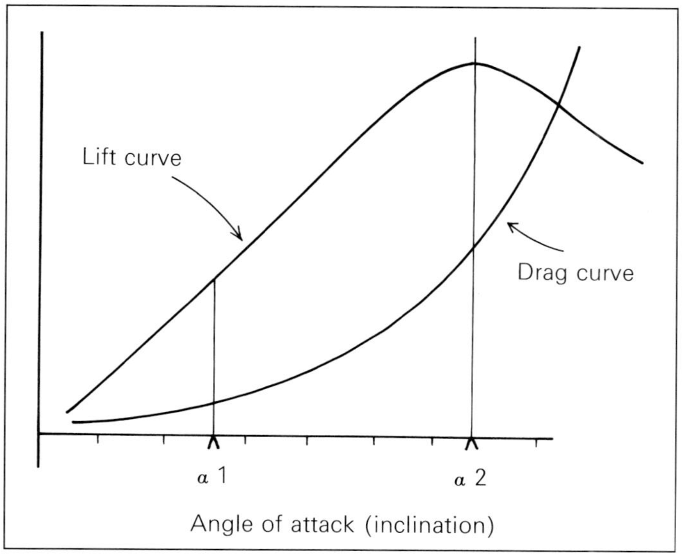

Fig 3.2 Variation of lift and drag with angle of attack

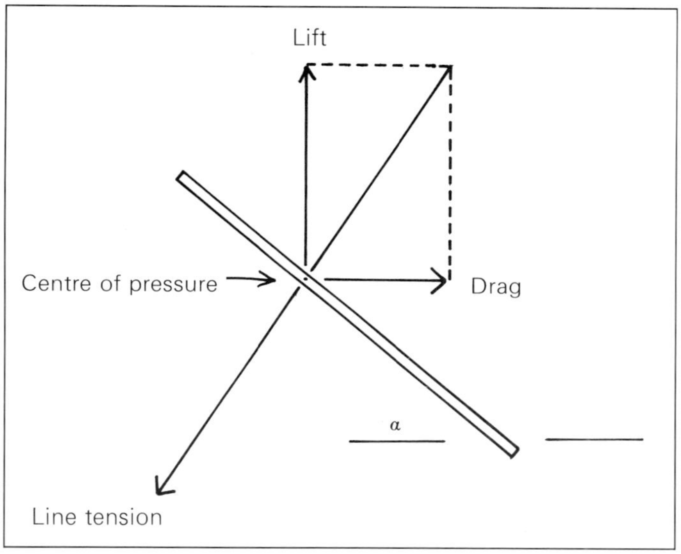

Fig 3.3 Forces balanced at the centre of pressure

centre of pressure. From a more detailed study of aerodynamics, we also find that the position of the centre of pressure and the angle of attack are interrelated. Any change in the position of the centre of pressure results in a change of the angle of attack, and vice-versa. Thus, by controlling the position of the towing point, the point of attachment of the flying line, we can control position of the centre of pressure and therefore both the angle of attack and the relative values of lift and drag.

It is, however, uncommon for the flying line to be attached directly to the kite. More often it is fixed via two or three intermediate lines collectively described as the 'bridle'. A bridle attached to the kite at two points, one below the other, is described as 'two leg'; one attached at three points is 'three leg', and so on (Fig 3.5).

In very light winds, to generate sufficient lift it may be necessary to increase the angle of attack, achieved by lowering the towing point, moving it towards the base of the kite. Looking back at Fig 3.1, however, we see that increased lift is only acheived at the expense of increased drag.

As the winds increase, however, we can bring the kite to its maximum elevation (maximum lift to drag ratio) and reduce the angle of attack, by moving the towing point towards the tip (Fig 3.4).

A word of caution here though. Moving the towing point up and down the bridle not only affects the angle of attack, but also stability. Too high a towing point may cause the kite to oscillate from side to side, like a pendulum, occasionally tipping over. A low towing point may produce a distinct wobble or twitching, produced by drag effects, or cause the kite to perform large circular motions, in gusty conditions, or indeed not to lift at all. The final position of the towing point, producing the 'best' performance, is consequently a compromise between all the forces affecting lift, drag and stability. So when you are out flying your kite, do not be afraid to bring it down to re-adjust the bridle to achieve maximum performance with changing wind conditions

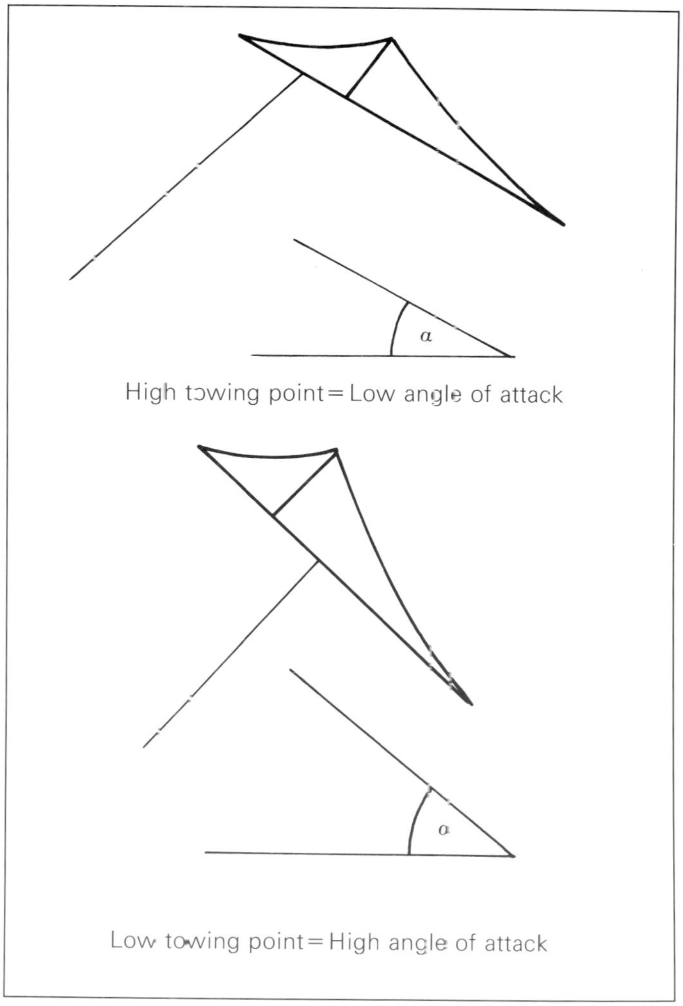

Fig 3.4 Changing the position of the towing point changes the angle of attack

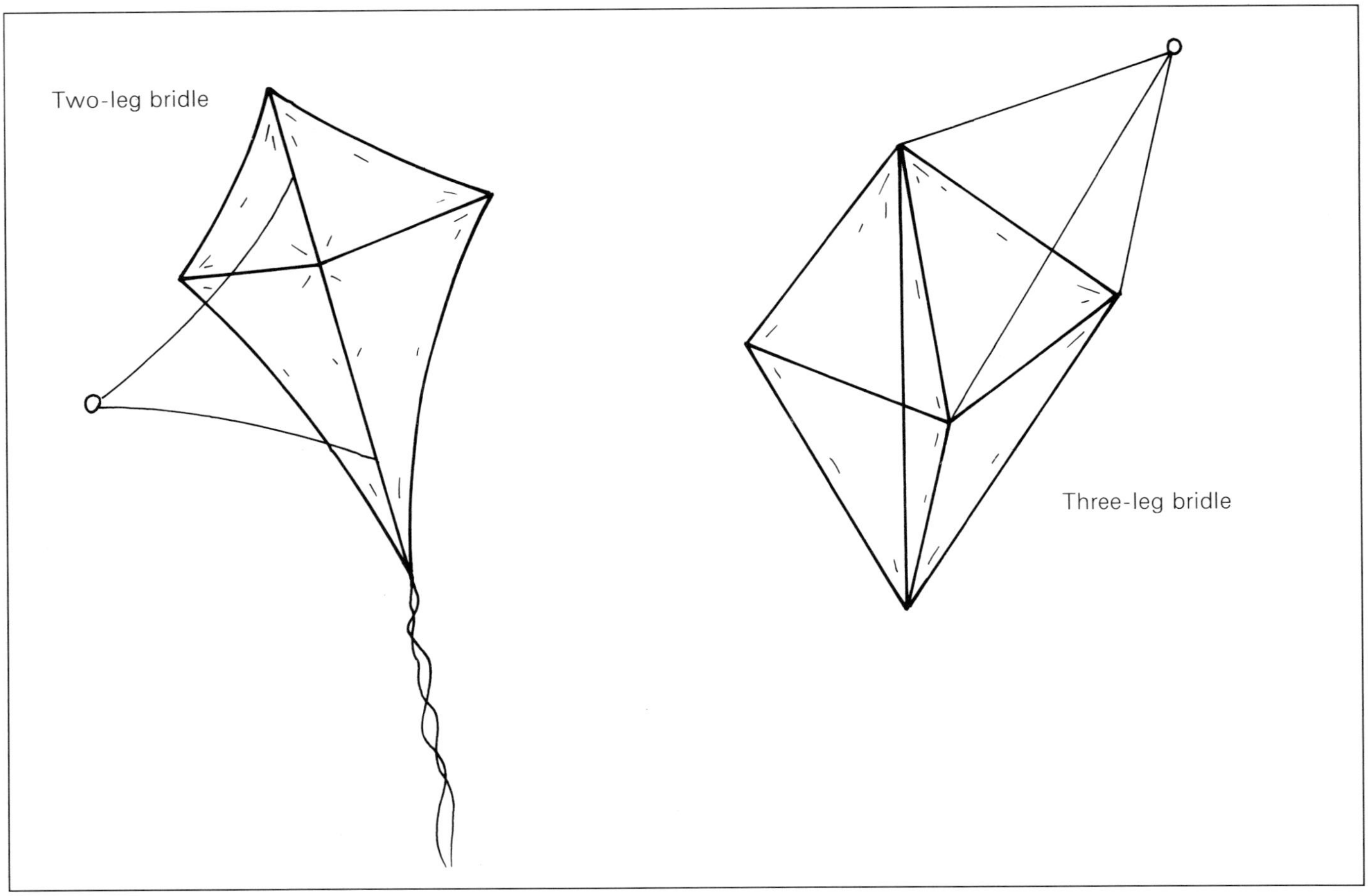

Fig 3.5 Two and three-leg bridles

PREPARING TO FLY

There are a few simple checks which are always worthwhile making before you attempt to fly a newly-made kite.

Firstly, make sure that all your knots are good and tight. If any seem insecure add a *small* spot of glue or, perhaps better still, tie another. Also check your kite for balance. Hold the kite at towing ring: is it too heavy on one side (Fig 3.6)?

Go fly your kite

Although novice fliers sometimes believe that kites need a good stiff breeze to get them into the air, most are actually designed for fairly light conditions, just strong enough to produce a rustle in the trees or a gentle swaying of the lighter branches. You can, of course, use all sorts of natural signs, such as smoke rising or grass swaying, to gauge the actual wind speed, but a simpler way of judging the wind for kiteflying is this: if you can feel the wind on your face, it is strong enough for lighter kites; if the wind is difficult and uncomfortable to stand in, it is too strong for any kite.

Safety must also be considered carefully: not only your own safety but that of people around you, so choose the place to fly your kites with care. Open moorland or wide flat beaches are the safest and best places to fly, but if you live in a town, miles from the sea, moorlands and beaches are understandably hard to find. Instead, look for a good sized playing field, relatively free of trees and a fair distance from roads, telephone and power cables.

Assisted launch

Most beginners start with the assisted launch. Tie the line to the towing point and unwind about 5–6 metres (15–20 feet) of line. Lightly take hold of the line in your stronger hand and ask your helper to hold the kite into the wind. When you feel a gust of wind, signal them to let go of the kite and, as it begins to rise, gradually pay out the line.

Single-handed launch

This is a more expert approach. Attach the line at the towing point and unwind about 4–5 metres (12–15 feet). Hold the line in your stronger hand, the kite in the other. When you feel a gust, drop the kite into the wind, tugging gently on the line. As it rises, gradually pay out more line.

Winch launch

The winch launch is usually the second stage of the first two launches. In light breezes, you may find that as you pay out the line it starts to slacken and the kite starts to fall, possibly turning out of the wind as it does so. If this starts to happen, give the line a good tug then, as the kite starts to rise again, pay out more line trying to maintain tension. You may have to do this several times to lift the kite into stronger air currents.

Fig 3.6 Hold the kite by the towing point and check that it is balanced

Long launch

In very light ground conditions when none of the other launches works, a long launch is the only remaining option. It is also the one and only occasion when you should run with your kite.

With the line attached to the towing point, set the kite in position or ask your helper to hold it 15–20 metres (40–60 feet) down wind. With both hands on the reel, tension the line, giving it a sustained tug, to lift the kite into the air. If you have to run at this stage, do so steadily, keeping control of the kite, and remain facing it as much as you can. As the kite rises into stronger air currents, continue with the winch launch.

Landing

Some people find landing a kite difficult, but, like launching, with the right technique and some practice it does come easier. What you are aiming to do is to bring the kite safely to the ground without damaging it and without causing any danger to people or property around you.

If the line is relatively slack, it should be possible to bring the kite in directly by winding the line slowly and carefully around the handle, keeping control of the kite as you do so.

If the line is quite taut and you are unable to effectively control the kite with one hand, you are clearly going to need the help of an assistant. Ask him or her to take control, gradually bringing down the kite arm over arm, as you wind the line on to the handle or reel.

CHAPTER FOUR

paperfold kites

To start you off, here is a selection of paperfold kites with a simple construction.

All four designs prefer sails made from a slightly stiffer paper, such as Kraft, or *Tyvek* 10, although in a group kitemaking session 80 gsm ($2\frac{1}{2}$ oz) copier or bond is adequate.

Also, remember that they are all quite fragile and should only be flown in relatively light winds.

WIZARD

Probably the simplest kite design ever developed, for those days when the wind is so light nothing else will fly.

Sail : A3 sheet of paper, *Tyvek* 10 or very light card ($16\frac{1}{2}$ inches × $11\frac{5}{8}$ inches)

Mark and cut out the sheet of paper as indicated in Fig 4.1, trim the corners and cut along the semicircular lines on each side.

Carefully fold the sail along the lines AB, CD, folding the outer triangular 'wings' underneath the central section, rather than vice versa (Fig 4.2) since folding this way will help to retain some stiffness in the semicircular rudders.

Reinforce the wing tips with some cellulose/PVC tape and punch holes on each side to accept the bridle, which, after tying, should be about 1.5 metres (5 feet) long. Finally, tie an overhand loop at the centre of the bridle line and attach the flying line (Fig 4.3).

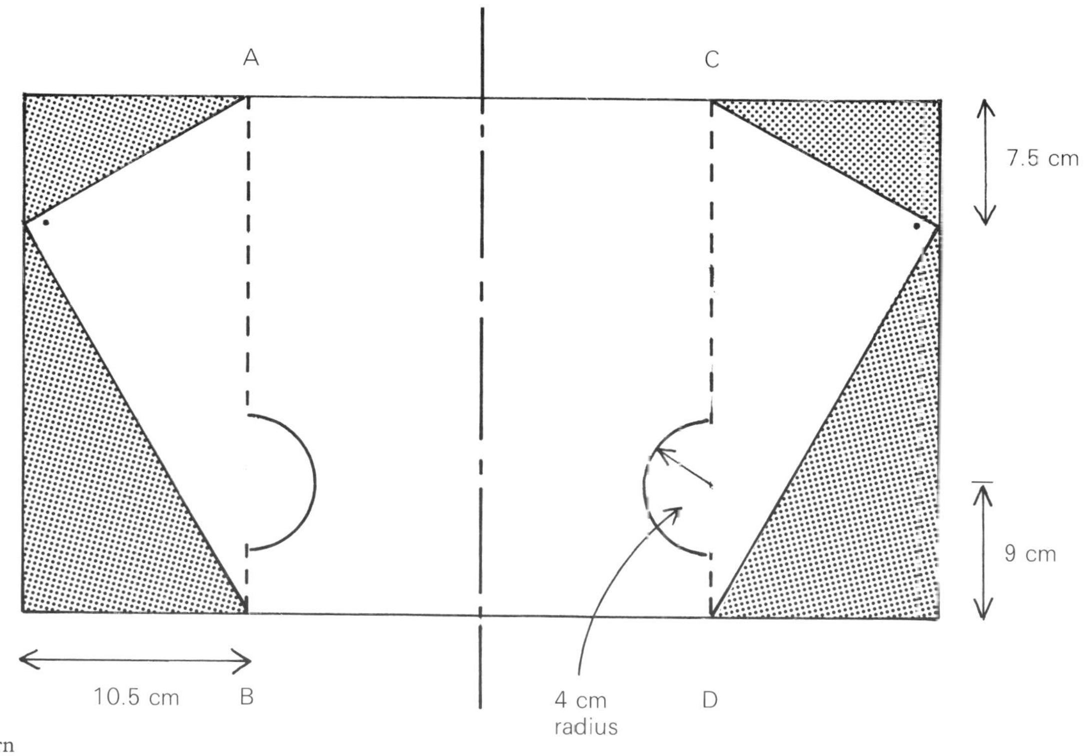

Fig 4.1 Wizard Pattern

Fig 4.2 Fold the wings under the central section

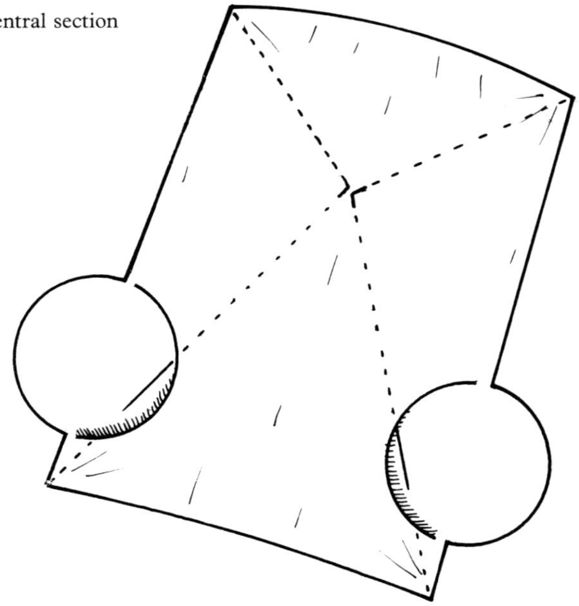

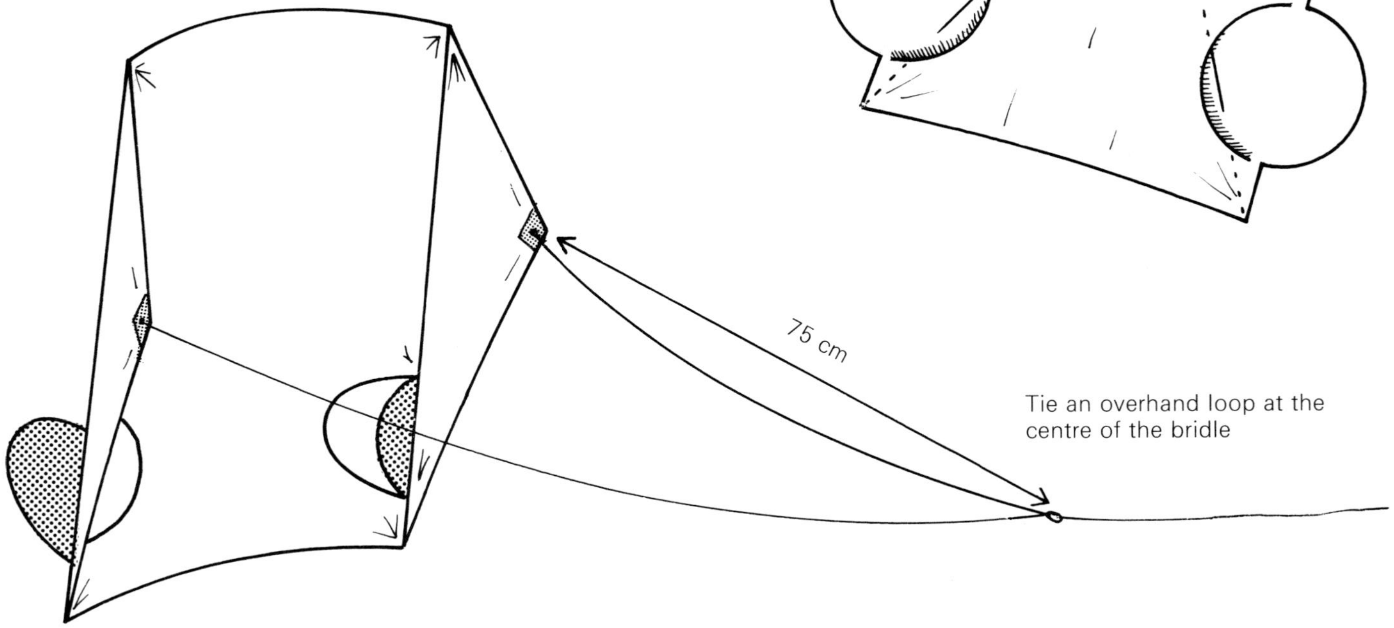

Fig 4.3 Wizard complete

DIAMANTE (PAPERFOLD DIAMOND)

Sail : A3 sheet of paper or *Tyvek* 10 ($16\frac{1}{2}$ inches × $11\frac{5}{8}$ inches)
Spars : Drinking straw or light bamboo skewer 28 cm (11 inches) long

Fold the paper in half to create a central reference line. Mark two further lines AB, A′B′, 1 cm ($\frac{3}{8}$ inch) each side of this line and, still folded, cut out the shape indicated in Fig 4.4. Fold the kite back along the lines AB, A^1B^1, and glue within the fold to create a wide 'T' section.

Make the triangular keel by gluing the two smaller triangles of paper each side of the central fold (Fig 4.5). Reinforce the tip and punch a hole to accept the flying line.

The cross spar is made from a drinking straw fitted to the back of the kite and taped at 4–6 points along its length (Fig 4.6). If your straws are not long enough, it is easy to join them by making a simple ferrule. Cut a length of straw about 10 cm (4 inches) and slit along its length, then, with some adhesive on its surface, slide it into the ends of two additional straws. To achieve proper balance, however, you should ensure that the ferrule and join are centrally placed across the sail.

Reinforce the tip of the keel and punch a hole for the flying line then, finally, add a light ribbon tail to the bottom point (Fig 4.7).

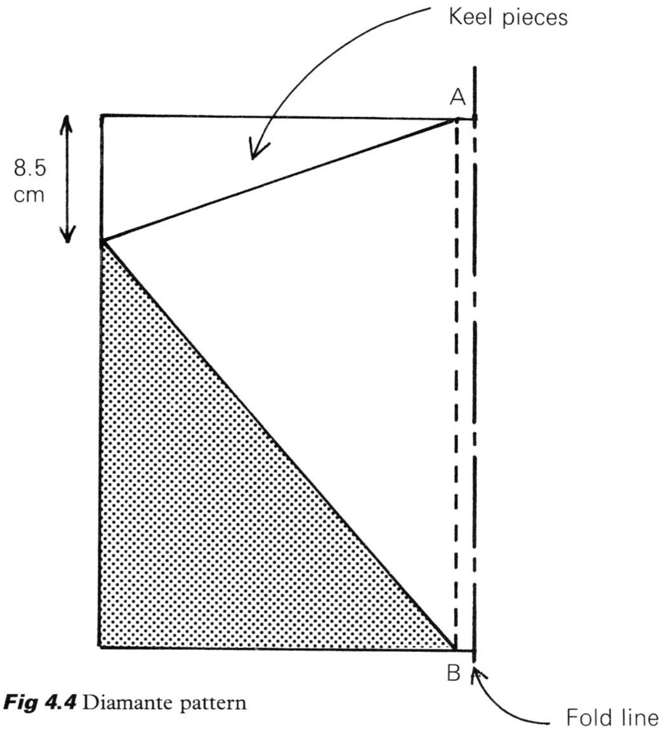

Fig 4.4 Diamante pattern

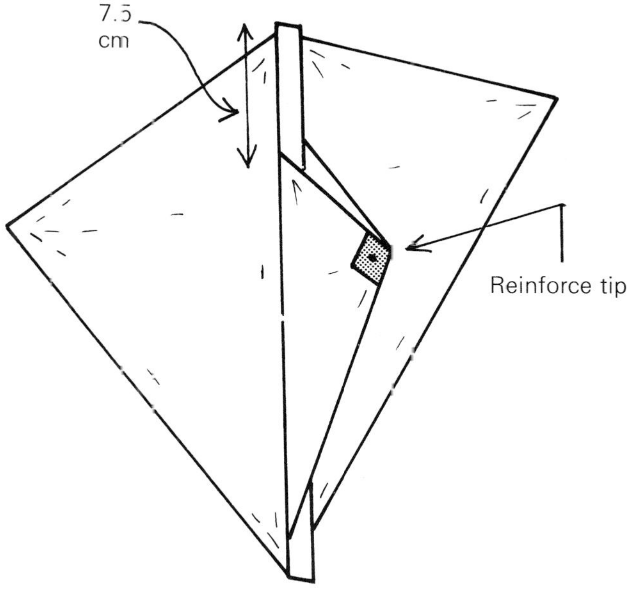

Fig 4.5 Tape the keels in place each side of the central fold

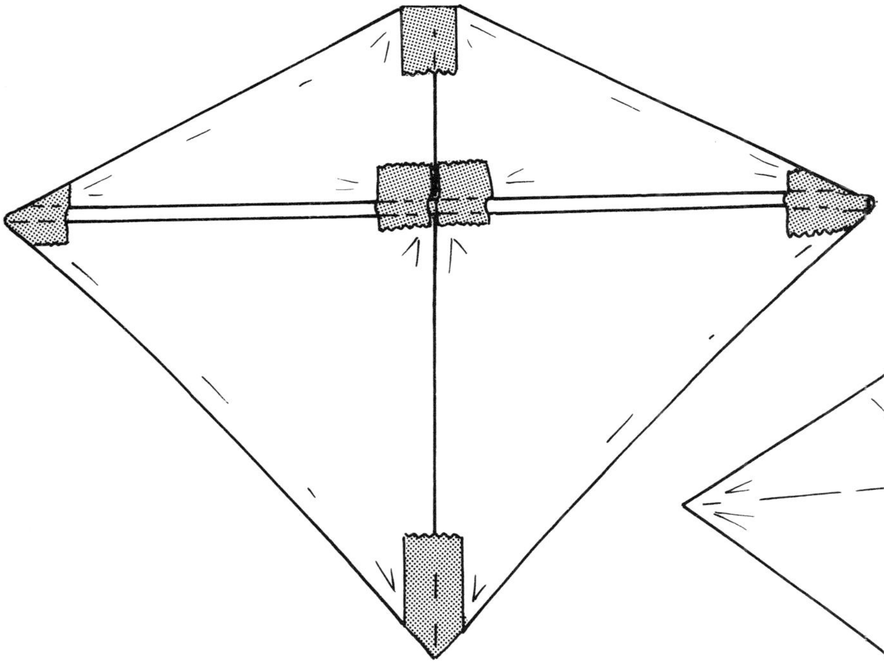

Fig 4.6 Tape the spar to the rear

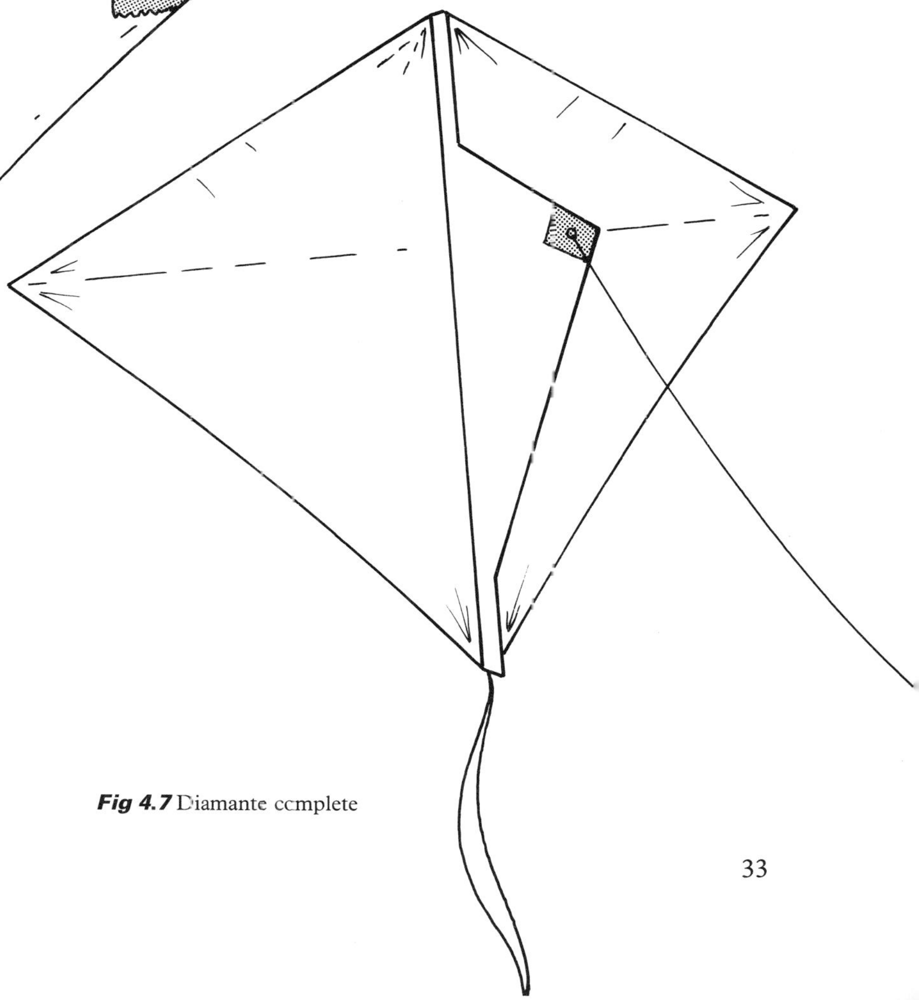

Fig 4.7 Diamante complete

TIGER DELTA

Sail : A3 sheet of paper or *Tyvek* 10 ($16\frac{1}{2}$ inches × $11\frac{5}{8}$ inches)
Spars : Drinking straw or light bamboo skewer 24 cm ($9\frac{1}{2}$ inches) long

Fold the paper in half, then mark and cut out the shape (Fig 4.8). Refold the sail back along the lines AB to create a sort of 'T' section, and glue the inner faces to make the forward keel (Fig 4.9). You can also add further reinforcement by running a length of tape along the keel fold at the back of the sail.

Tape the spar at the back of the kite at the points X–X¹ only (Fig 4.10). The spar will seem short but is fitted such that the wings form a dihedral (swept back) angle.

Reinforce the tip of the keel with some tape, punch a hole to accept the flying line and finally add a long (2 metres – 7 foot) ribbon tail made from crepe paper to the base of the keel (Fig 4.11).

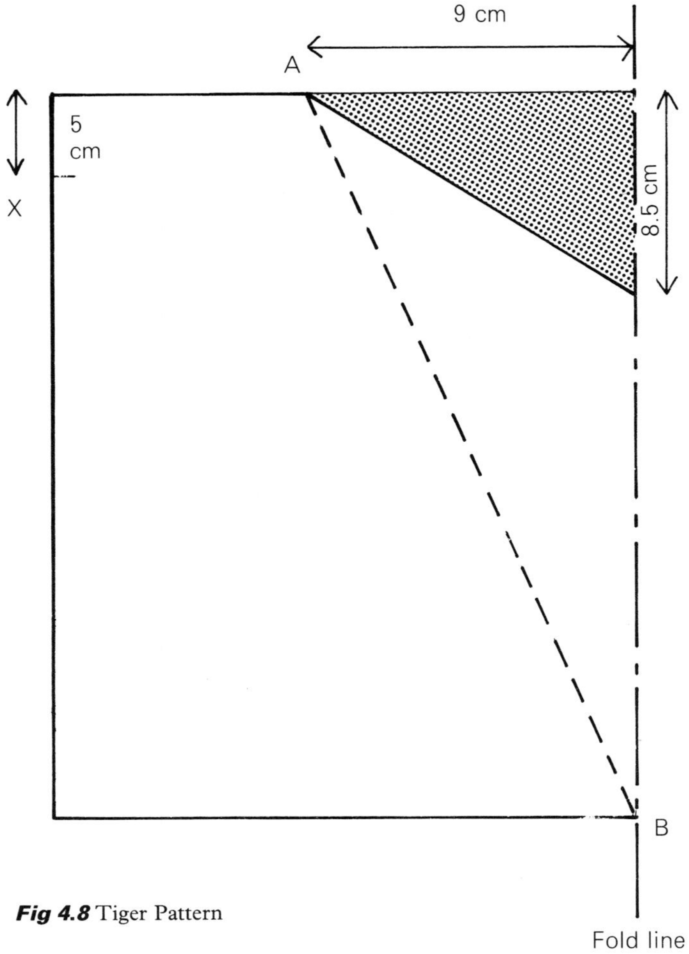

Fig 4.8 Tiger Pattern

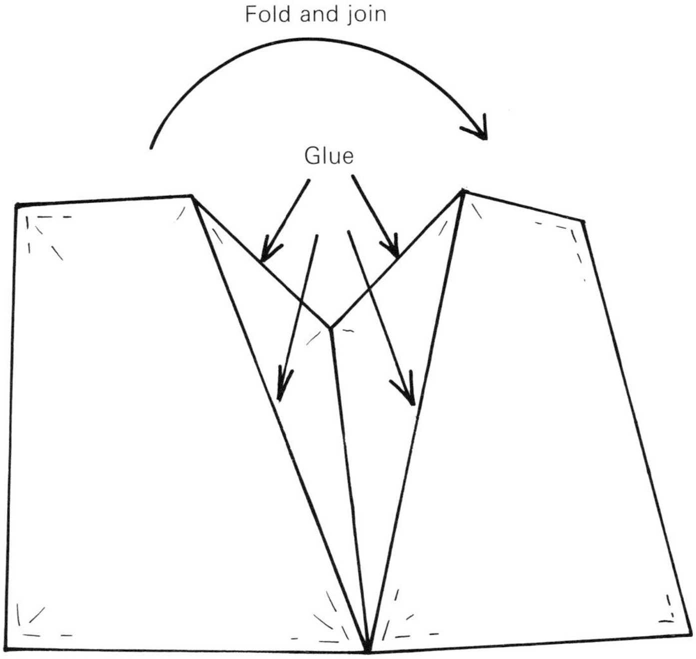

Fig 4.9 Glue both sides within the keel fold

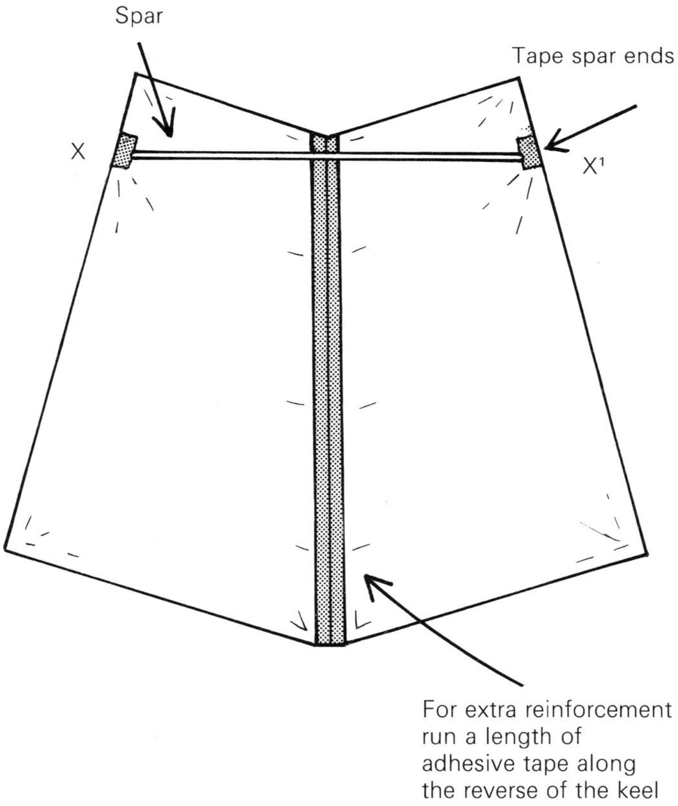

Fig 4.10 Tape the spar to the rear of the sail

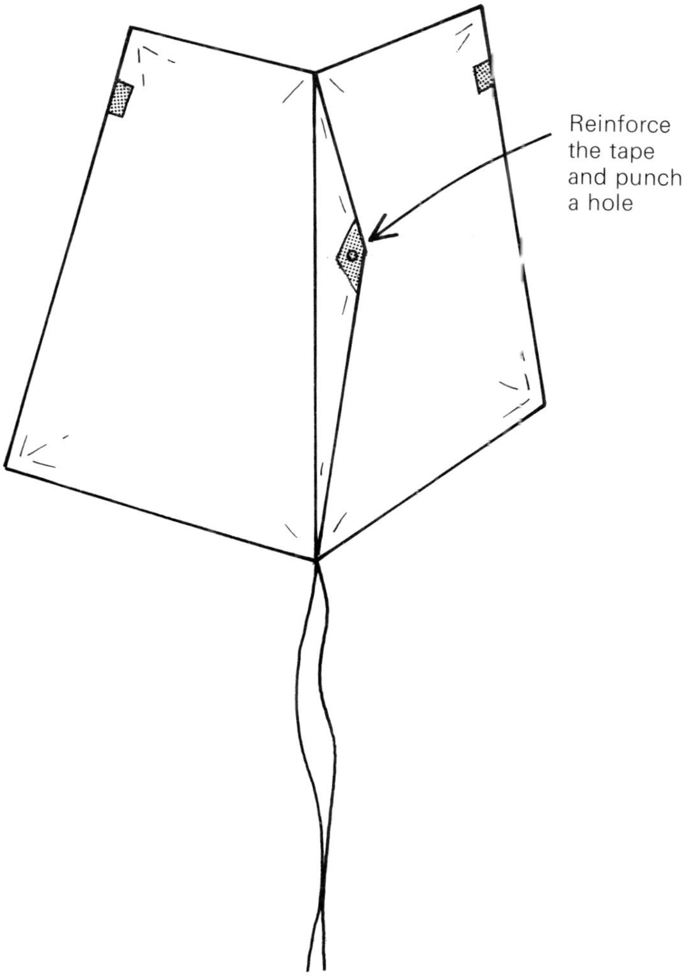

Fig 4.11 Reinforce the keel tip and add a long tail

SKIPPER

Sail : A3 sheet of paper or *Tyvek* 10 ($16\frac{1}{2}$ inches × $11\frac{5}{8}$ inches)
Spars : Drinking straw or light bamboo skewer 28 cm (11 inches) long

Fold the sheet of paper in half, carefully matching the corners, to create a central reference line. Then, with the paper still folded, mark and cut out the pattern in Fig 4.12. Next, fold the paper back along the lines AB to create a central 'V' shaped box (Fig 4.13).

Tape the spar to the rear of the sail at three or four points to form the triangular box front (Fig 4.14).

Reinforce the front of the triangular box 8 cm ($3\frac{1}{4}$ inches) from the tip and punch a hole to accept the flying line, tied direct. Finally, add two long crepe paper tails to the bottom points (Fig 4.15).

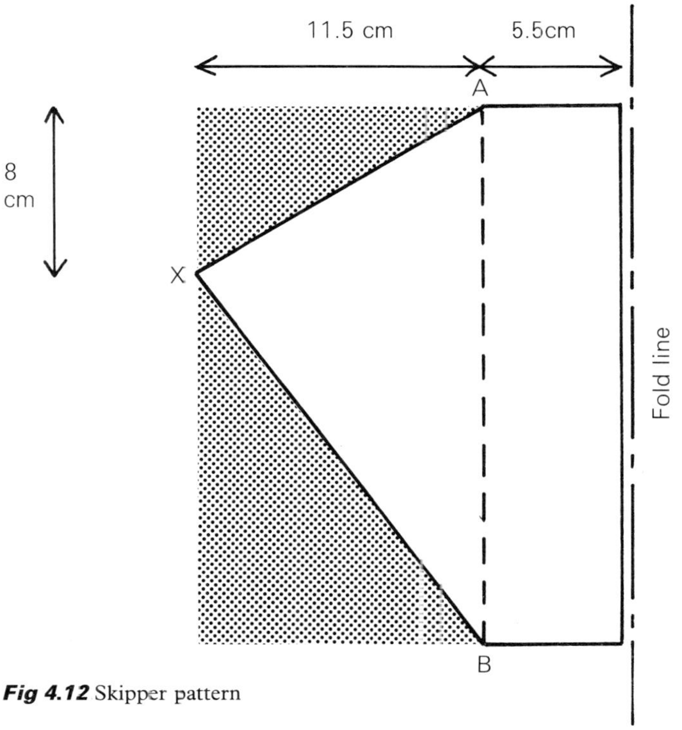

Fig 4.12 Skipper pattern

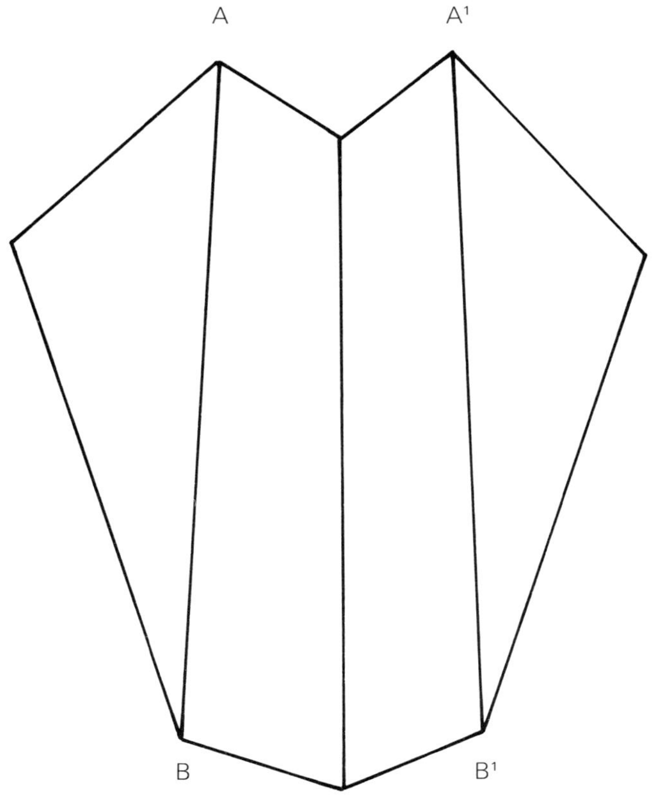

Fig 4.13 'V' box shape

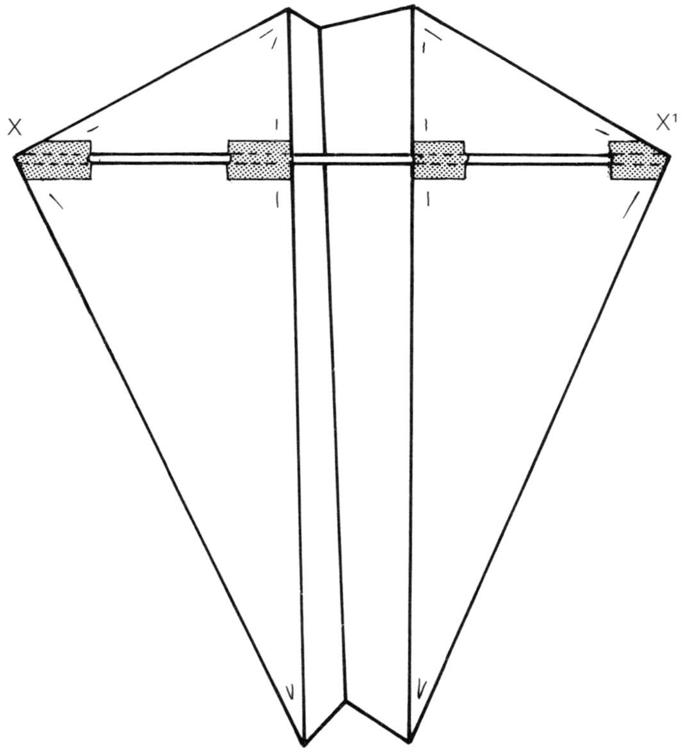

Fig 4.14 Tape the spar to the reverse of the sail

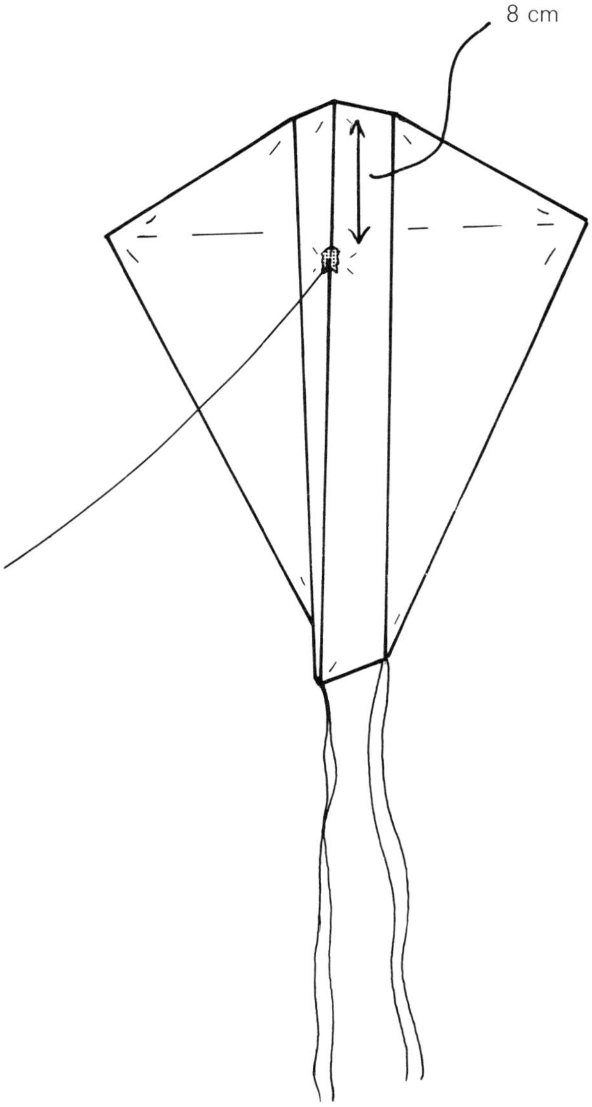

Fig 4.16 Add long crepe paper tails and tie the line to the box front

CHAPTER FIVE

sleds

As with the paperfolds, sleds are great kites for group projects. They are simple to make, and only rarely do they let you down.

VENTED SLED

To maintain stability, sleds do not normally have tails but use a number of other devices, such as rudders, stabilising tubes, or, as in this case, vents.

Sail : Polythene, paper, polyester film or *Tyvek*
Spars : 2 pieces 5 mm ($\frac{3}{16}$ inch) dowel, 58 cm ($22\frac{1}{2}$ inches) long

Cut a piece of sail material roughly 60 cm × 84 cm ($23\frac{1}{2}$ inches × 34 inches), fold it along the centre line, parallel to the shorter side and cut out the pattern Fig 5.1. Cutting in this way will ensure a good degree of symmetry.

Tape the spars in position at perhaps four or five points along their length (Fig 5.2), using a stronger tape at the tips to protect the spars during a crash.

Reinforce and punch holes at the wing tips and attach a bridle 3 metres (10 feet) long. Tie an overhand loop at the centre of the bridle to accept the flying line (Fig 5.3).

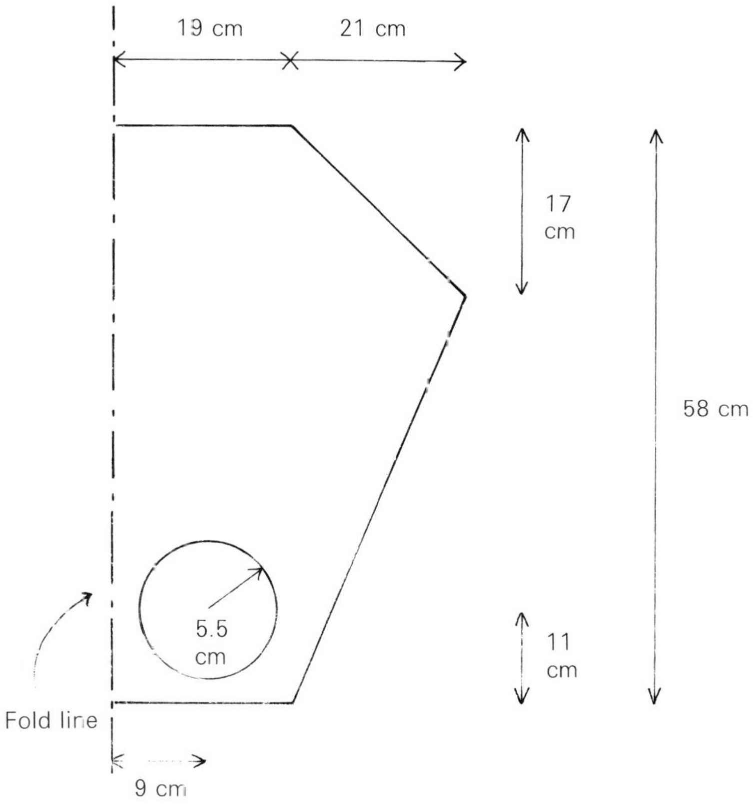

Fig 5.1 Vented sled pattern

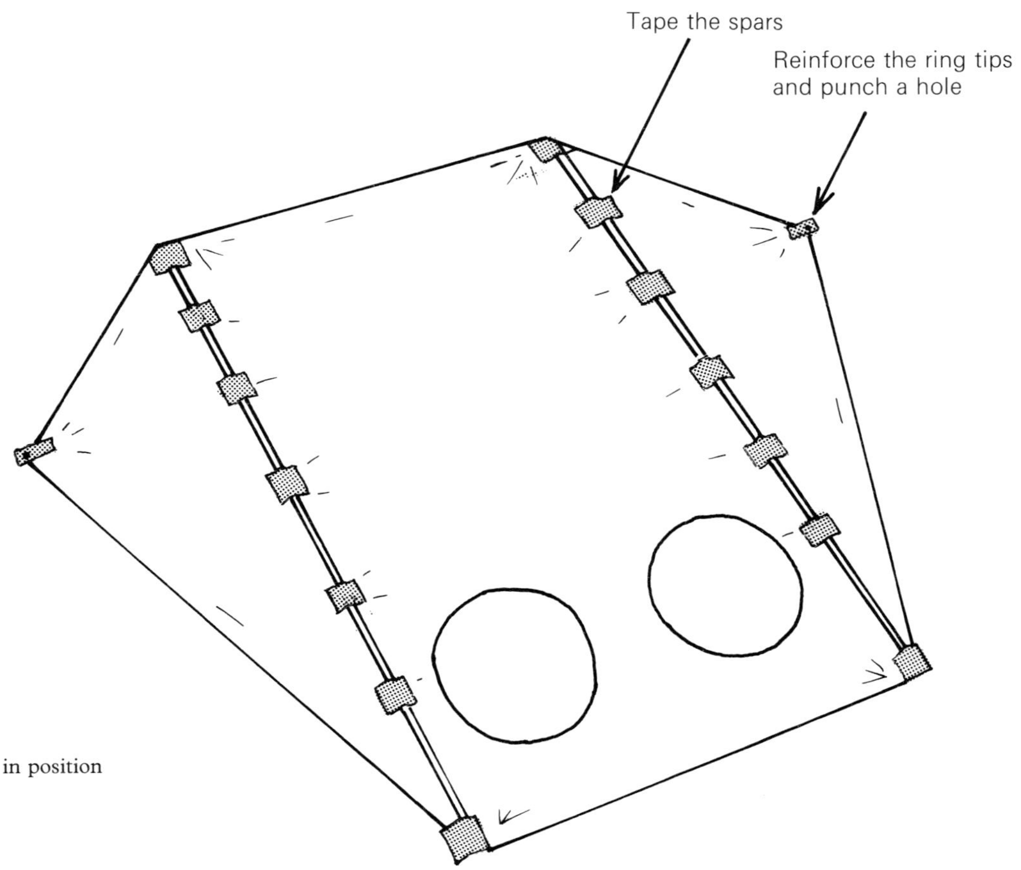

Fig 5.2 Tape the spars in position

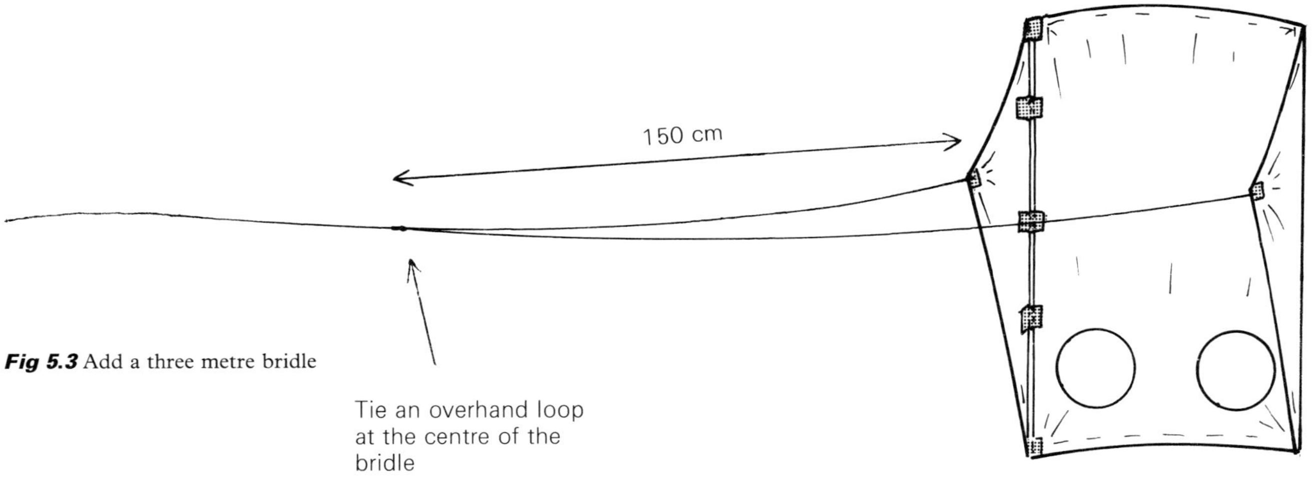

Fig 5.3 Add a three metre bridle

POCKET SLED

This little design is ideal as a first kite for a junior kitemaker or as a fun lightweight for the adult traveller.

Sail : Polythene, wrapping paper, *Tyvek*, Polyester film

Like the vented sled, to achieve good symmetry the sail is best cut from a piece of material 64 cm × 52 cm (25 inches × 20 inches) folded along the centre. Mark and cut the sail pattern (Fig 5.4a).

To make the stabilising 'tubes', cut out two pieces of material (Fig 5.4b) and tape them to the sail, matching the lines AB–CD on each half of the main sail (Fig 5.5).

Reinforce and punch holes at the wing tips and attach the bridle, which after tying should be 2.5 metres (9 feet) (Fig 5.6). Lastly, tie an overhand loop at the centre of the bridle to accept the flying line.

Fig 5.4a Pocket sled pattern

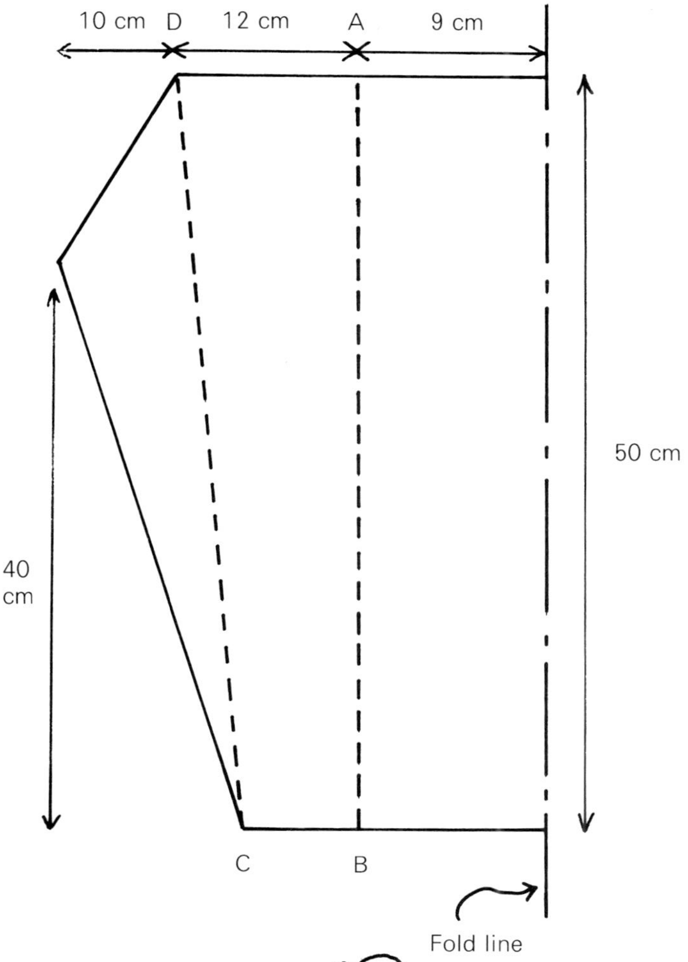

Fig 5.4b Tubes pattern

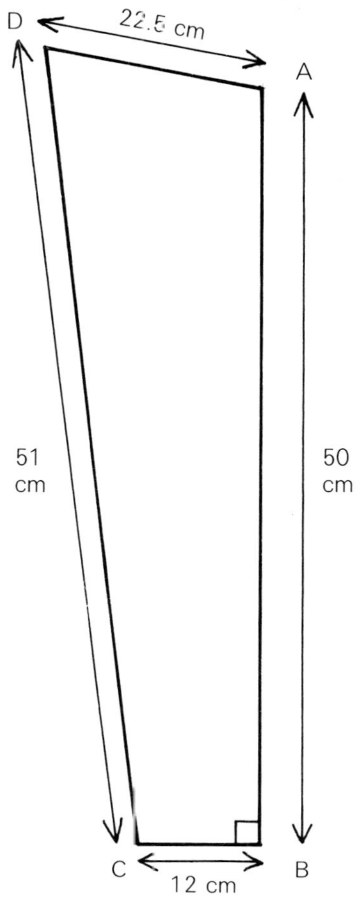

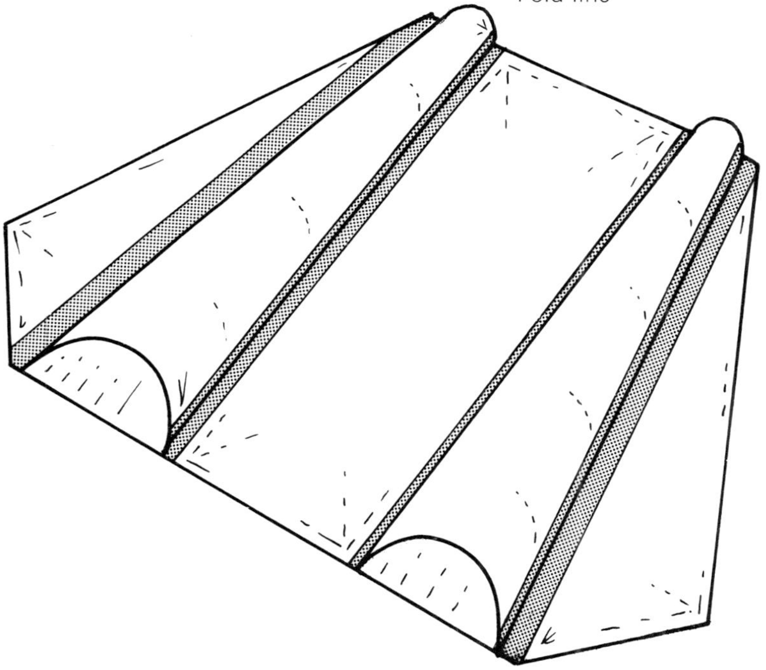

Fig 5.5 Tape the tubes to the rear of the sail matching the lines AB and BC on the sail

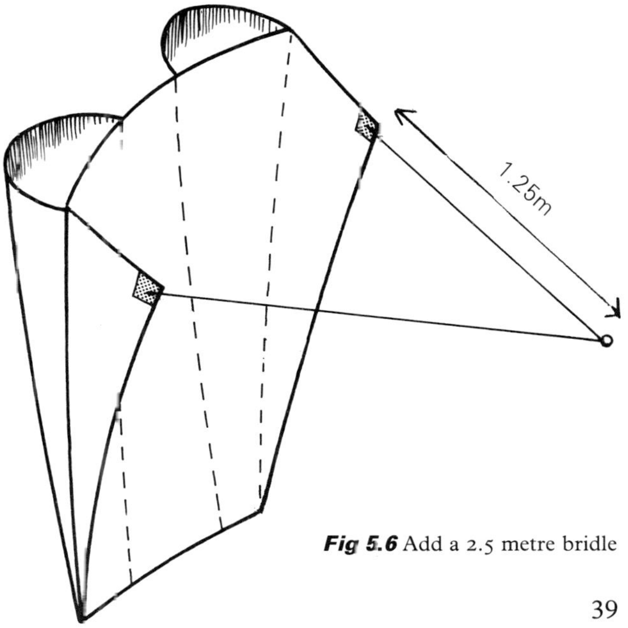

Fig 5.6 Add a 2.5 metre bridle

HYBRID

This is another novel 'soft kite', a little more difficult than the simple 'Pocket' sled but nonetheless, quite satisfying to fly.

Sail : Wrapping paper, *Tyvek*, polyester film, polythene

Cut two pieces of sail material (Fig 5.7) and mark the lines AB and CD on each. Crease and fold both pieces along the lines AB, folding one left and the other right-handed, then tape them together (Fig 5.8a,b).

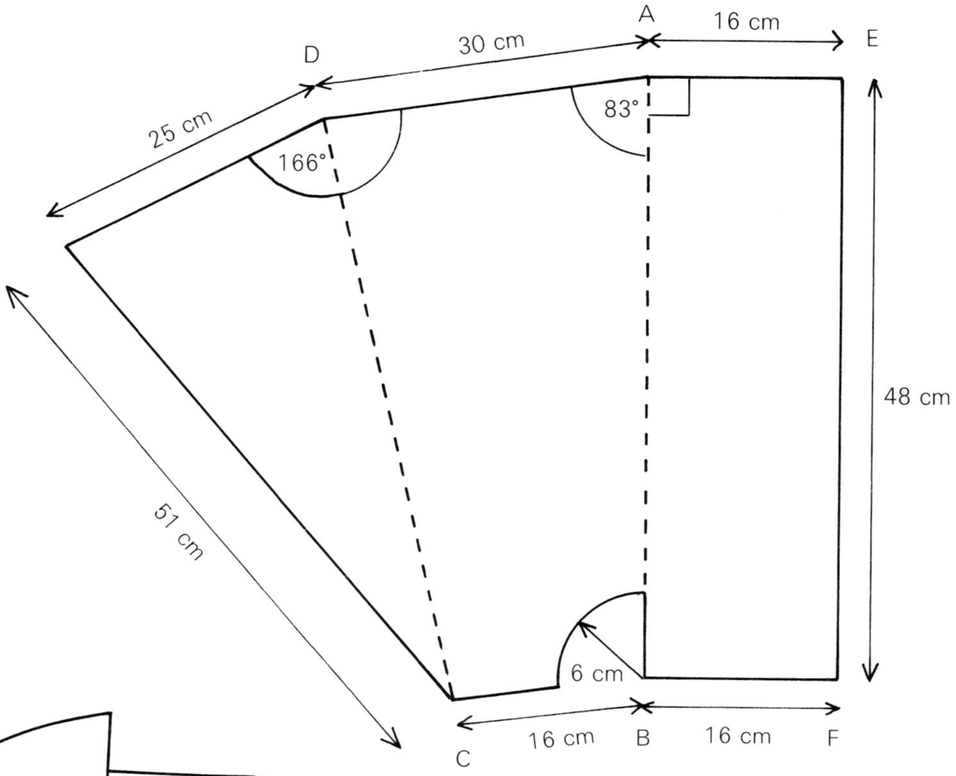

Fig 5.7 Hybrid pattern

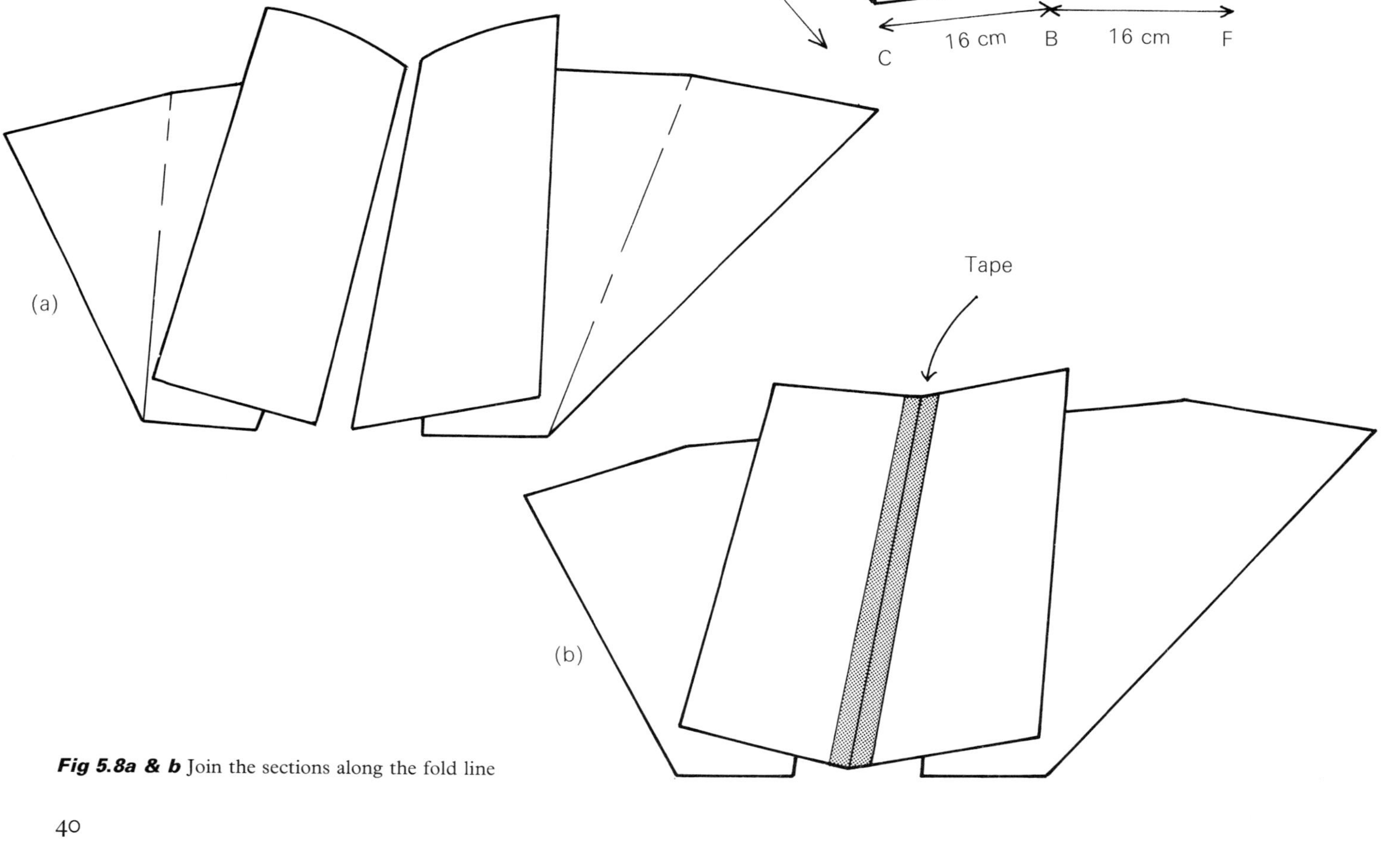

Fig 5.8a & b Join the sections along the fold line

Bring the free edges EF across and tape them along the lines CD to create a tube on each half (Fig 5.9). Finally, tape along the bottom edge to close the tubes (Fig 5.10).

The Hybrid requires a much longer bridle; 4 metres (13 feet) tied to the wing tips as previous designs (Fig 5.11).

Fig 5.9 Fold and tape the loose sections to create two tubes

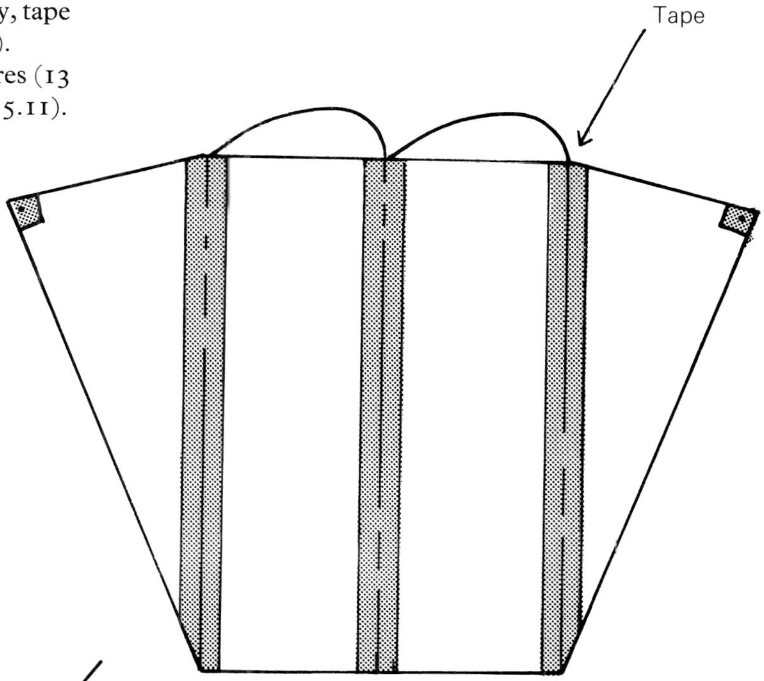

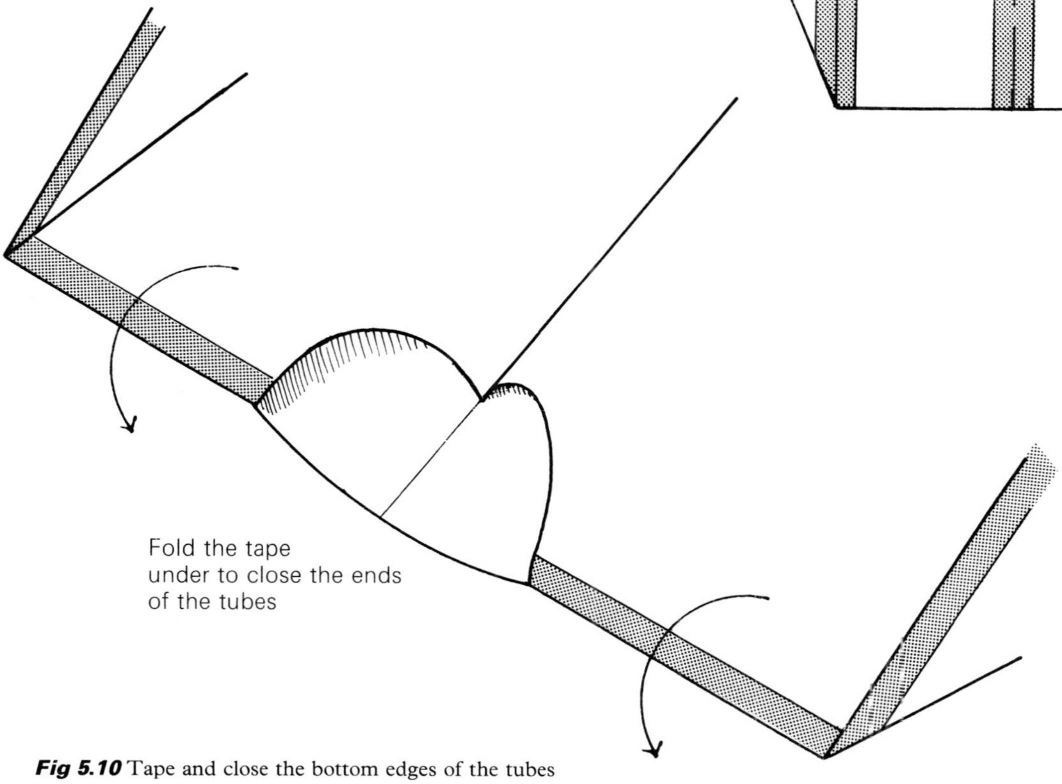

Fig 5.10 Tape and close the bottom edges of the tubes

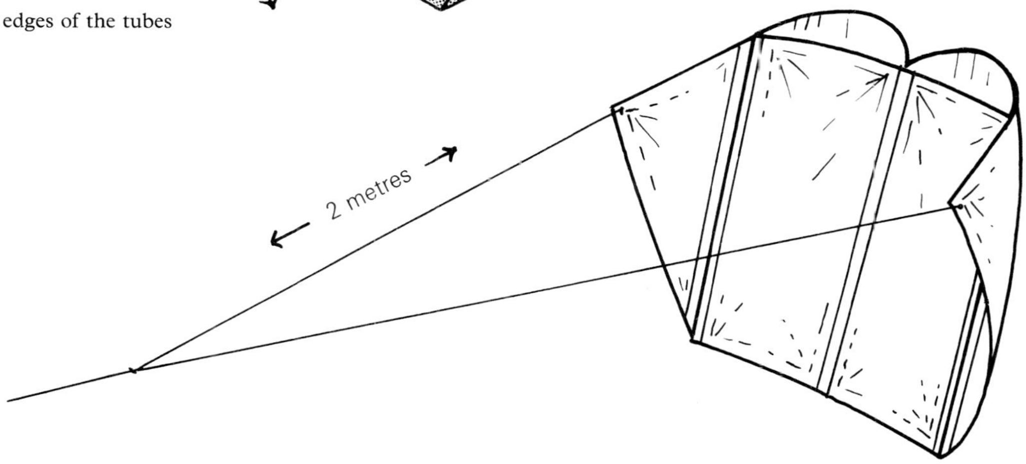

Fig 5.11 Fit a four-metre bridle

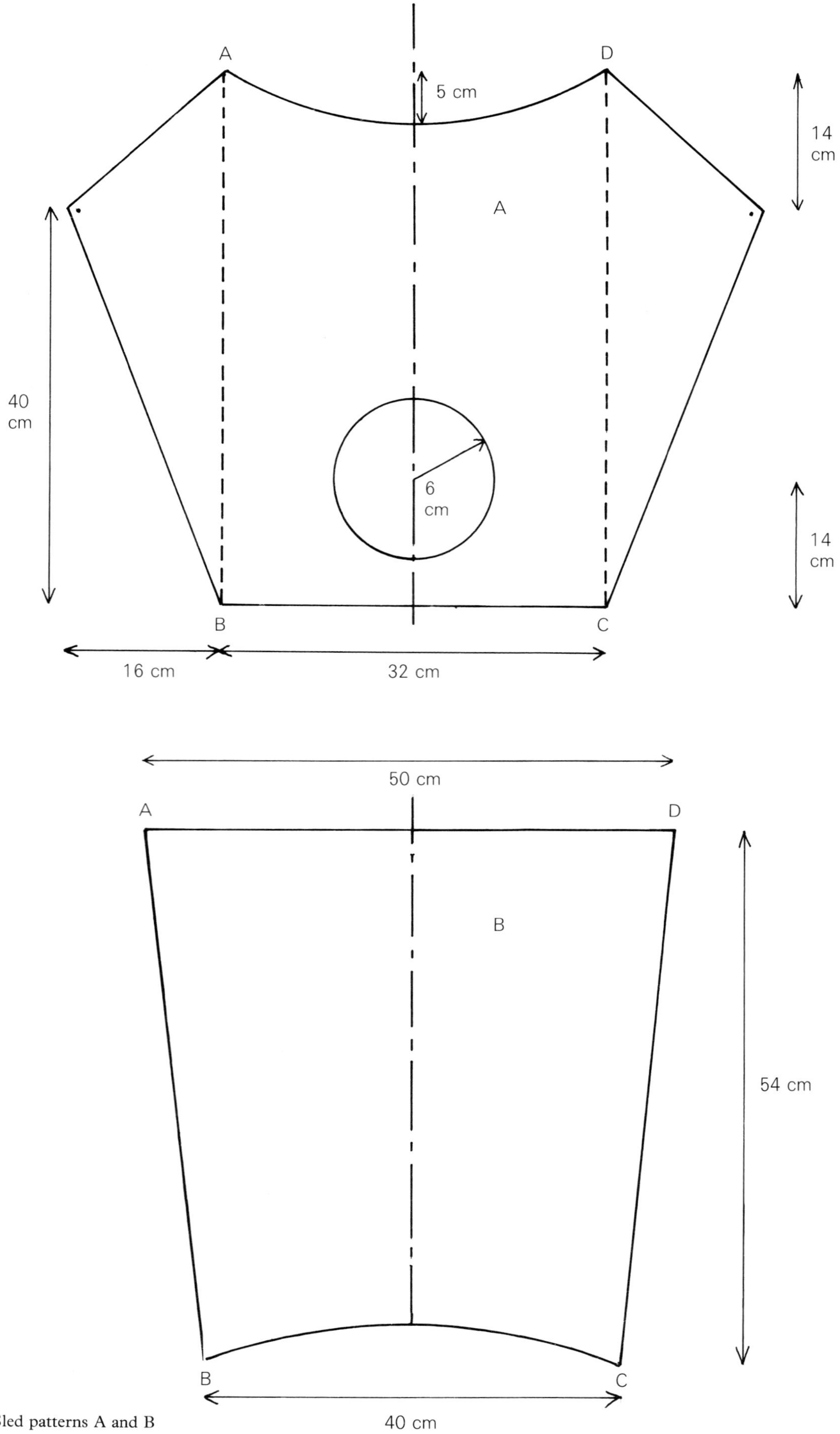

Fig 5.12 Tube Sled patterns A and B

TUBE SLED

The origin of this particular type of sled is unclear, though many attribute it to Takeshi Nishibayashi, an elderly and extremely amiable Japanese kitemaker, who has paid numerous visits to Britain, bringing with him a host of new and amazingly simple ideas for kites.

Sail : Polythene, wrapping paper, *Tyvek*, polyester film

Spars : 2 pieces 5 mm ($\frac{3}{16}$ inch) dowel 54 cm ($21\frac{1}{4}$ inches) long

Cut out two pieces of sail (Fig 5.12a,b) and tape or glue the edges AB and CD of piece A along the corresponding edges of piece B to create the 'tube'.

Although it is much neater to fit the spars on the inside of the tube, it is certainly easier to tape them to the front along the lines AB, CD. Either way, the flying qualities of the kite seem unaffected (Fig 5.13).

Reinforce the wing tips and tie the bridle, which after tying should be 3 metres (10 feet) long. As above, attach the flying line to an overhand loop at the centre of the bridle (Fig 5.14).

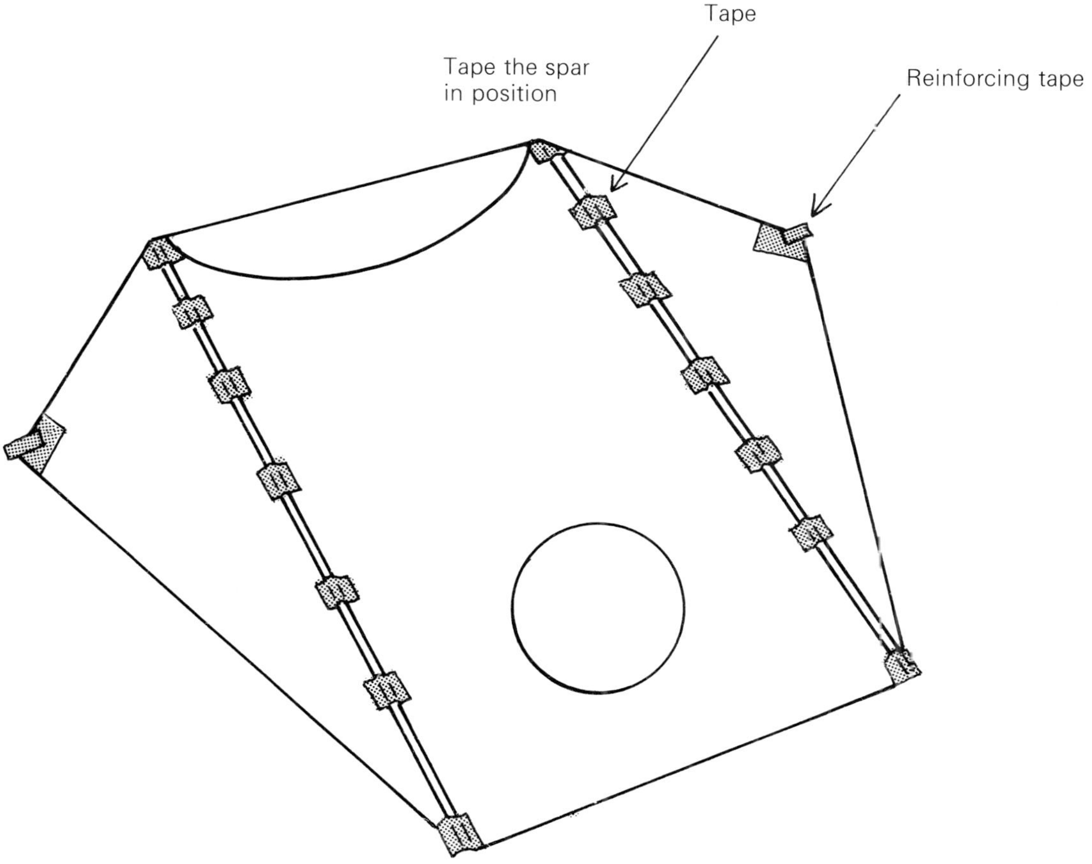

Fig 5.13 Join the two sails and tape the spars in position

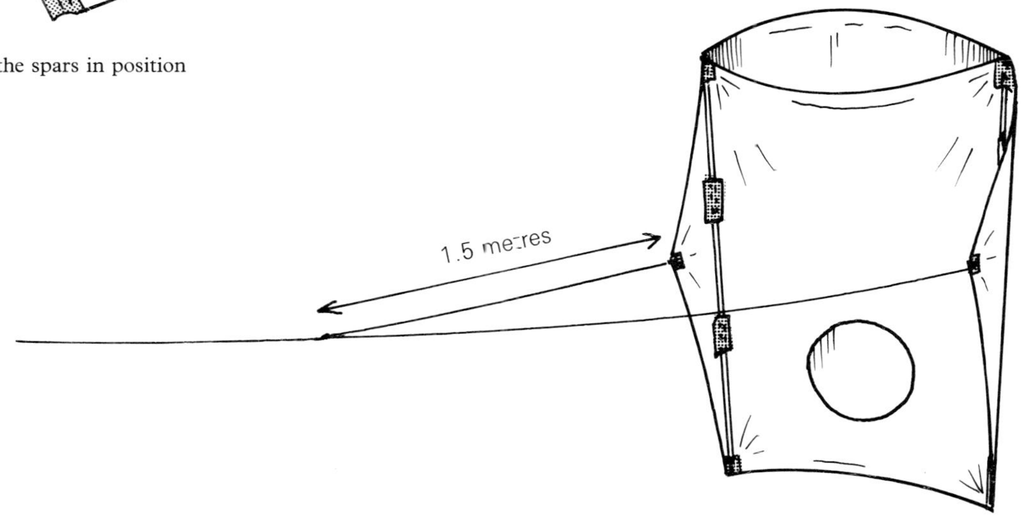

Fig 5.14 Add a three-metre bridle

CHAPTER SIX

delta kites

Unlike many other kites, whose origins go back hundreds of years, deltas have only been flown for about thirty. They derive from the gliding parachute wing developed by Francis Rogallo. Generally they have a triangular wing shape, with four spars: two along the wing edges; one down the middle of the triangle (spine) and the 'spreader bar', loosely fitted across the back of the kite, holding it all in shape.

The wing, or leading edge, spars, as they are known, are not taped to the sail, but are housed in tubes created along the wing edge by folding and gluing an additional narrow flap of sail. If you are using glues, this extra flap should be about three times the diameter of the spars wide, or, if using adhesive tape, twice the diameter should be sufficient (Fig 6.1).

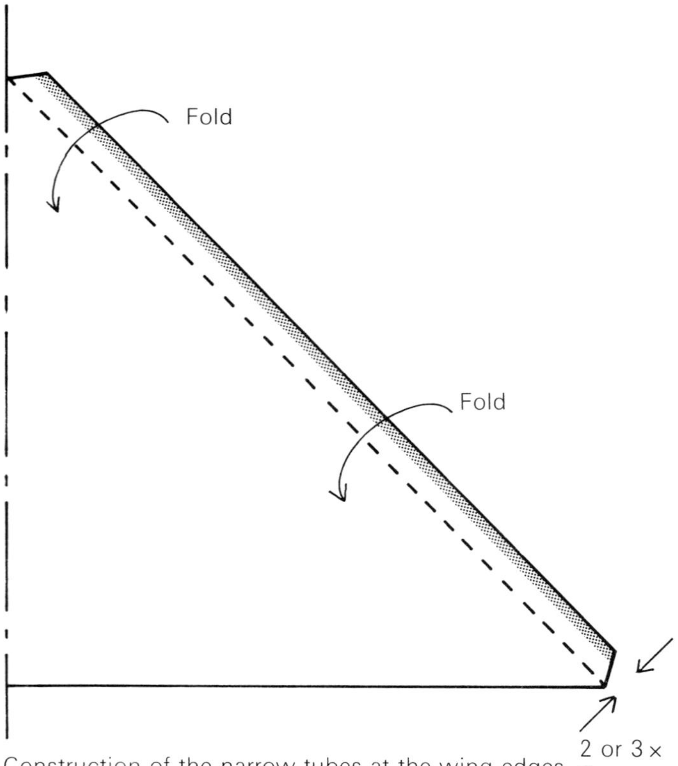

Construction of the narrow tubes at the wing edges

Fig 6.1 Fold the wing flaps over to make the spar tubes

SQUARE DELTA

Although as a rule deltas do have triangular wing shapes, this simple design, with its square sail, is the exception. Also, rather than having a keel, it flies better with a small rudder placed towards the lower end of the spine.

Sail	:	Light paper, *Tyvek*, polythene, polyester film
Spars	:	Spine and leading edges 5 mm ($\frac{3}{16}$ inch) dowel 44 cm ($17\frac{3}{8}$ inches) long; spreader bar 6.3 mm ($\frac{1}{4}$ inch) 48 cm (19 inches) long

Cut out a rectangular piece of material, roughly 45 cm × 55 cm ($17\frac{3}{4}$ inches × $21\frac{1}{2}$ inches). Fold and crease it at the centre, parallel to the shorter edges and cut out the sail shape as a half (Fig 6.2a). Next, cut out a rudder (Fig 6.2b) and reinforce it along the two outside edges.

With the sail still folded, tape or glue the rudder along the centre line, and tape a small ring or punch a hole at its tip (Fig 6.3).

Make spar tubes at the wing edges as described above. Thread the wing spars into these tubes and tape them at the top and bottom. Next, tape the spine along the centre line with extra reinforcing at the tip and base (Fig 6.4).

There are numerous different methods of attaching the spreader bar, and of course any of these may be used with almost any design. Use one of the simplest by attaching small rings or loops of line just slightly larger than the spreader bar diameter, 7 cm from each upper corner. Next, thread an elastic band, or wind a few (folded) layers of adhesive tape, 1 cm ($\frac{3}{8}$ inch) from each end. Finally, thread the spreader bar through the loops at the wing edges (Fig 6.5).

The line is not attached directly, but via a two-leg bridle 95 cm (37 inches) long, one end of which is tied to the spine through the small hole cut in the sail and the other to the rudder tip.

For average conditions the upper bridle leg should be approximately 48 cm (19 inches) (Fig 6.6).

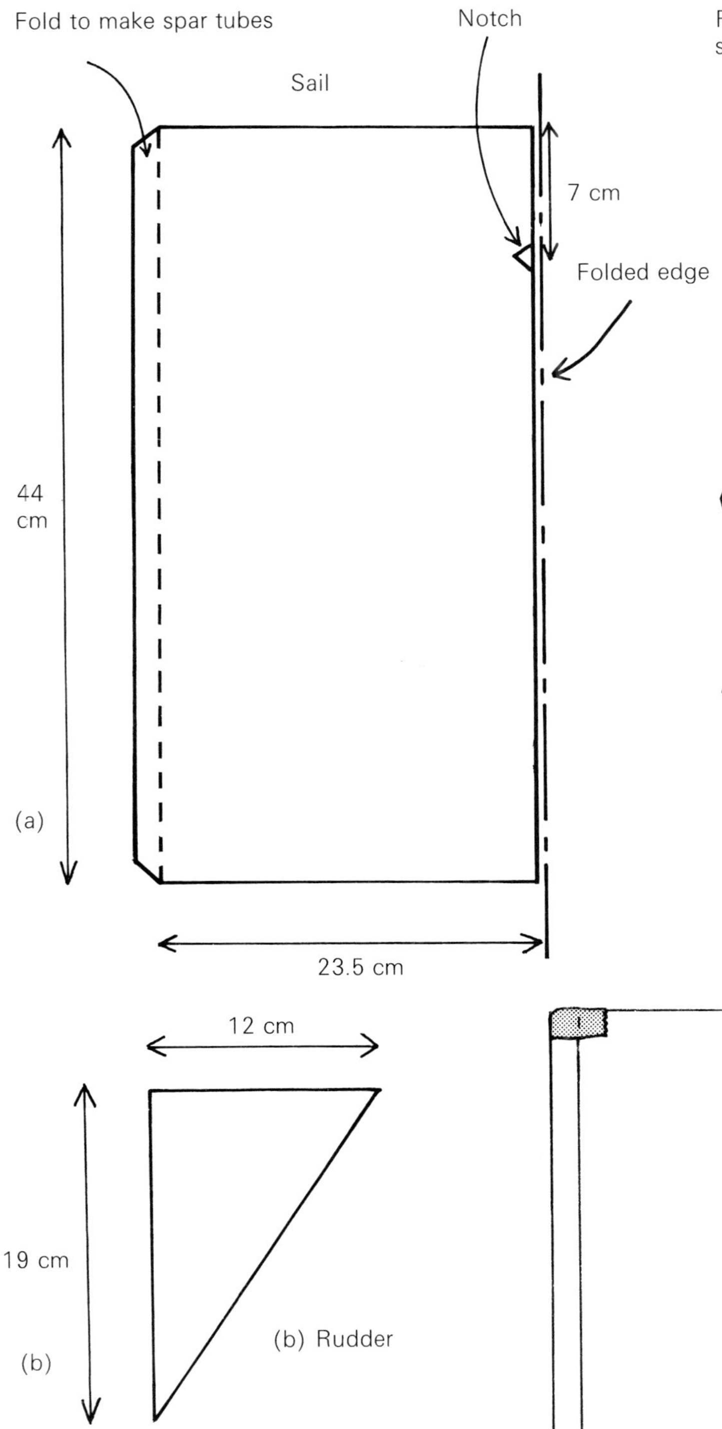

Fig 6.2 Square Delta pattern

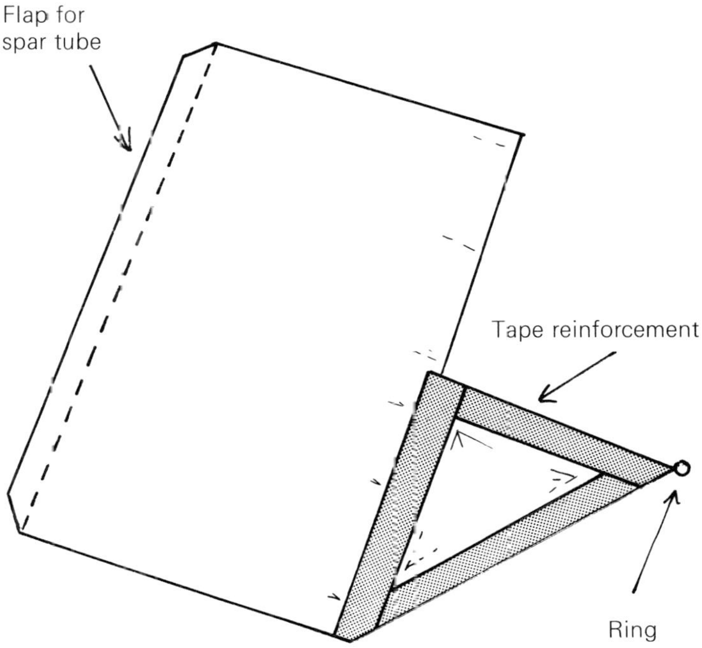

Fig 6.3 Tape the rudder along the fold line

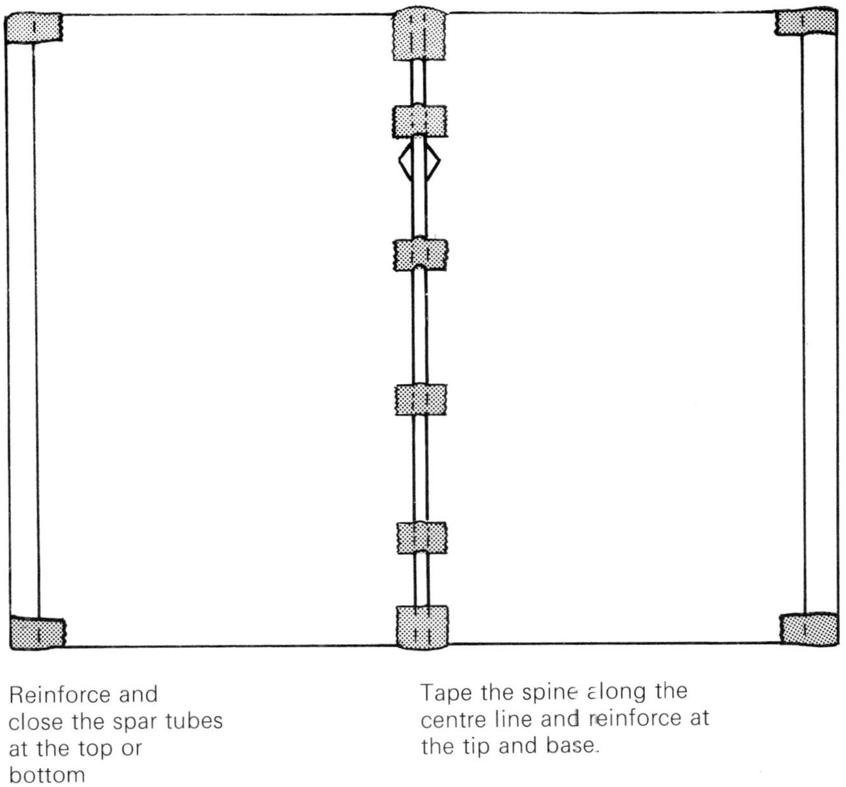

Fig 6.4 Thread the spars along the wing edges and tape the spine in position

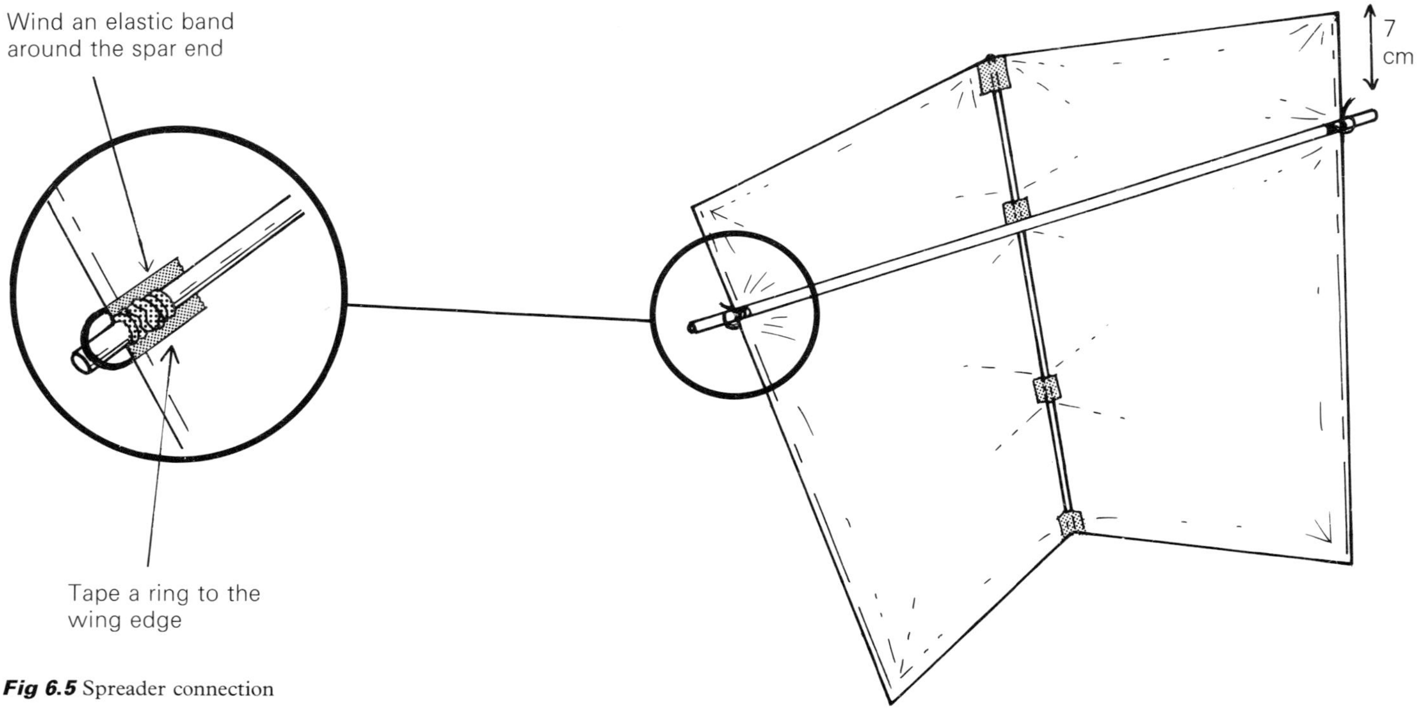

Fig 6.5 Spreader connection

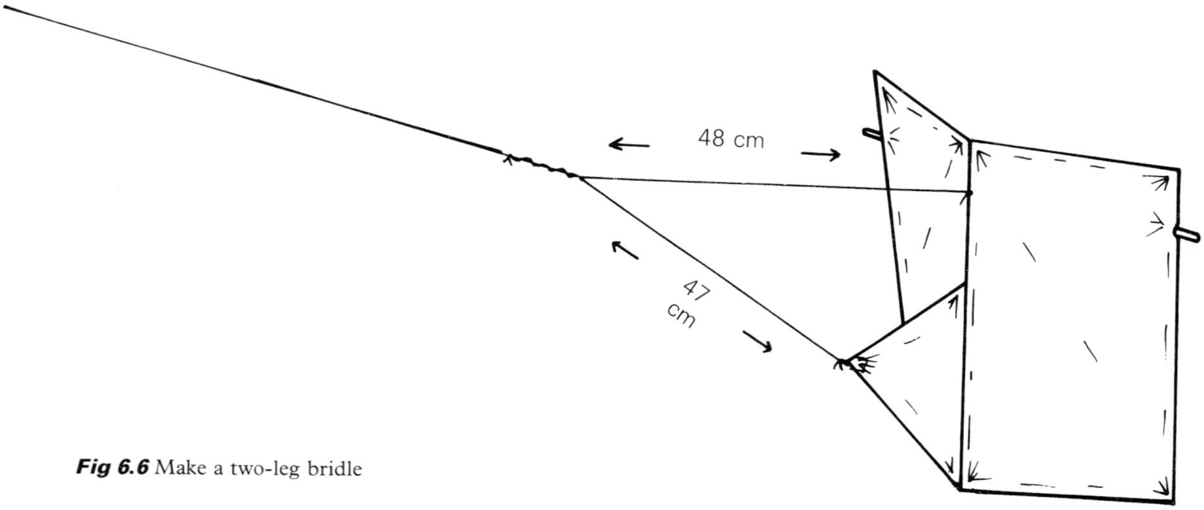

Fig 6.6 Make a two-leg bridle

ARROWHEAD DELTA

Sail : Polythene, wrapping paper, polyester film, *Tyvek*

Spars : Spine 5 mm ($\frac{3}{16}$ inch) dowel 58.5 cm (23 inches) long;
wing spars 2 pieces 5 mm ($\frac{3}{16}$ inch) dowel 35.5 cm (14 inches) long;
spreader 6.3 mm ($\frac{1}{4}$ inch) dowel 46 cm (18 inches) long

Cut a rectangular piece of sail material at least 80 cm × 60 cm (26 inches × 24 inches), then, as before, fold it along the centre parallel to the shorter side and cut out the pattern indicated (Fig 6.7a).

The keel (Fig 6.7b) can be cut from one of the scrap pieces. Reinforce the two outer edges of the keel and tape it along the centre folded edge in a fashion similar to the Square Delta.

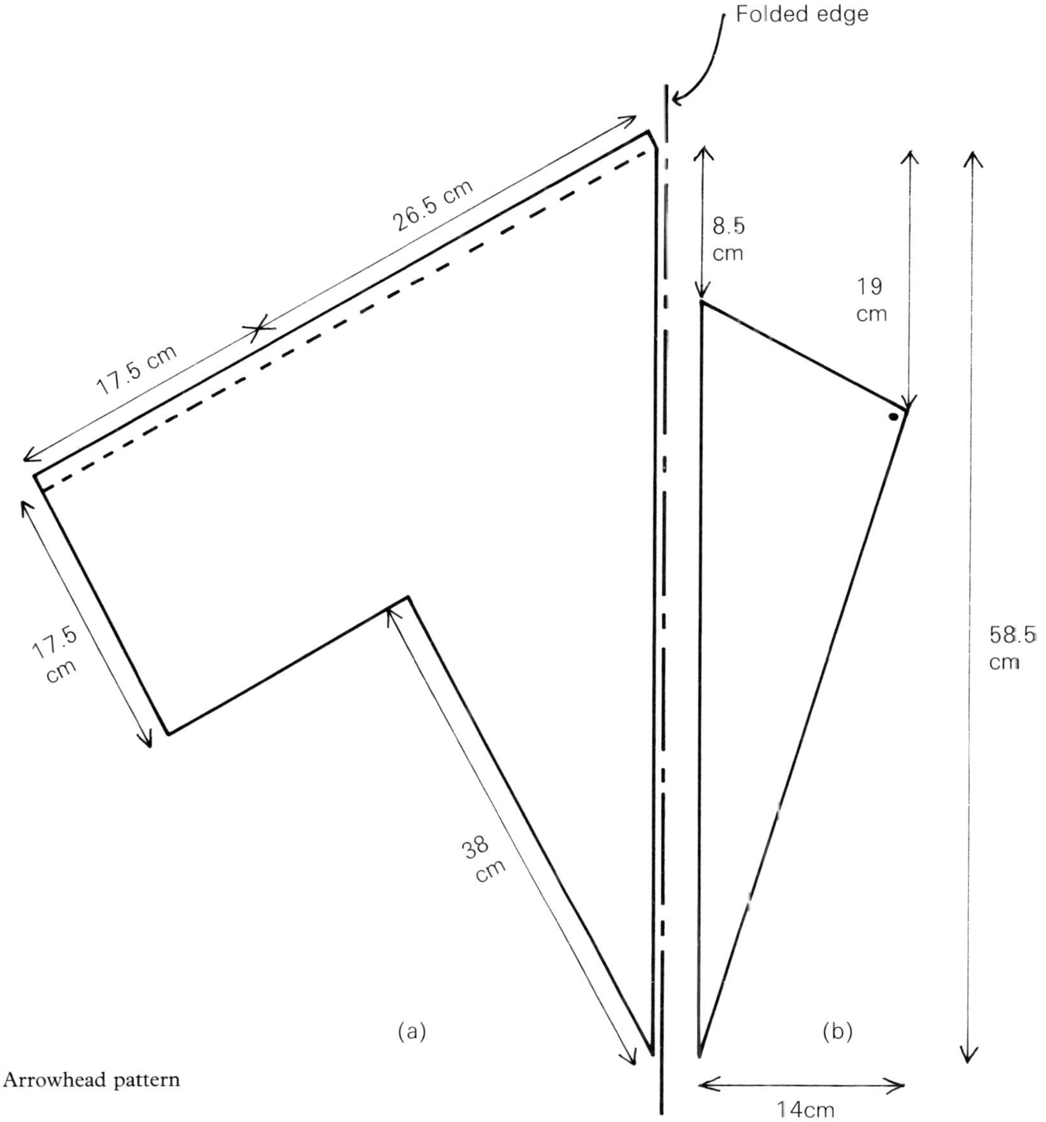

Fig 6.7 Arrowhead pattern

There are two methods of attaching the flying line to the keel tip: either reinforce the keel enclosing a thin dowel or bamboo (Fig 6.8a) and punch holes, or tape a ring or loop of line at the keel tip (Fig 6.8b).

Make the tubes for the wing spars as described above and tape the spine along the centre line at the back of the kite with extra reinforcing at the wing tips, and the spine tip and base.

The wing spars seem short at first, but are not. Tape them so that they just stick out (about 2 mm or $\frac{1}{16}$ inch) at the wing tips and staple the sail just above the spar, to prevent it sliding upwards (Fig 6.9).

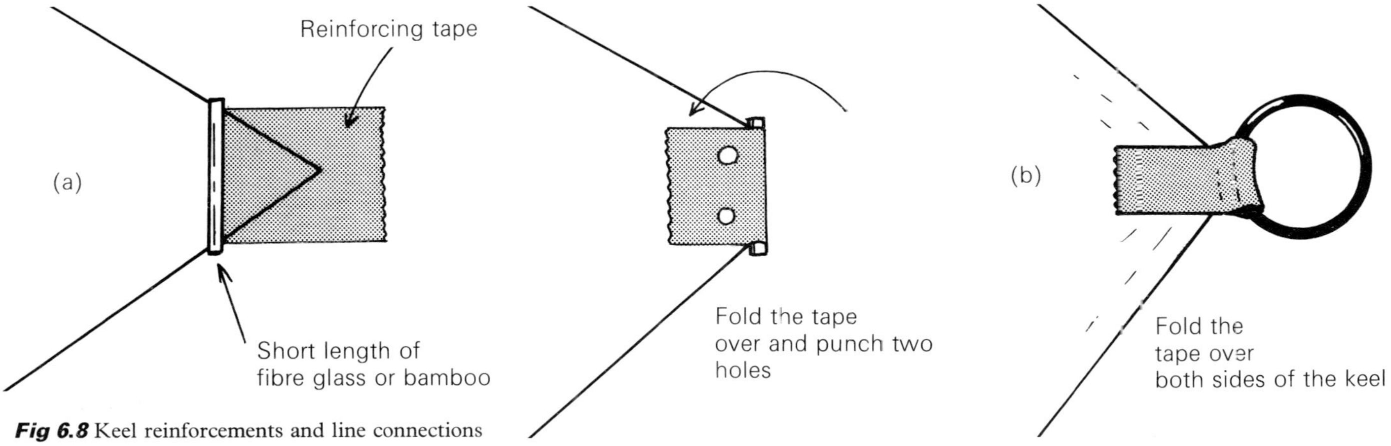

Fig 6.8 Keel reinforcements and line connections

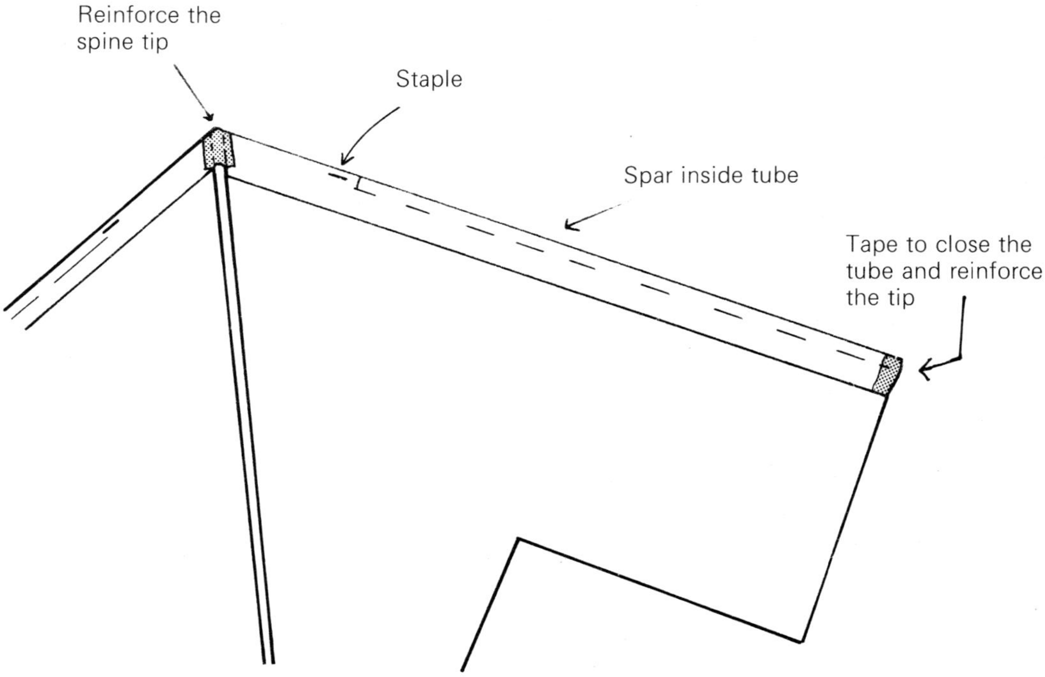

Fig 6.9 Staple the tube at the upper end of the spar and reinforce the tip

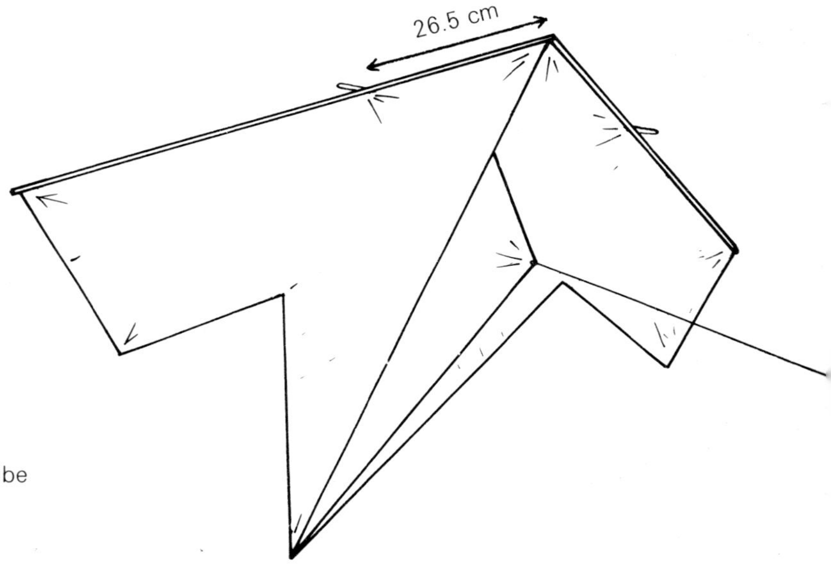

Fig 6.11 Add the spreader bar and tie the line to the keel tip

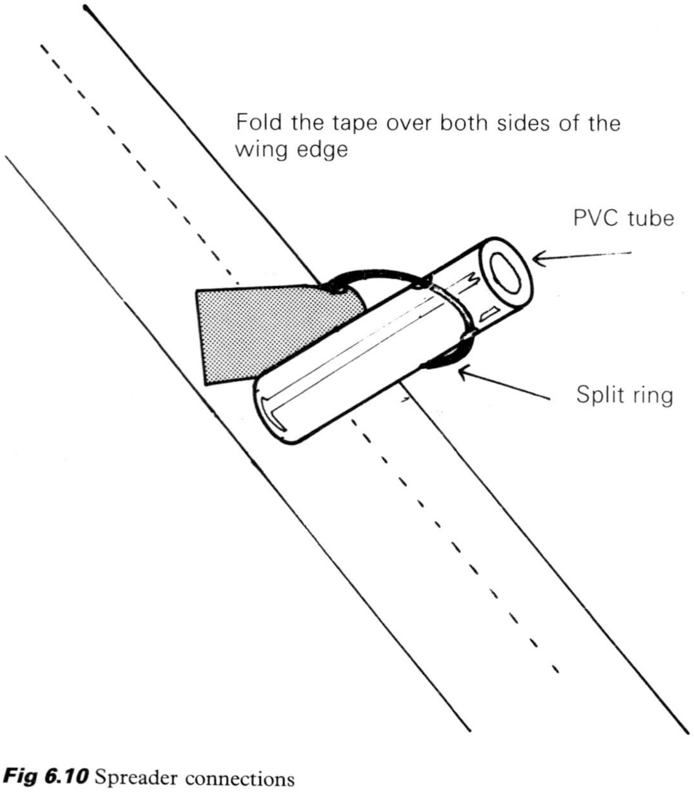

Fig 6.10 Spreader connections

The Arrowhead introduces a second, much stronger method of securing the spreader bar to the leading edges. Thread a split ring through a hole punched towards the end of short length of 6.3 mm ($\frac{1}{4}$ inch) diameter PVC tube and tape it to the wing edges 26.5 cm ($10\frac{1}{2}$ inches) from the spine tip (Fig 6.10).

Finally, fit the spreader bar across the back of the kite, each end fixed into the PVC connections (Fig 6.11). If the kite has been cut and made correctly, the wings will hang at an angle of about 160 degrees.

▲ Four-wing corner kite

▲ Wine-rack box kite

Fringe delta kite ▼

Gull delta kite ▼

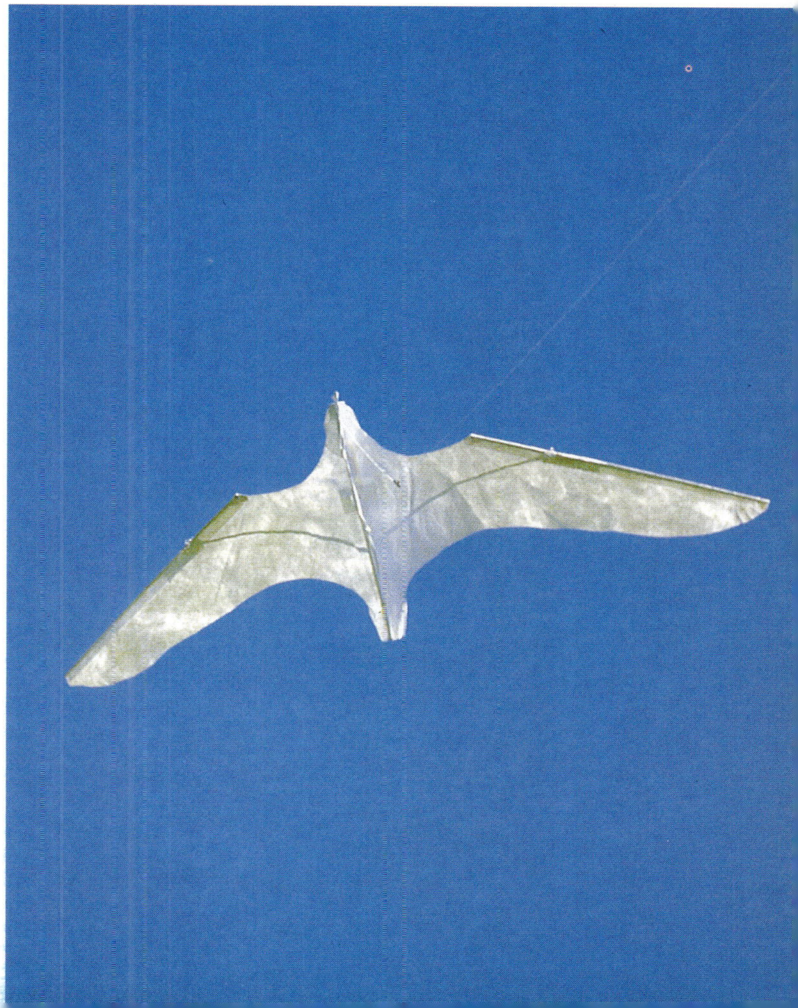

▲ Sentinel – folded keel delta kite

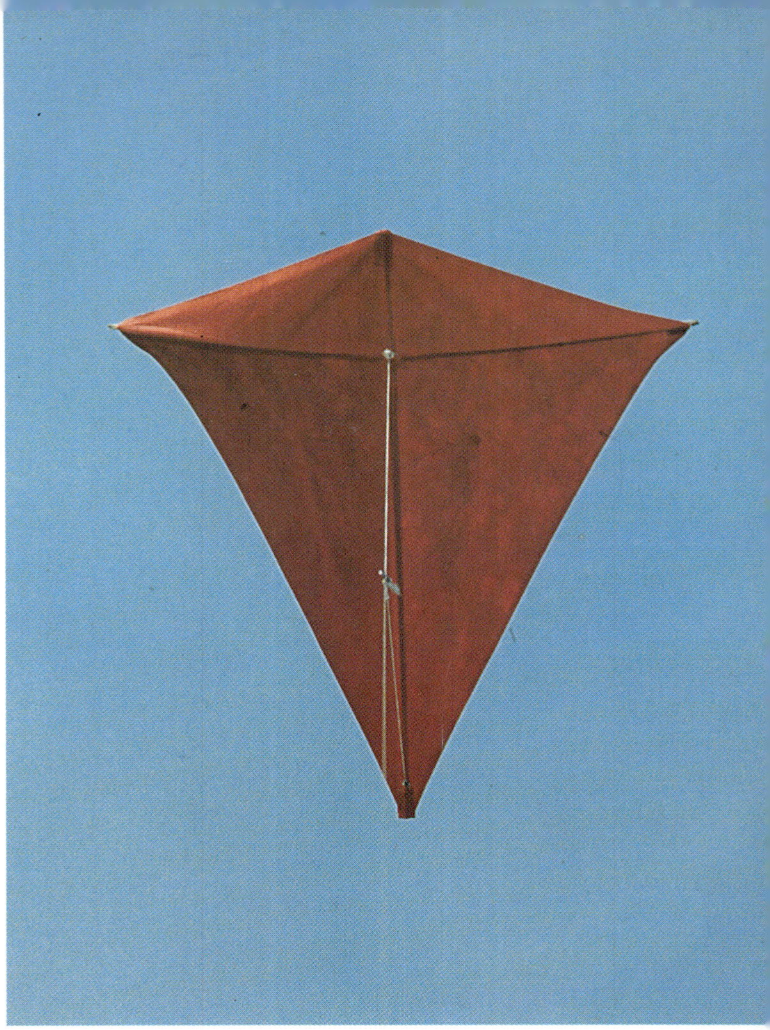

▲ Eddy kite

Jib-sail kite ▼

Arrowhead kite ▼

▲ Pocket sled kite

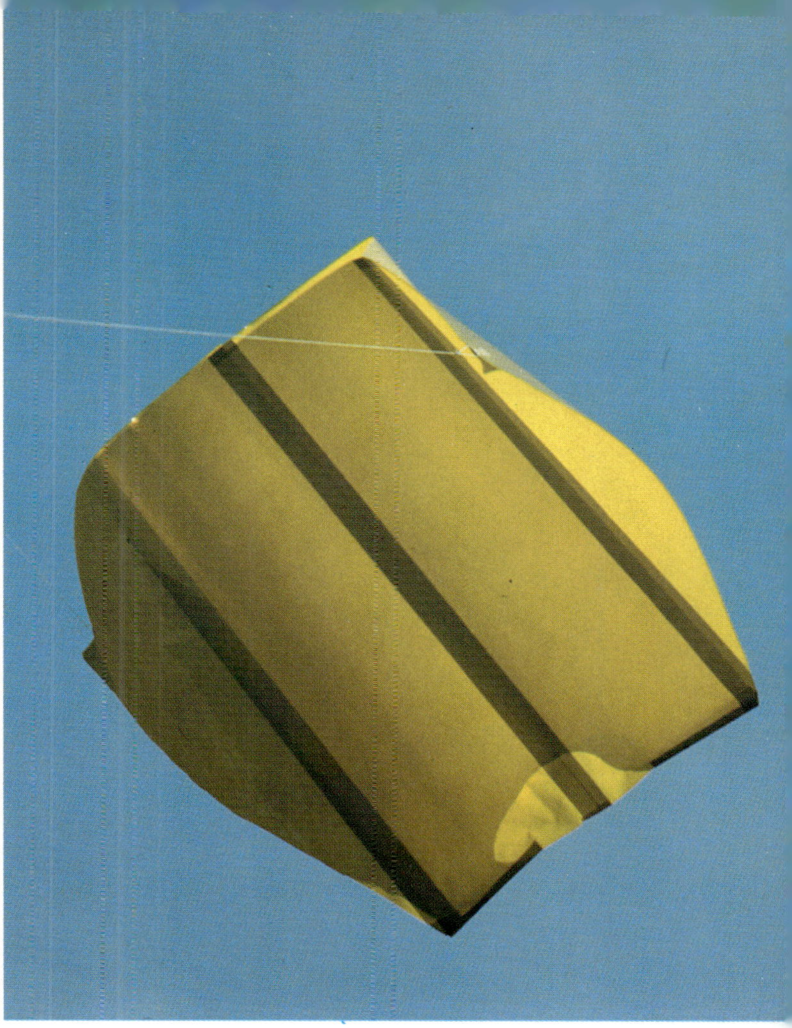

▲ Hybrid

Diamante kite ▼

Delta dart stunter kite ▼

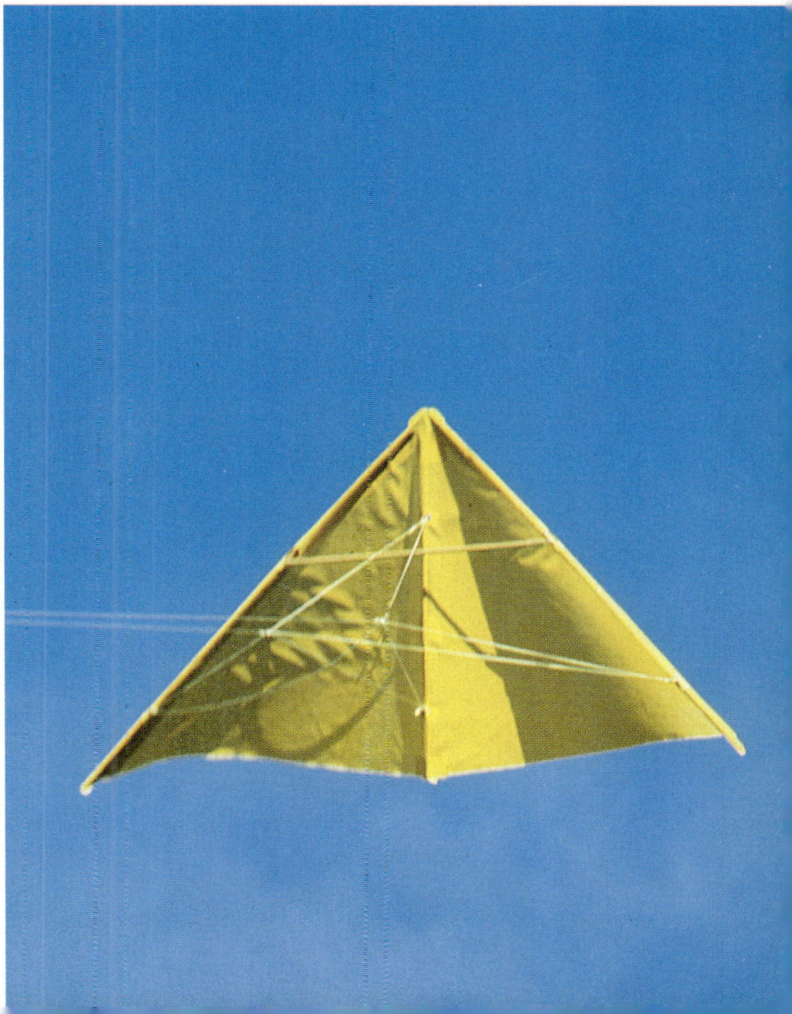

▲ Crusader stunter kite

▲ Skipper kite

Yakko kite ▼

SENTINEL – FOLDED KEEL DELTA

Sail : Polythene, *Tyvek*
Spars : Spine 6.3 mm ($\frac{1}{4}$ inch) dowel 61 cm (24 inches) long;
spreader, 6.3 mm dowel approximately 57 cm ($22\frac{1}{2}$ inches) long;
wing spars 2 pieces 5 mm ($\frac{3}{16}$ inch) 62 cm (25 inches) long

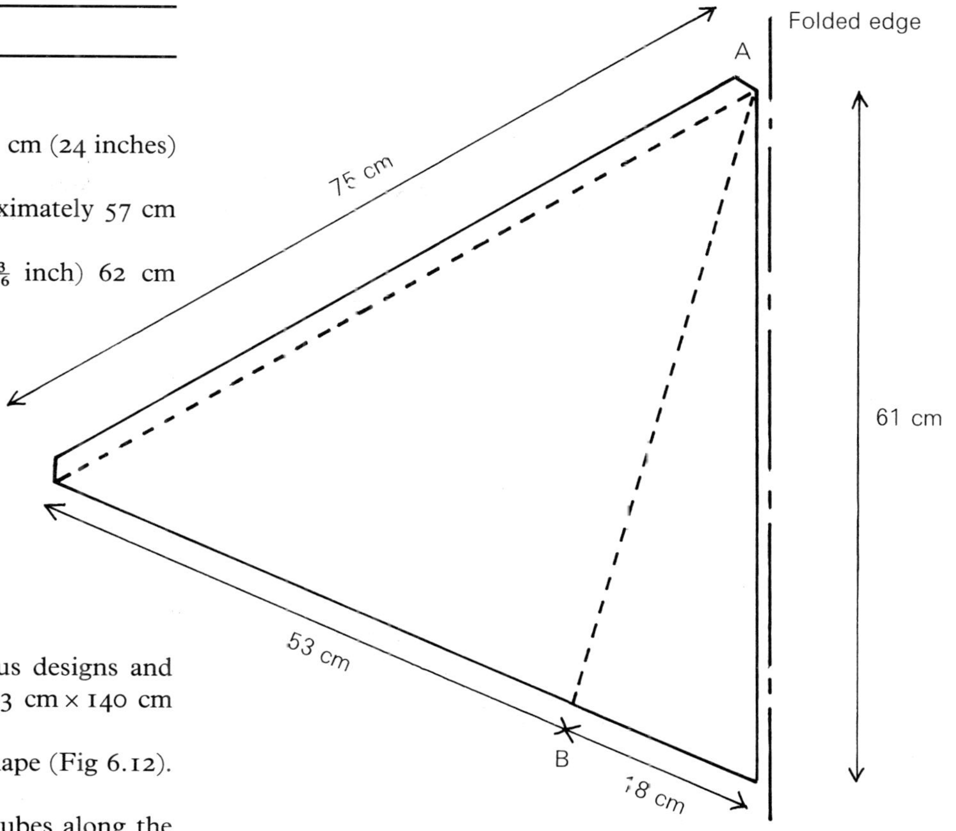

Fig 6.12 Sentinel pattern

The Sentinel is much larger than previous designs and requires a piece of sail material at least 63 cm × 140 cm (25 inches × 55 inches)

Fold the sail material and cut out the shape (Fig 6.12). Mark the lines AB on both sides.

Lay the sail out flat and make narrow tubes along the wing edges to house the spars as previous kites. It is also convenient at this stage to fit the spine along the centre line, giving the sail a slight tension as you do so, although don't worry too much about reinforcing just yet (Fig 6.13).

Refold the sail material along the centre line AC and fold and make creases along the lines AB on both sides. Now join

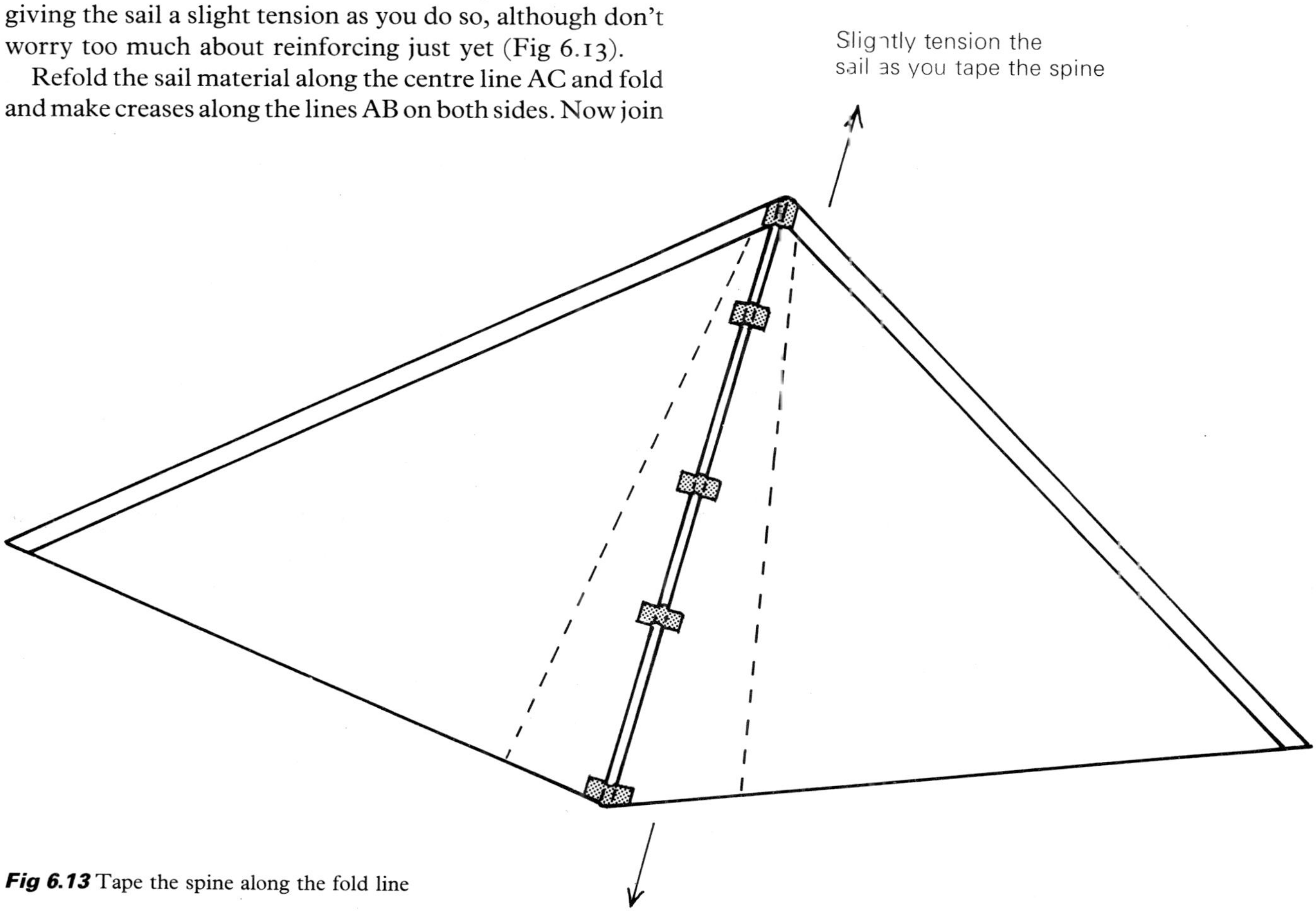

Fig 6.13 Tape the spine along the fold line

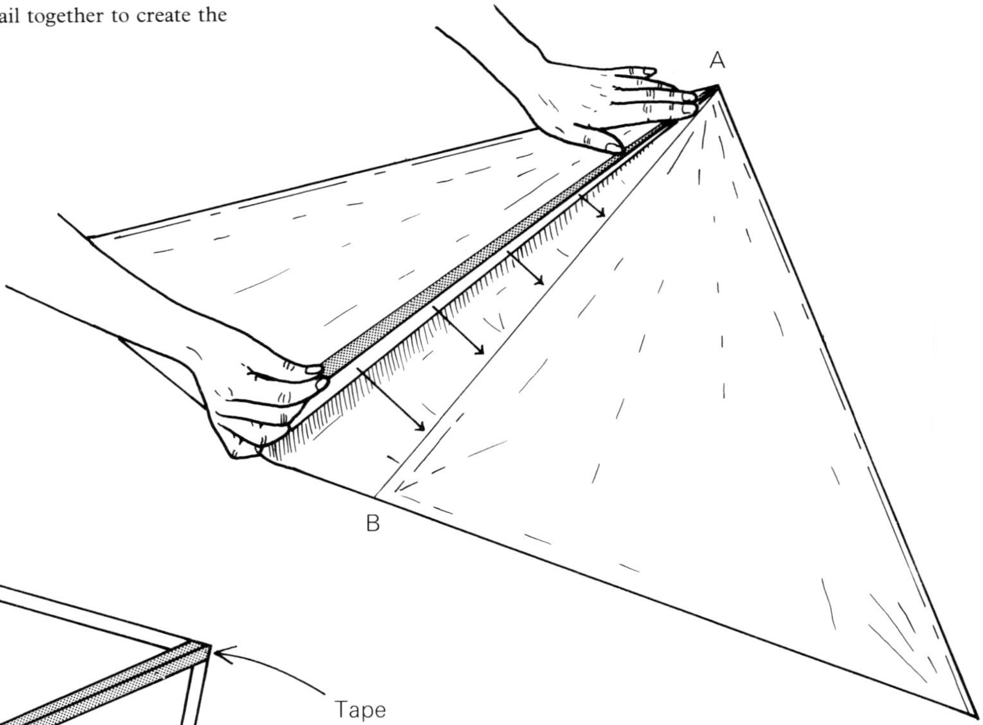

Fig 6.14 Fold and tape both halves of the sail together to create the forward 'folded keel'

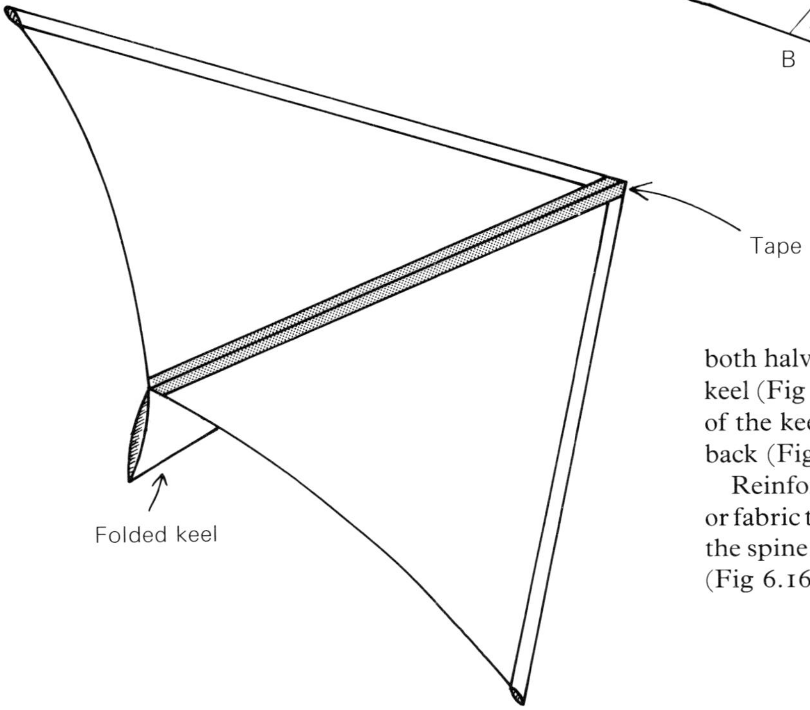

Fig 6.15 Also tape along the rear of the junction

both halves of the sail along these lines to create a forward keel (Fig 6.14). You can either glue over the whole surface of the keel or just run a length of adhesive tape along the back (Fig 6.15).

Reinforce the tip and base of the spine with strong PVC or fabric tape. Also reinforce a point 34 cm ($13\frac{1}{2}$ inches) from the spine base and punch two holes to accept the flying line (Fig 6.16).

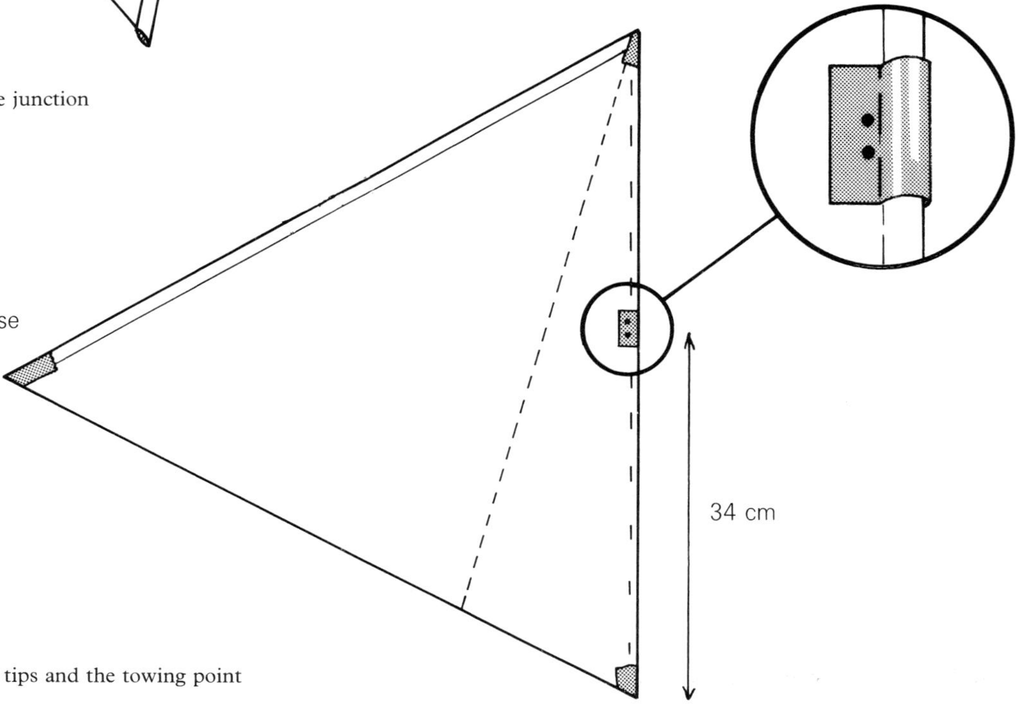

Fig 6.16 Reinforce the spine and wing tips and the towing point

Make the spreader bar connections as with the Arrowhead, fitted 36 cm (14 inches) from the spine tip, and add the spreader bar (Fig 6.17).

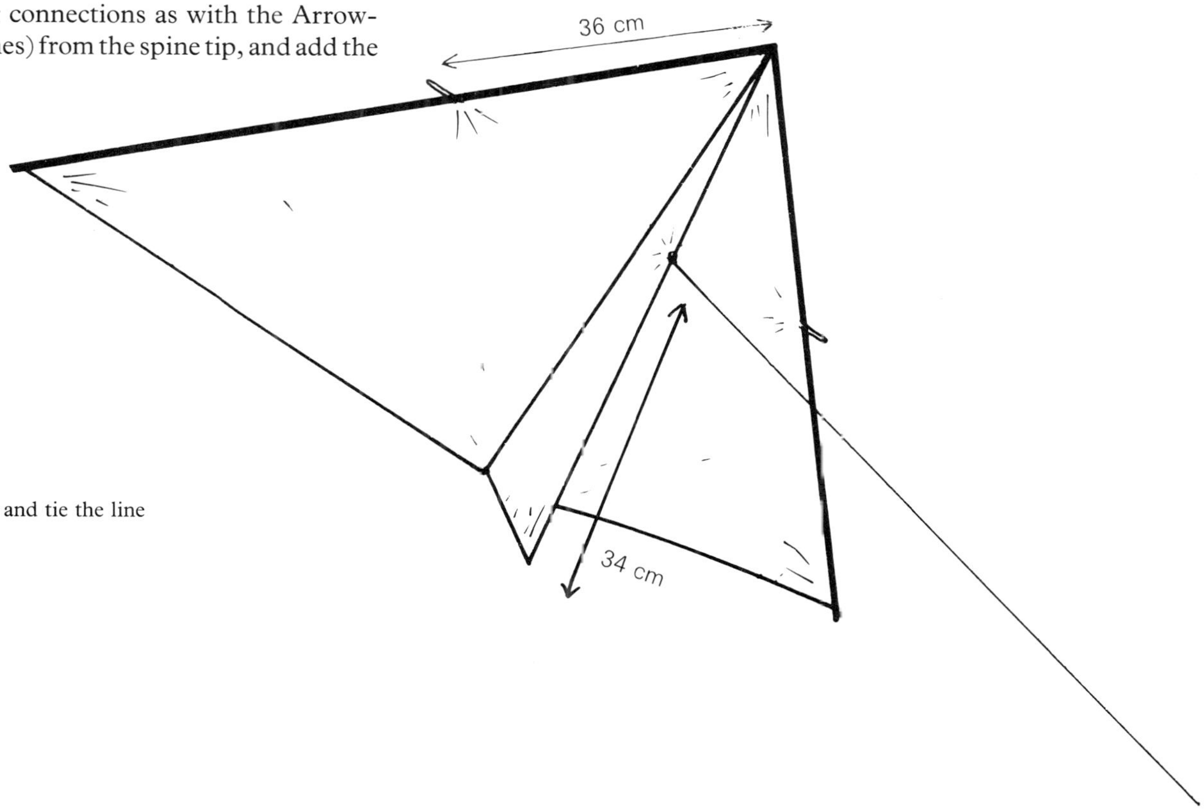

Fig 6.17 Add the spreader bar and tie the line

FRINGE DELTA

Sail : Polythene
Spars : Spine 6.3 mm ($\frac{1}{4}$ inch) dowel 55 cm ($21\frac{1}{2}$ inches) long;
spreader, 6.3 mm dowel approx 56 cm (22 inches) long;
wing spars 2 pieces 5 mm ($\frac{3}{16}$ inch) dowel 68 cm ($26\frac{3}{4}$ inches) long

The Fringe Delta is a superb poly-bag kite which has been very successful in workshops.

Fold the sail material and cut out the pattern shown in Fig 6.18 to create the symmetrical shape.

Cut out the keel from one of the scrap pieces and reinforce

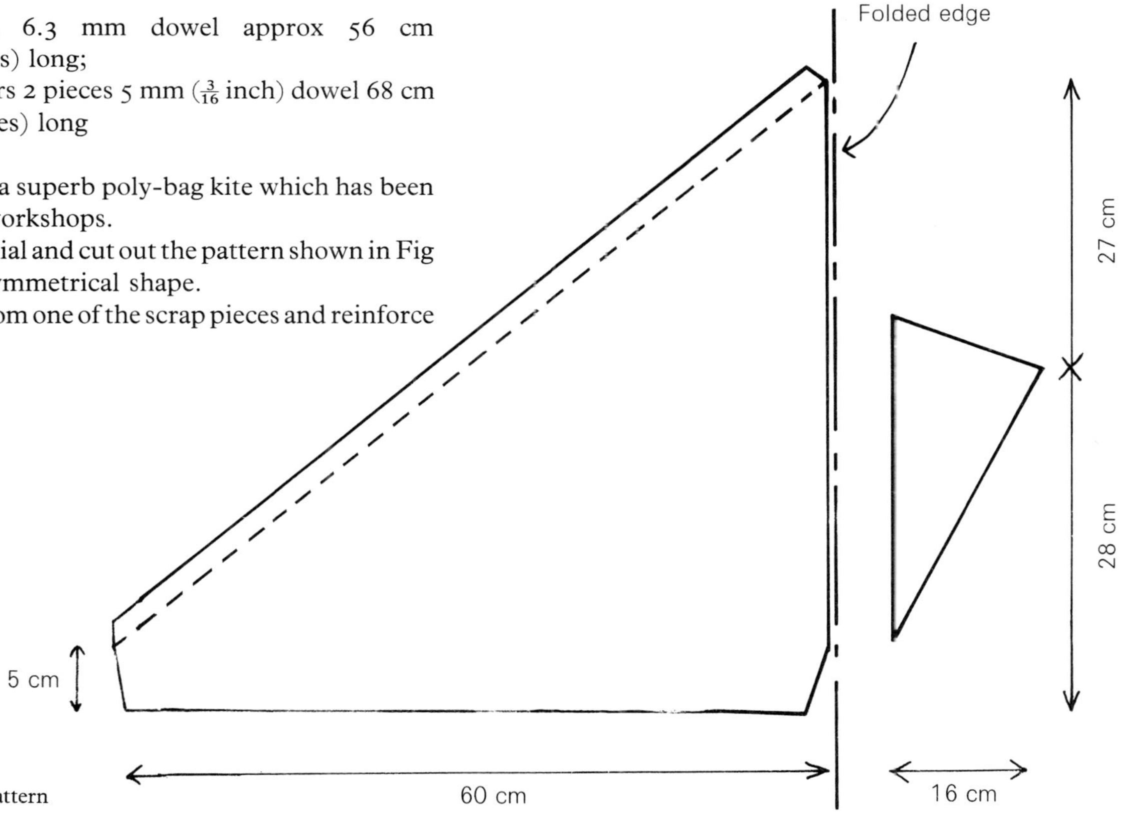

Fig 6.18 Fringe Delta pattern

it along the two outer edges and at the tip, then with the sail still folded tape it along the fold line (Fig 6.19).

Fold and make the spar tubes at the wing edges as previous designs, then cut the fringes to a depth of about 5 cm ($2\frac{1}{2}$ inches) along the lower edges.

Tape the spine to the back of the kite along the central fold line, with some extra reinforcing at the tip (Fig 6.20).

Make and fit the spreader bar connections as with the Arrowhead, 47 cm ($18\frac{1}{2}$ inches) from the wing tip. Finally add the wing spars and the spreader bar (Fig 6.21).

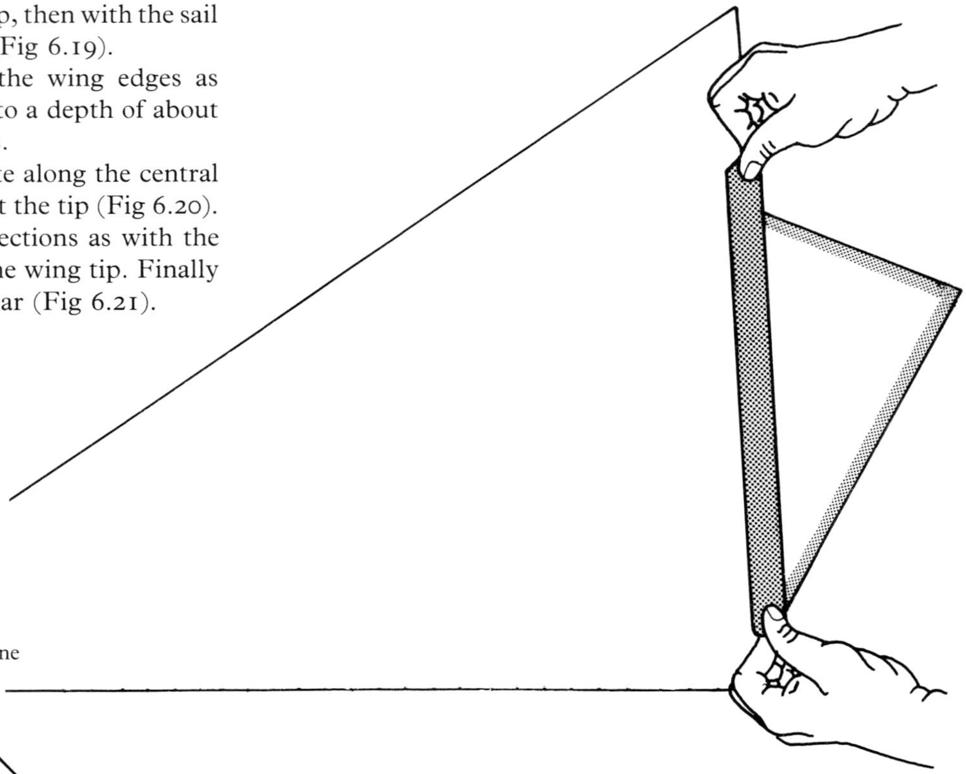

Fig 6.19 Tape the keel along the central fold line

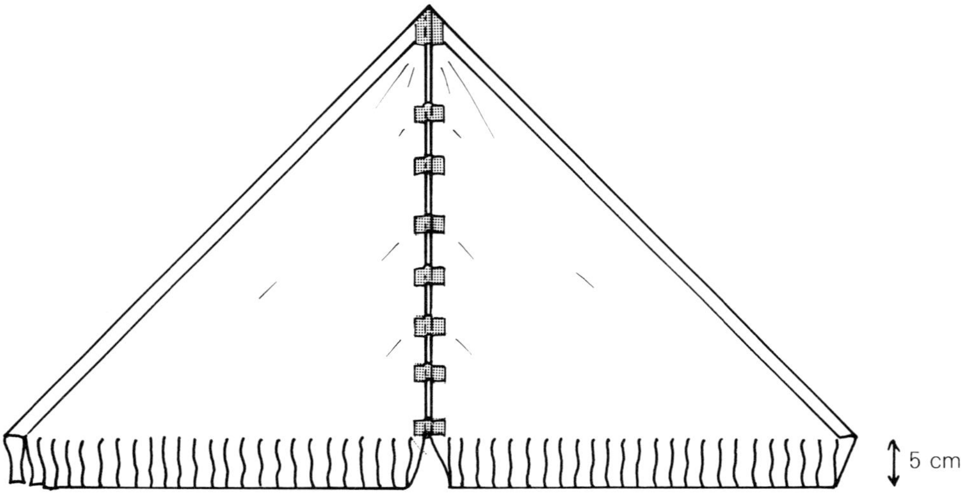

Fig 6.20 Tape the spine to the rear of the sail

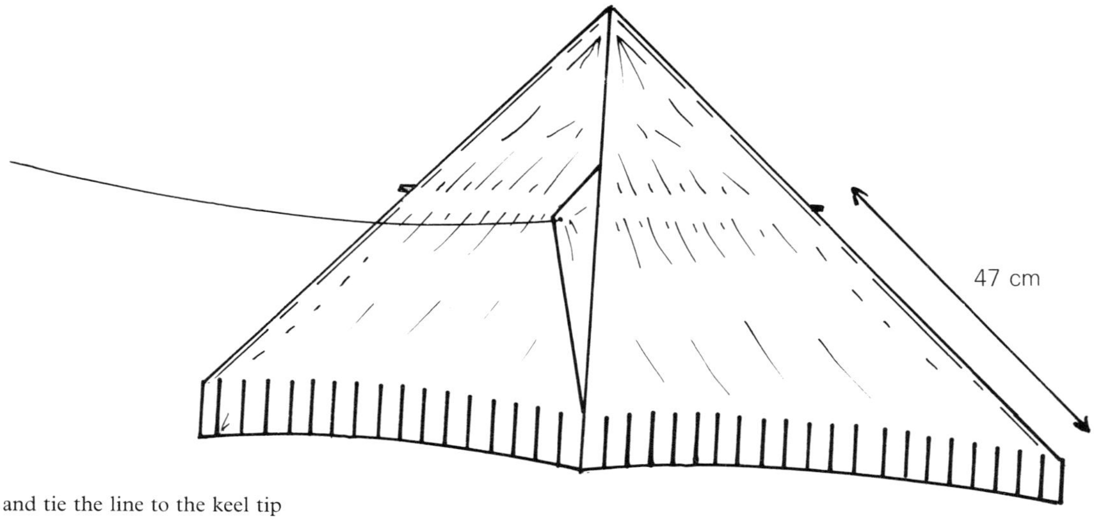

Fig 6.21 Add the spreader bar and tie the line to the keel tip

CONCORDE

Sail : Wrapping paper, *Tyvek*
Spars : Spine 6.3 mm ($\frac{1}{4}$ inch) dowel 95 cm (39 inches) long;
wing spars 2 pieces 5 mm ($\frac{3}{16}$ inch) dowel 72 cm ($28\frac{1}{2}$ inches) long;
spreader, 6.3 mm dowel, approximately 56 cm (22 inches) long

The Concorde derives from a kite designed by Martin Powell called the Tunnel Keel Delta, which was popular in the 1970s. Martin's original design has a more common triangular wing shape, but, with what seems to be a revival of aeroplane forms for kites, Concorde was designed specifically for a workshop with adults.

As with previous designs, cut out a triangle of sail material, 115 cm ($46\frac{1}{2}$ inches) base and 98 cm ($38\frac{1}{2}$ inches) height. Fold it along the centre and cut out the sail shape illustrated in Fig 6.22a.

Unfold the sail to lay it flat and mark the lines XX¹ on each side of the central fold. Mark, fold and glue the spar tubes at the wing edges as in previous designs.

It is also probably easier to fix the spine in place at this point, rather than when the keel back is in position. Tape it along the central fold (Fig 6.23).

Cut out the keel shape (Fig 6.22b), fold the edges on both sides to make gluing flaps, then glue it along the lines XX² on the sail piece (Fig 6.24).

Slide the spars along the wing tubes and tape/staple them in position. Reinforce the spine at the tip since, it will undoubtedly have to endure a number of crashes.

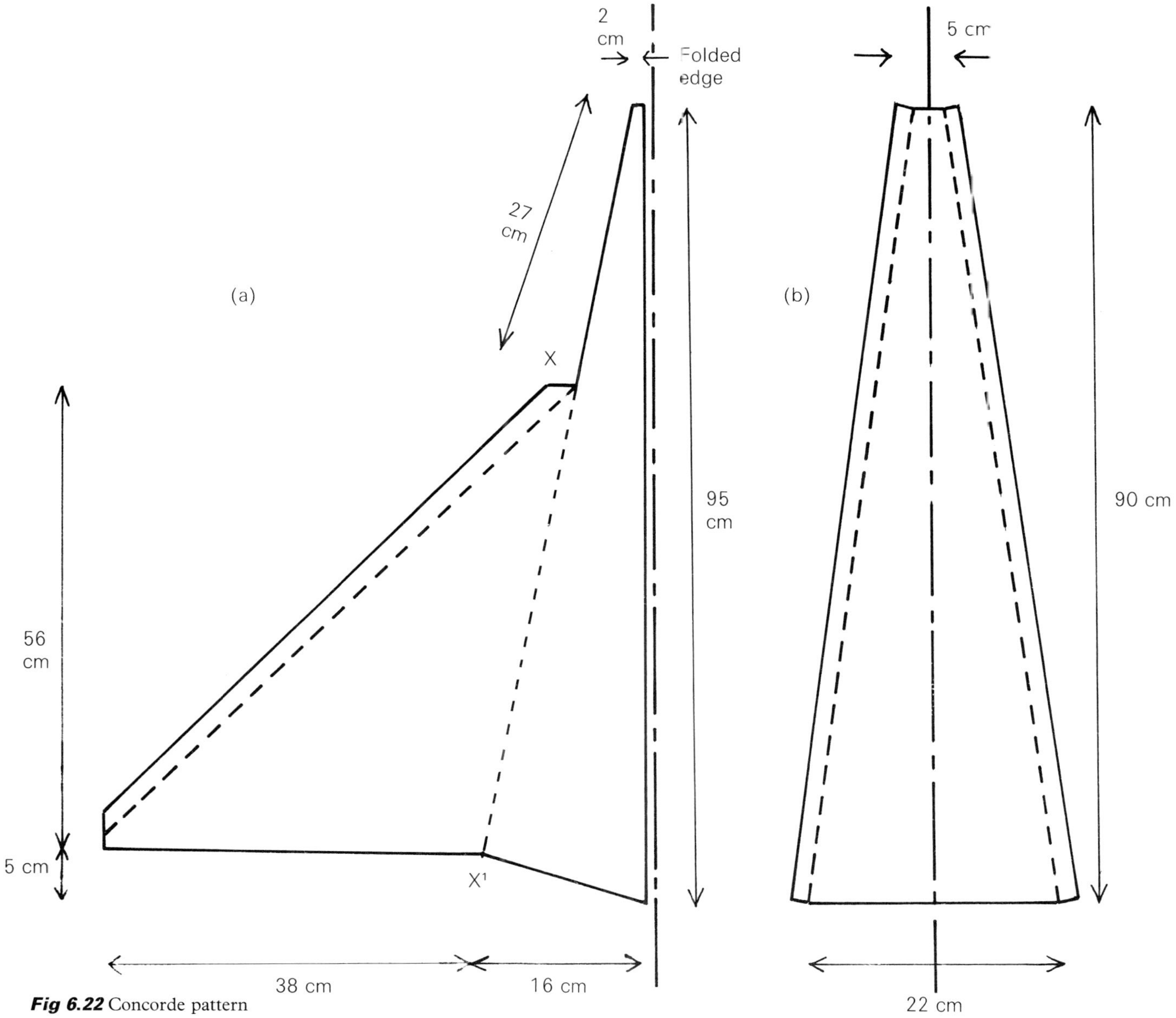

Fig 6.22 Concorde pattern

Make the spreader bar connections as with the Arrowhead, 36 cm (14 inches) from the wing tips and fit the spreader bar, trimmed so that the wings 'hang' at about 160 degrees.

Reinforce two sections of the sail 14 cm and 60 cm ($5\frac{1}{2}$ and $23\frac{1}{2}$ inches) from the spine base, and punch holes as described with the Sentinel. Finally, tie a two leg bridle 110 cm (43 inches) long.

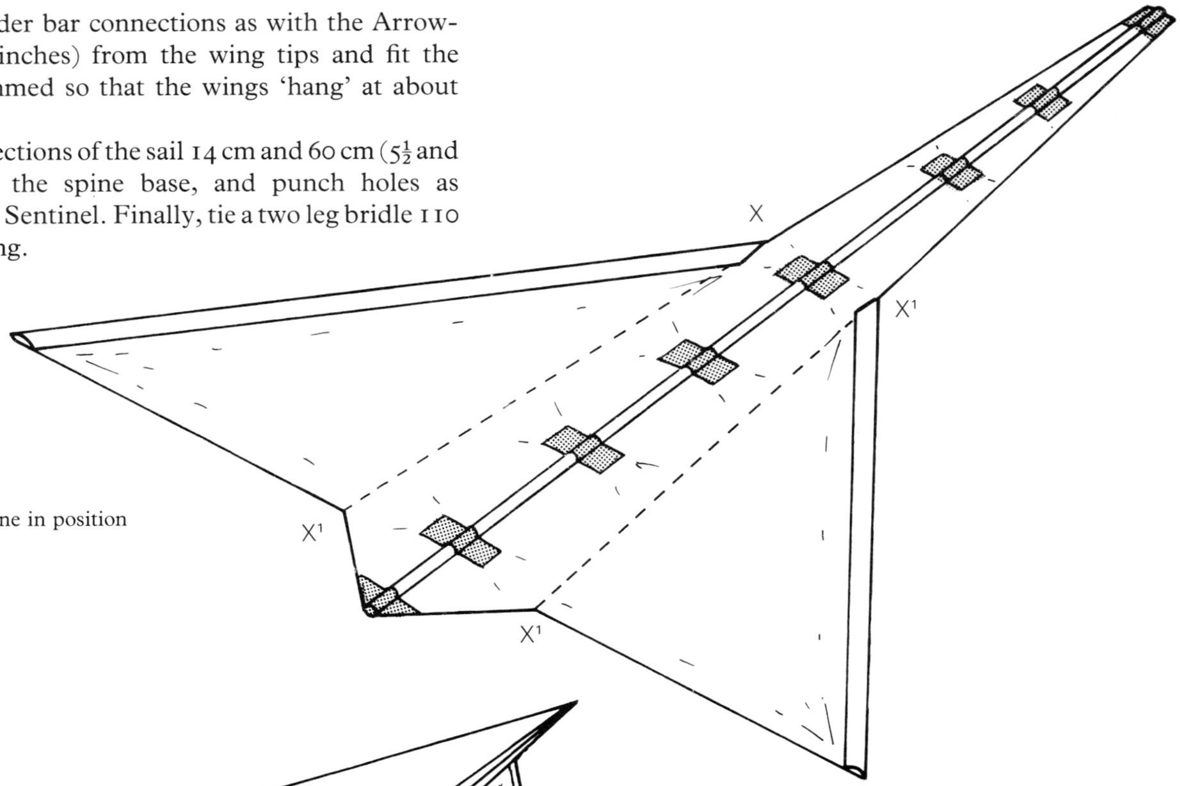

Fig 6.23 Tape the spine in position

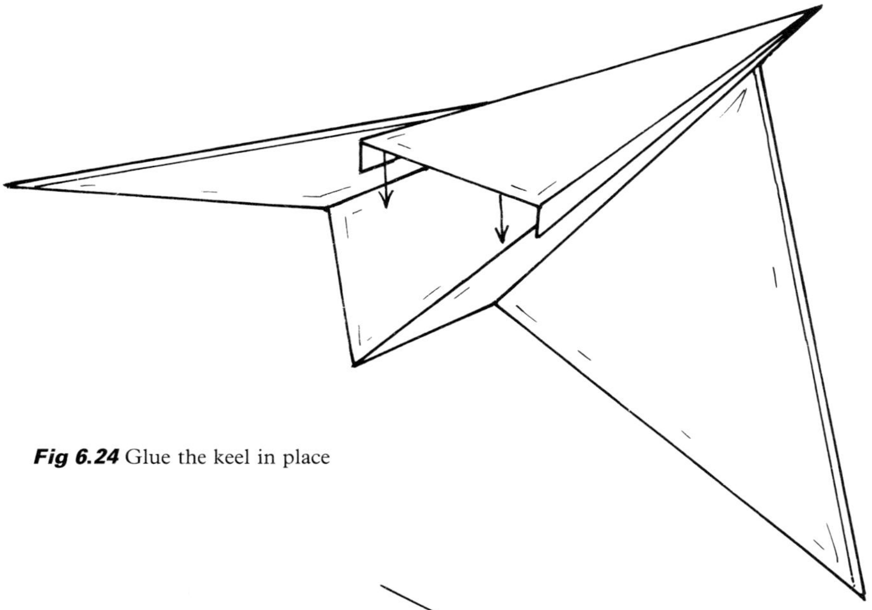

Fig 6.24 Glue the keel in place

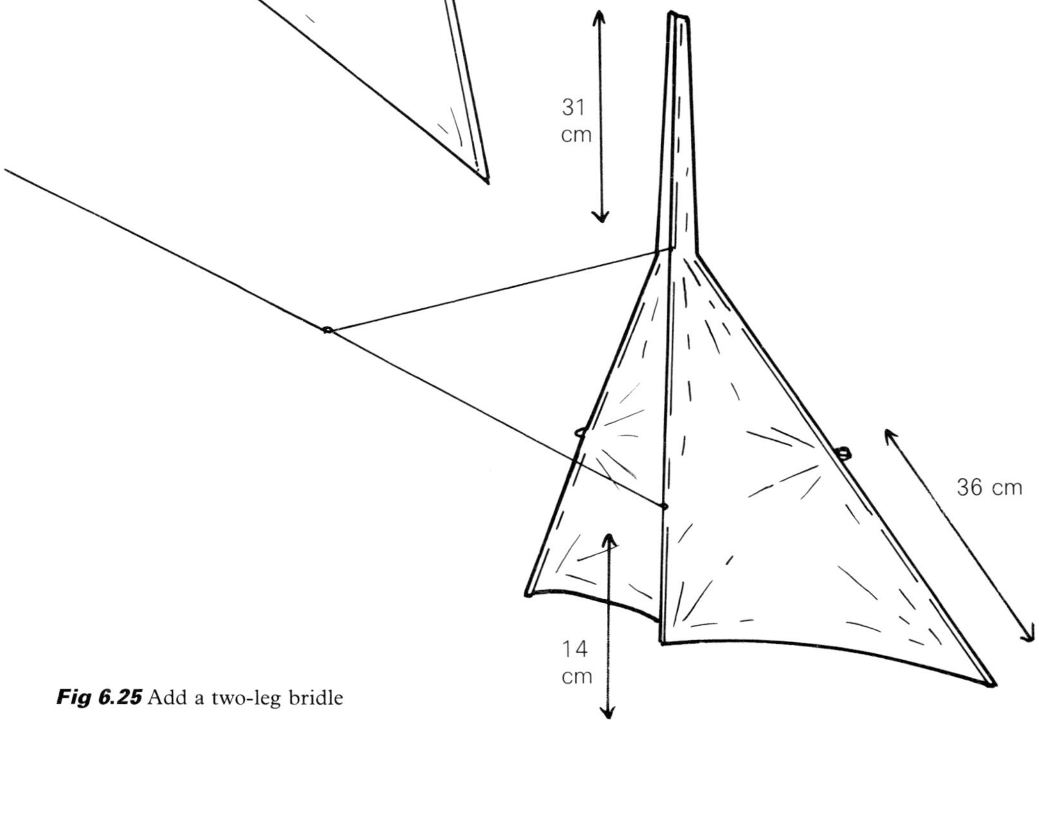

Fig 6.25 Add a two-leg bridle

GULL

Bird shapes have been popular for kites since their beginning and there are hundreds, if not thousands, of different types. The 'Gull' is an interesting variation on the standard delta form, again designed for an adult workshop.

Sail : *Tyvek* (white of course)
Spars : Spine 5 mm ($\frac{3}{16}$ inch) dowel 50 cm ($19\frac{1}{2}$ inches) long;
wing spars 2 pieces 5 mm dowel 65 cm (24 inches) long;
spreader 6.3 mm ($\frac{1}{4}$ inch) dowel 76 cm (30 inches) long

As the wing shape is a little awkward, it is much easier to start by making a template, even if you are only making one kite. Mark out the basic reference lines on a piece of card or paper 50 cm × 104 cm ($19\frac{1}{2}$ inches × 41 inches), then mark out the wing shape (Fig 6.26).

Using the template, mark and cut out two pieces of sail.

Fold each piece along the line AB, one left-handed, one right-handed, and glue them together over the whole surface of the keel/body shape (Fig 6.27). As you glue them, also fit a short length of 2 mm ($\frac{1}{16}$ inch) fibreglass or thin bamboo 15 cm (6 inch) long sandwiched between the two layers (Fig. 6.28).

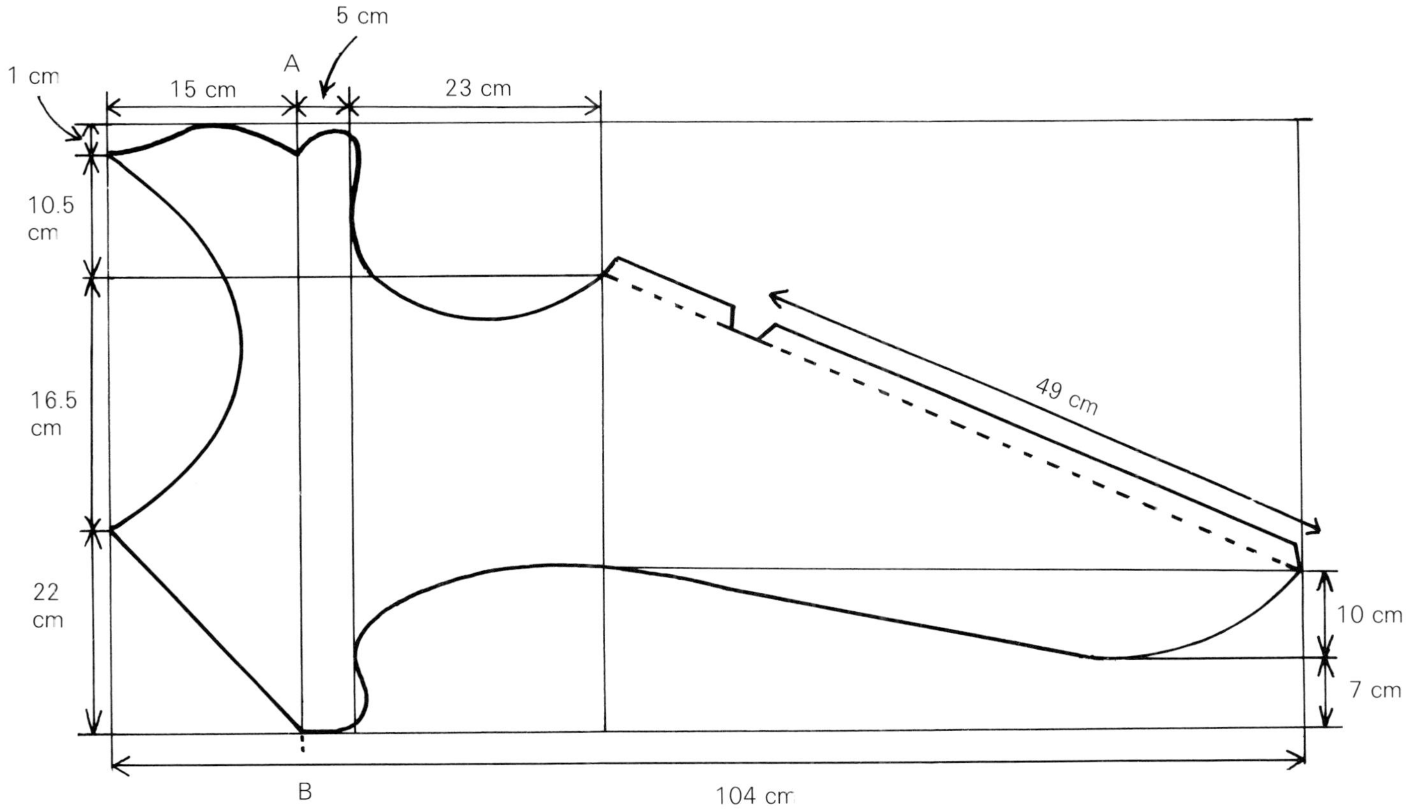

Fig 6.26 Gull pattern

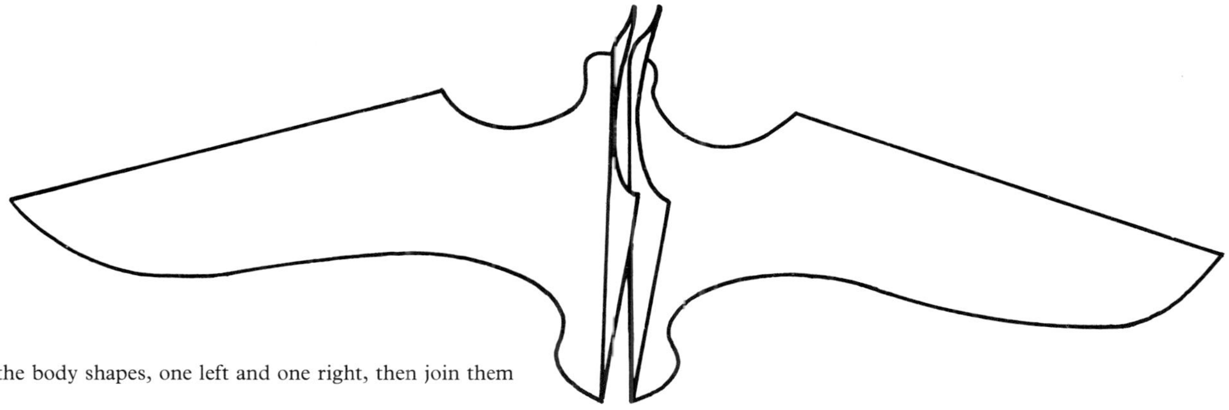

Fig 6.27 Fold the body shapes, one left and one right, then join them together

The wing tubes are made in a similar way to previous kites, except that you should cut a narrow notch in the wing flap, 49 cm (19¼ inches) from the tip, before folding and gluing.

Tape the spine in position to the rear, along the intersection of the wings and reinforce it at the tip and base.

The Gull introduces a third type of spreader bar connection. Slide each spar along the wing edges and, as you do so, also thread it through a hole in a short length of 6.3 mm (¼ inch) PVC tube at the notch (Fig 6.29). Tape or staple the wing spars to prevent them from moving and fit the spreader bar.

The Gull prefers a two-leg bridle, 80 cm (31½ inches) long, attached to the keel tip and the point X under the neck. For stability, it also likes to sit at a relatively high angle of attack with the upper bridle leg 44 cm (17½ inches) long (Fig 6.27).

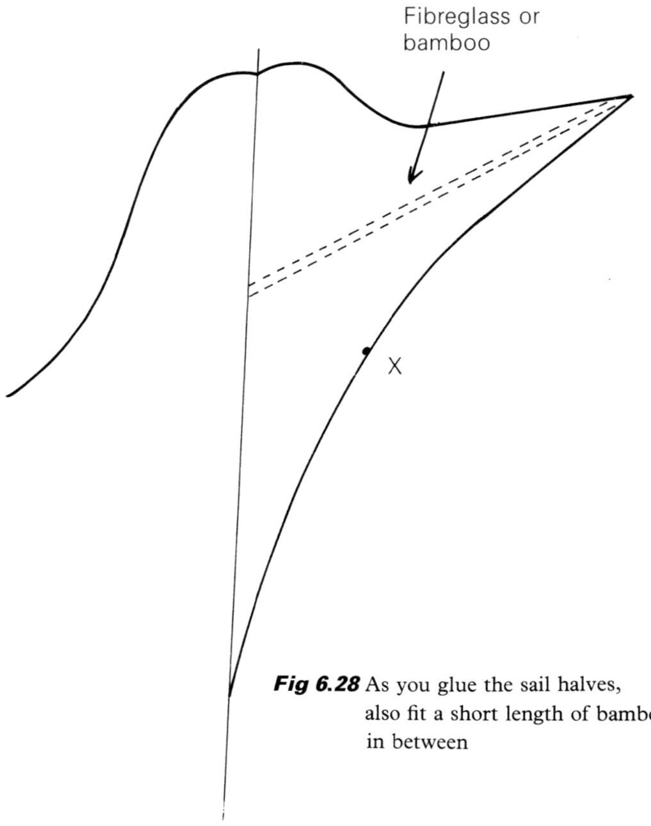

Fig 6.28 As you glue the sail halves, also fit a short length of bamboo in between

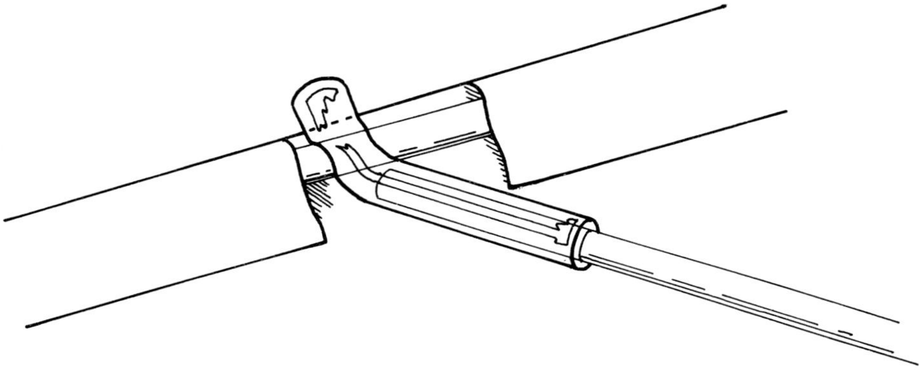

Fig 6.29 Spreader connection

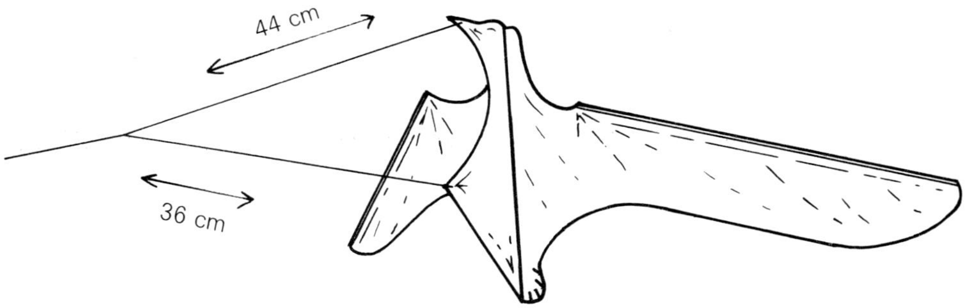

Fig 6.30 Add a two-leg bridle

flexible kites

In all previous designs, the frame of the kite is held rigid and should bend only in extreme conditions. Those featured below, however, all include spars designed to flex even in the lightest winds, helping them to remain stable.

JELLYFISH

A very popular workshop kite and great fun to fly.

Sail : Polythene, *Tyvek*, wrapping paper, polyester film

Spars : 2 mm ($\frac{1}{16}$ inch) fibreglass 130 cm ($51\frac{1}{4}$ inches) long;
5 mm ($\frac{3}{16}$ inch) dowel 51 cm (20 inches) long

Cut out a square of material approximately 55 cm ($21\frac{1}{2}$ inches) side as indicated in Fig 7.1. Mark the centre (reference) line, two points A,B 20 cm (8 inches) each side and a third point C, on the centre line, 51 cm (20 inches) from the bottom edge. Next punch or make holes along the centre line 10 cm and 40 cm (4 inches and 16 inches) from the bottom edge.

Mark the centre of the fibreglass rod and thread it through a hole punched towards the end of a short length of 5 mm ($\frac{3}{16}$ inch) PVC tube. Bend the rod into the arch shape (Fig 7.2) and tape it tightly to the sail at the ends, points A and B. Also tape the PVC tube at C and ensure that the

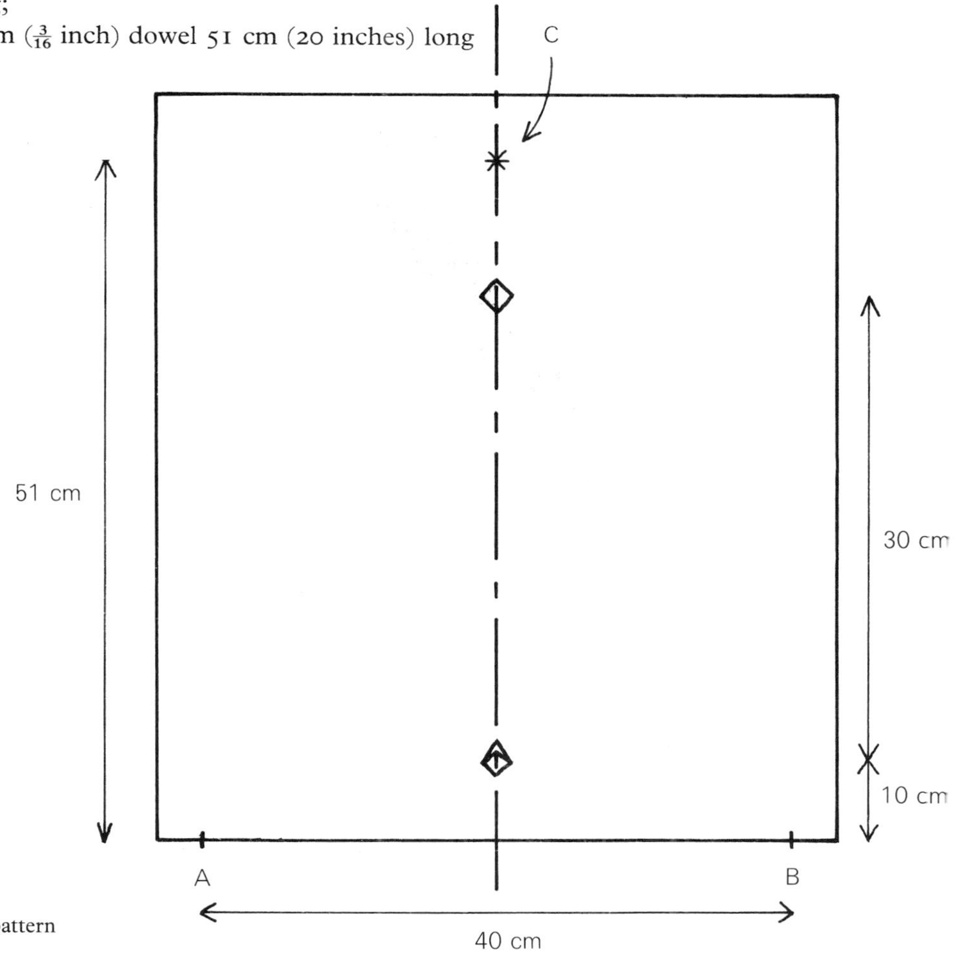

Fig 7.1 Jellyfish pattern

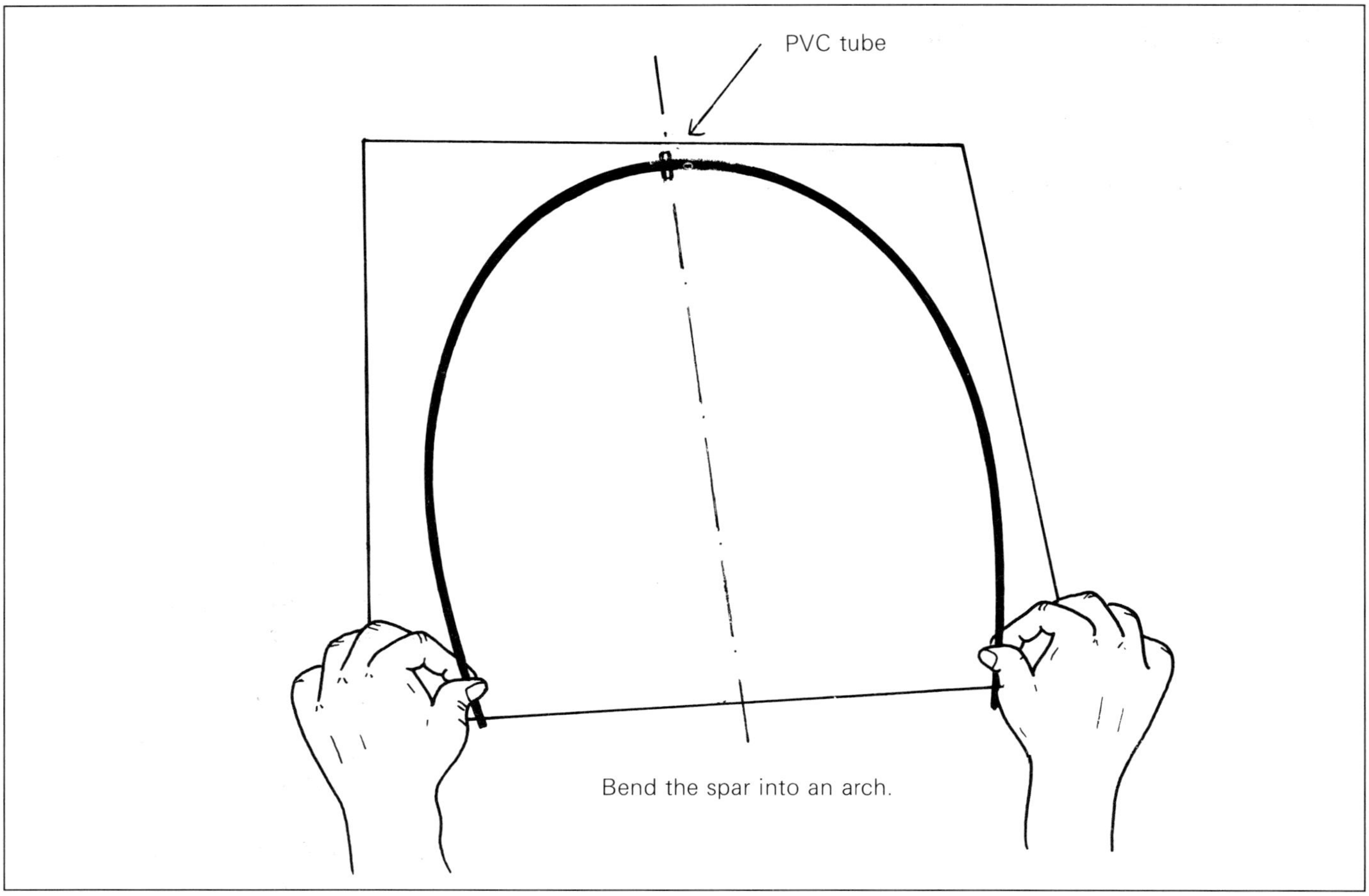

Fig 7.2 Fold the spar into an arch

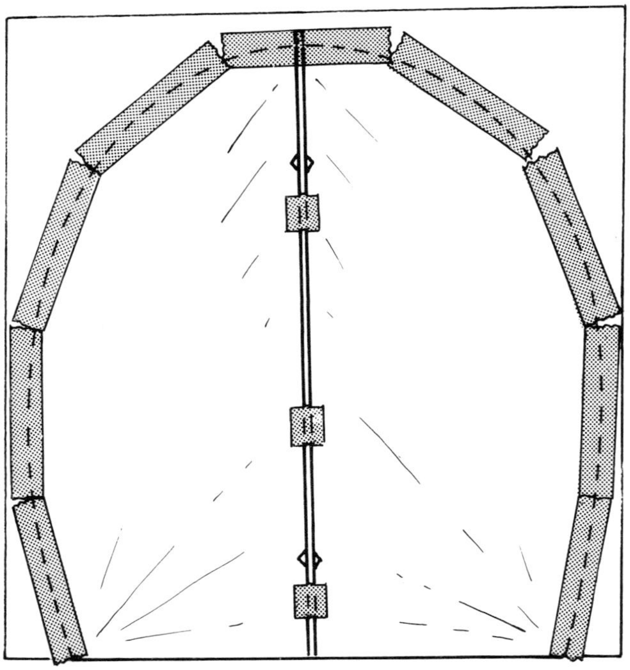

Fig 7.3 Tape construction

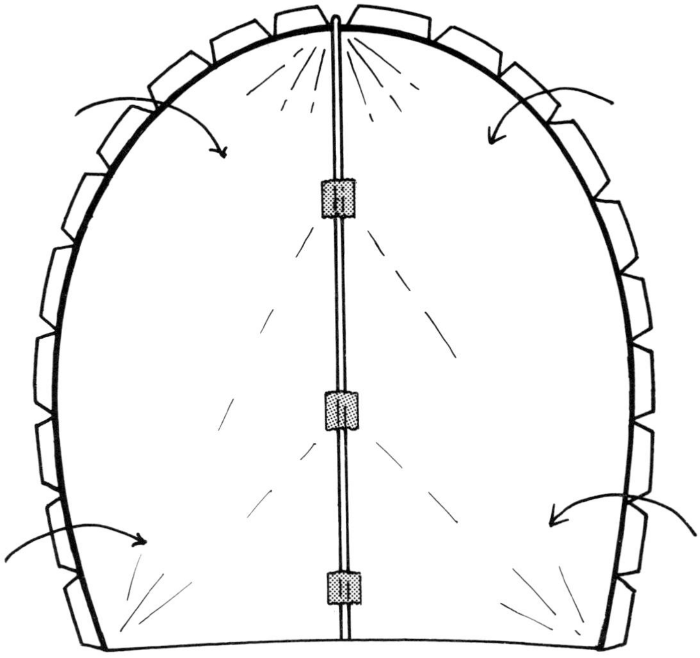

Fig 7.4 Make and fold flaps

centre of the fibreglass sits on the marked centre line of the sail.

The construction method varies here depending whether you are using glued materials or polythene. With polythene, cut strips of adhesive tape to fix the spar to the sail (Fig 7.3). If you are using glued materials, trim the sail to about 3 cm (1 inch) of the arch, creating small flaps (Fig 7.4). Fold and glue the flaps over the arched spar.

Fit the spine into the PVC tube at the tip and tape it to the sail along the centre line. Tie the bridle, 155 cm (61 inches) to the spine through the holes previously cut. Finally, fit long streamer tails, each about 3 metres long, symmetrically along the lower edge (Fig 7.5).

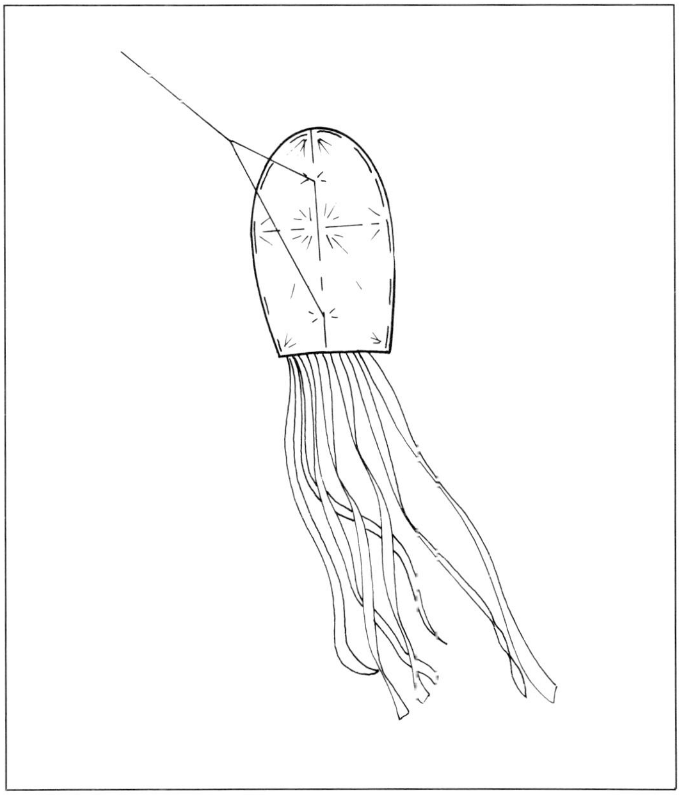

Fig 7.5 Add a two-leg bridle

ARCH-TOP KITE

Sail : Polythene, *Tyvek*, polyester film
Spars : 5 mm ($\frac{3}{16}$ inch) dowel 60 cm ($23\frac{1}{2}$ inches) long; 2 mm ($\frac{1}{16}$ inch) fibreglass 76 cm (30 inches) long

Cut out a rectangular piece of sail 50 cm × 65 cm ($19\frac{1}{2}$ inches × $25\frac{1}{2}$ inches). Fold it at the centre, parallel to the longer side, then mark and cut out the pattern (Fig 7.6). Reinforce and cut two small holes along the centre line, 12 cm and 46 cm ($4\frac{3}{4}$ inches and 18 inches) from the bottom point.

Unfold the sail and tape the spine at three or four points in position along the centre line.

As with the Jellyfish, mark the centre of the fibreglass rod and thread it through a small hole cut towards one end of a short length of PVC tube.

To create the arch, fit the PVC tube over the tip of the spine, then slide the fibreglass rod through such that the

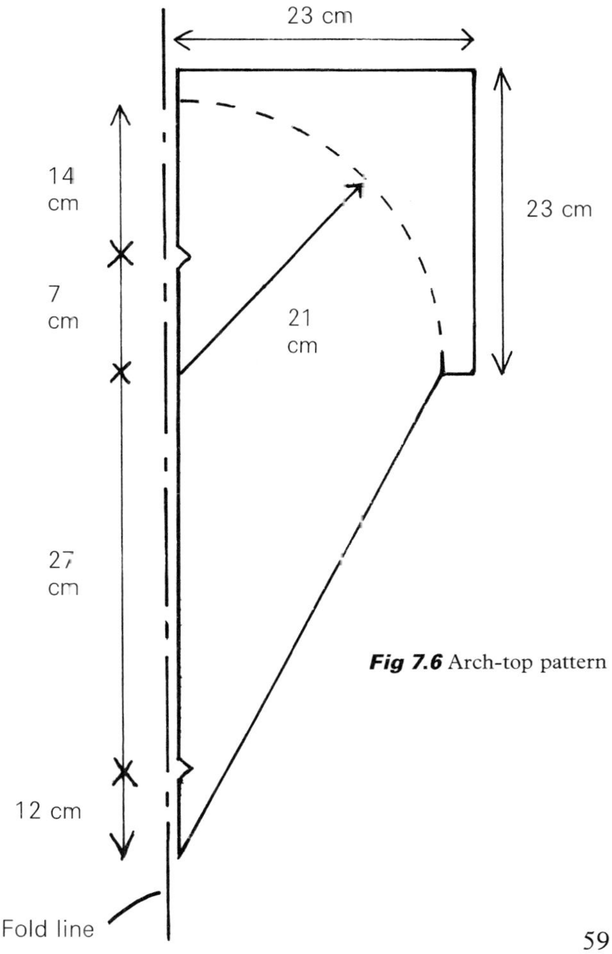

Fig 7.6 Arch-top pattern

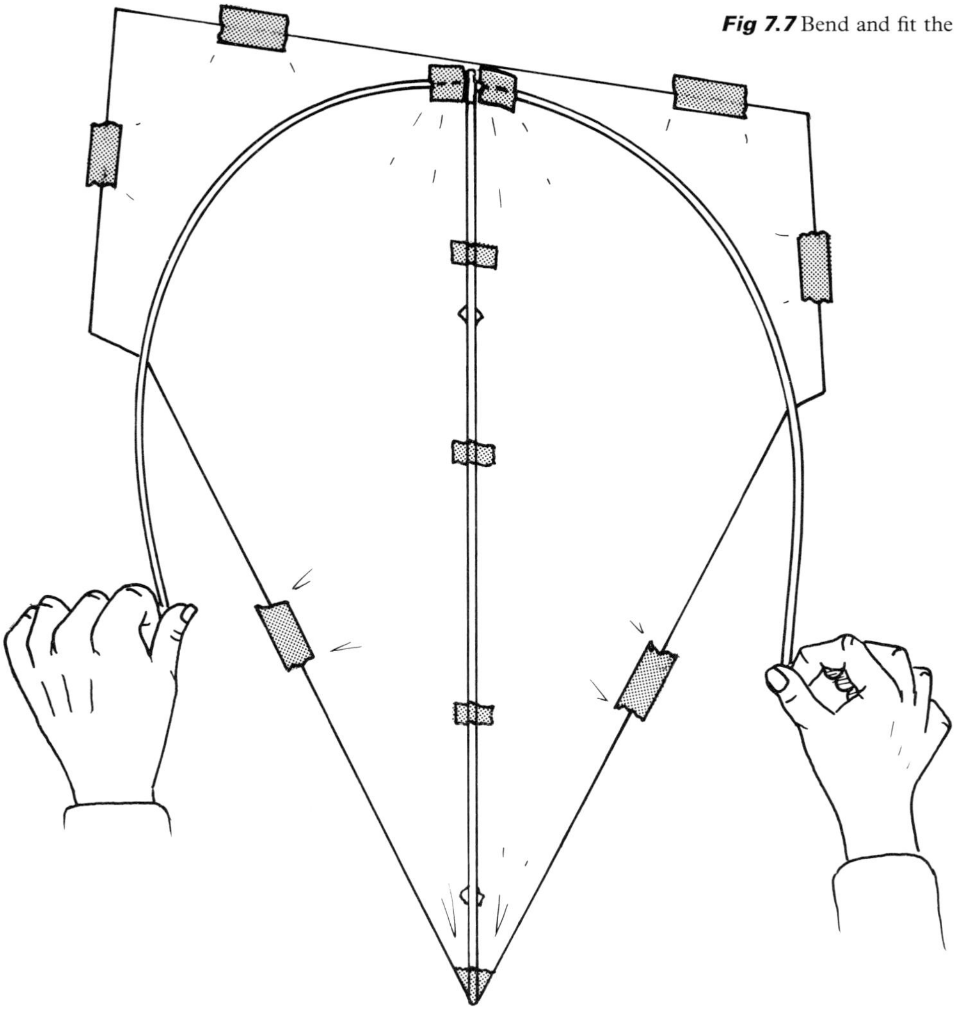

Fig 7.7 Bend and fit the arch

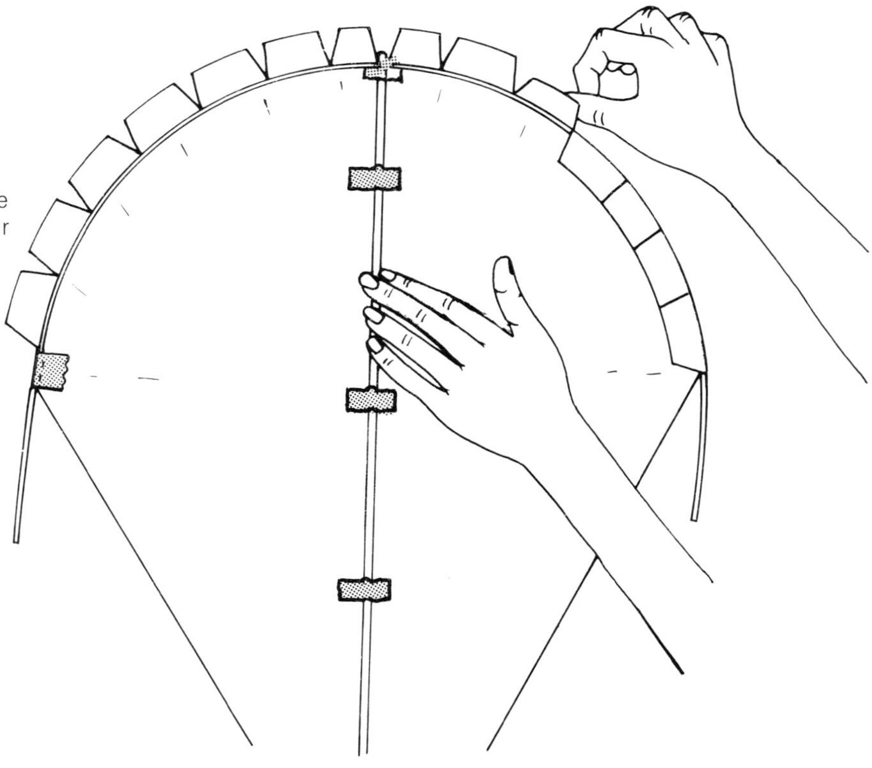

Fig 7.8 Tape the flaps over the arch

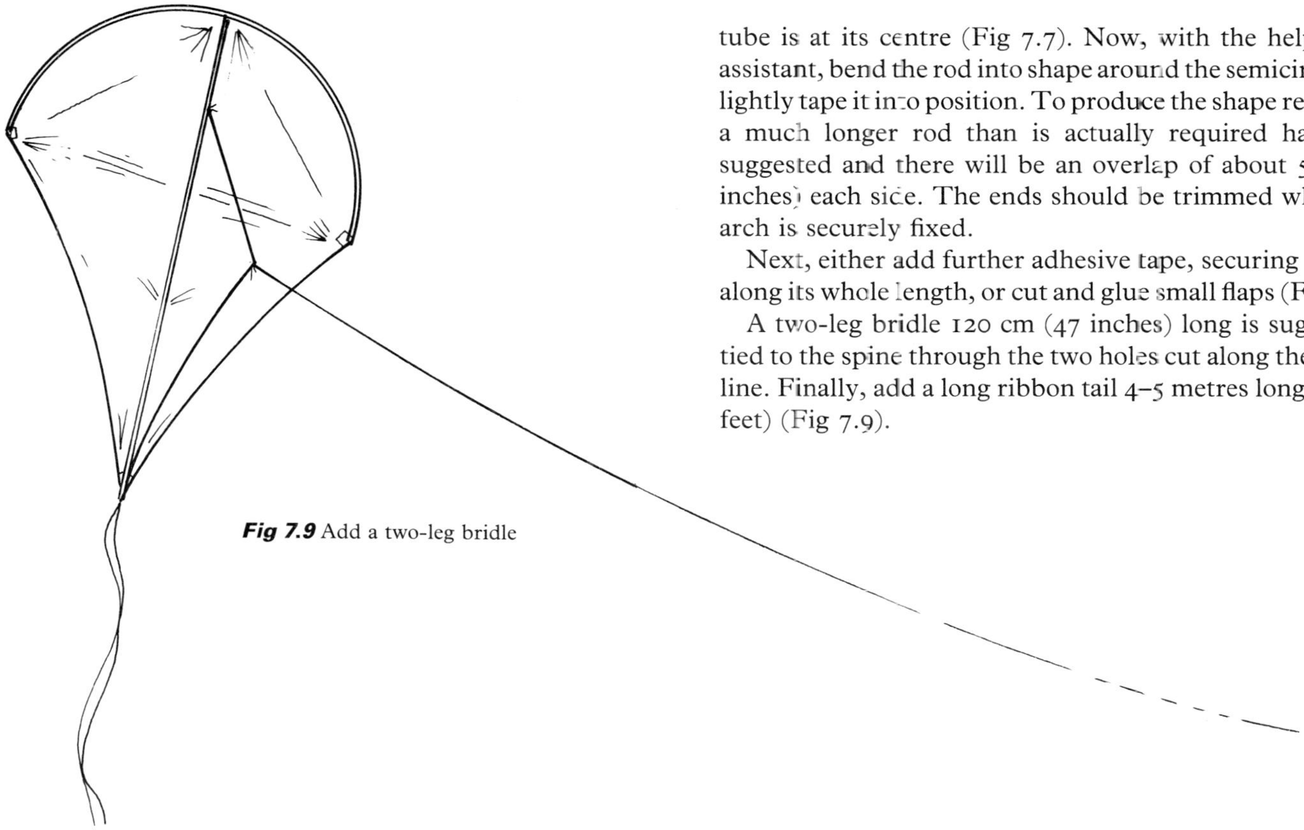

tube is at its centre (Fig 7.7). Now, with the help of an assistant, bend the rod into shape around the semicircle and lightly tape it into position. To produce the shape required, a much longer rod than is actually required has been suggested and there will be an overlap of about 5 cm (2 inches) each side. The ends should be trimmed when the arch is securely fixed.

Next, either add further adhesive tape, securing the rod along its whole length, or cut and glue small flaps (Fig 7.8).

A two-leg bridle 120 cm (47 inches) long is suggested, tied to the spine through the two holes cut along the centre line. Finally, add a long ribbon tail 4–5 metres long (12–15 feet) (Fig 7.9).

Fig 7.9 Add a two-leg bridle

YAKKO KITE

The Yakko is a traditional Japanese design also known as the 'Footman' kite, which in its original form would measure up to two or three metres tall. This version is, of course, much smaller, and has proved extremely popular in workshops. It also introduces the construction of a 'three-leg' bridle.

Sail : Polythene, *Tyvek*, wrapping paper, polyester film

Spars : 2 mm ($\frac{1}{16}$ inch) fibreglass 150 cm (59 inches) long

The Yakko requires a single rectangle of sail material roughly 85 cm × 40 cm (34 inches × 16 inches). Cut out the pattern indicated in Fig 7.10.

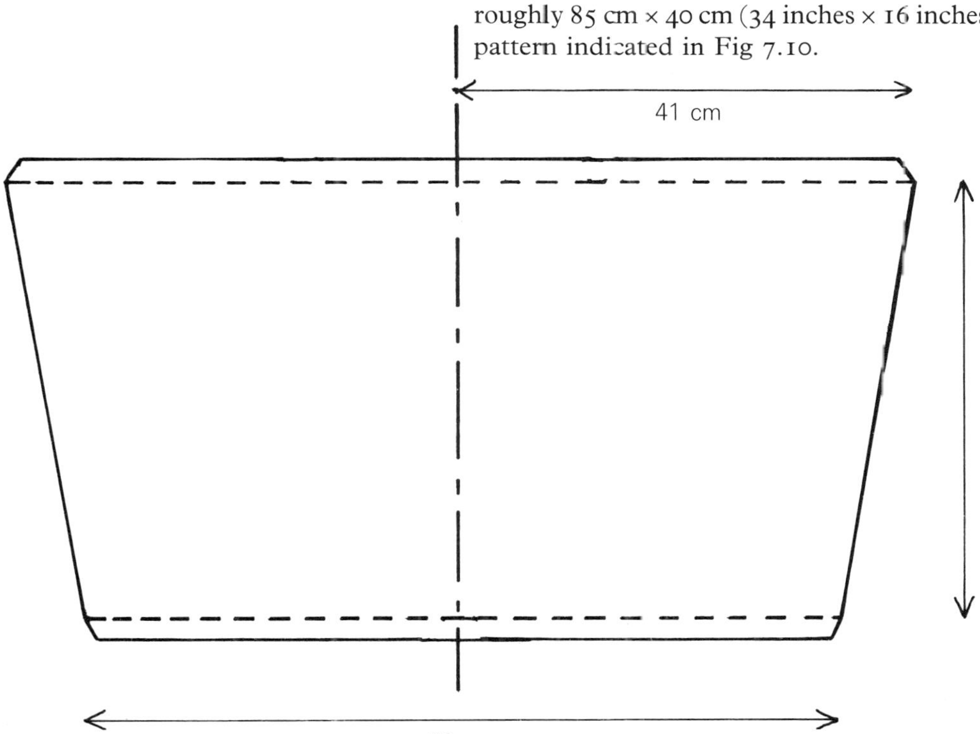

Fig 7.10 Yakko pattern

Fold and tape or glue the top and bottom flaps to create narrow tubes, similar to the construction of delta kites. Then reinforce and cut narrow notches in the top tube 10 cm (4 inches) each side of the centre line, and a much wider notch at the bottom centre (Fig 7.11).

Thread the fibreglass through the tubes at the edges of the sail, to create the hoop as shown (Fig 7.12). Next tape the upper and lower parts of the sail together at the outer edges (Fig 7.13). If necessary, reposition the fibreglass so that the ends overlap at the centre bottom, and, with a slight tension in the hoop, tape them together.

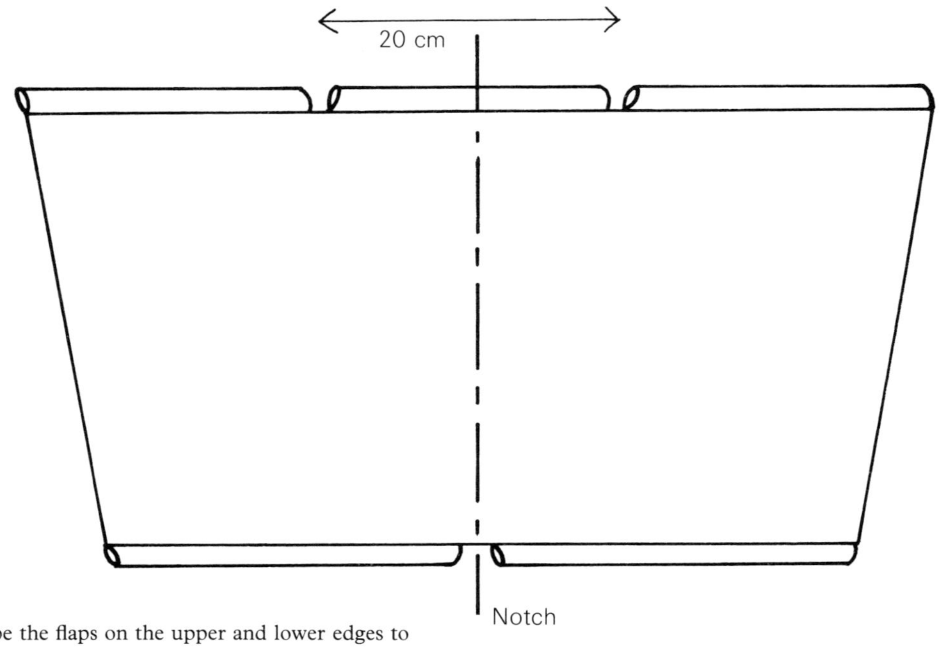

Fig 7.11 Fold and tape the flaps on the upper and lower edges to make the spar tubes

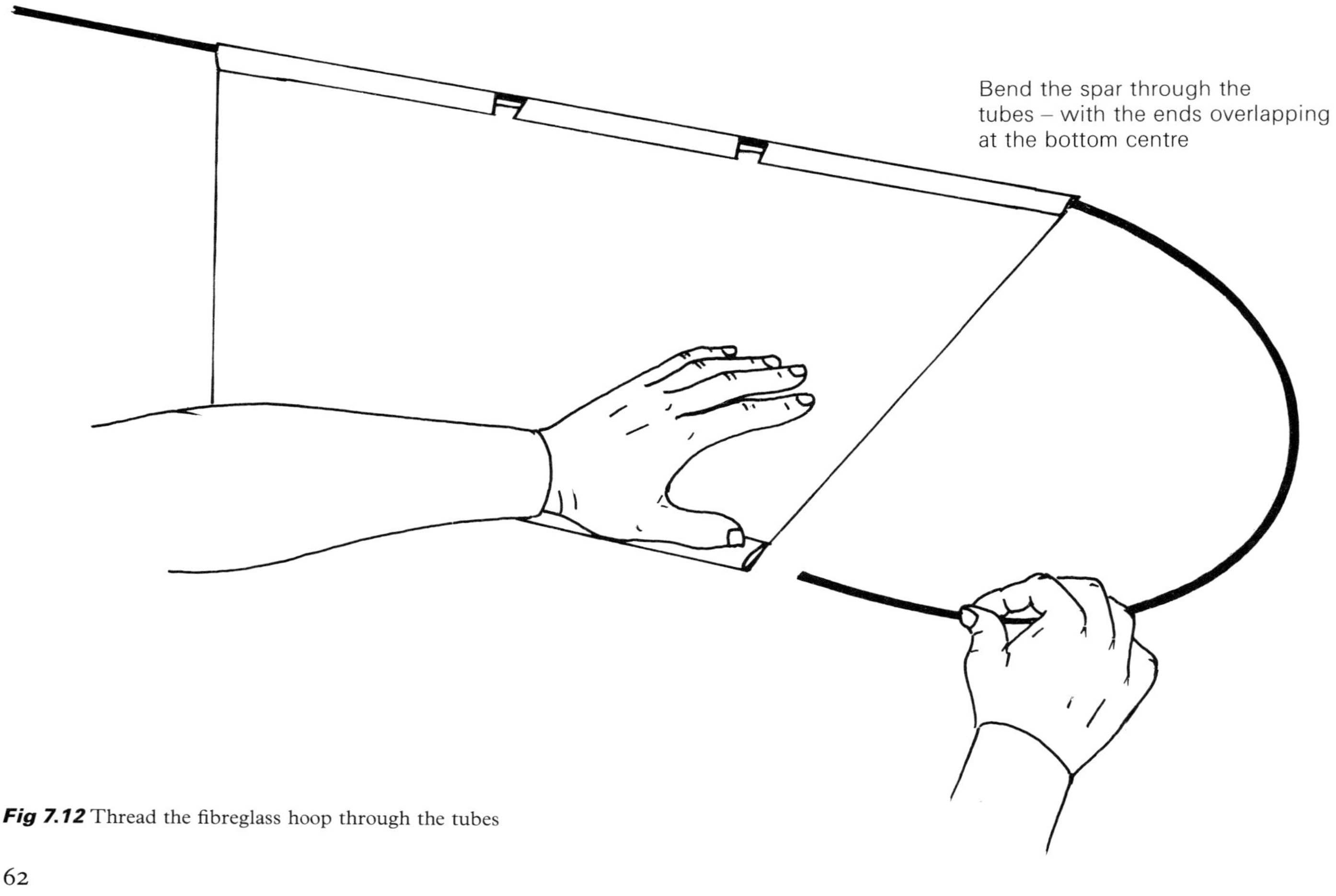

Fig 7.12 Thread the fibreglass hoop through the tubes

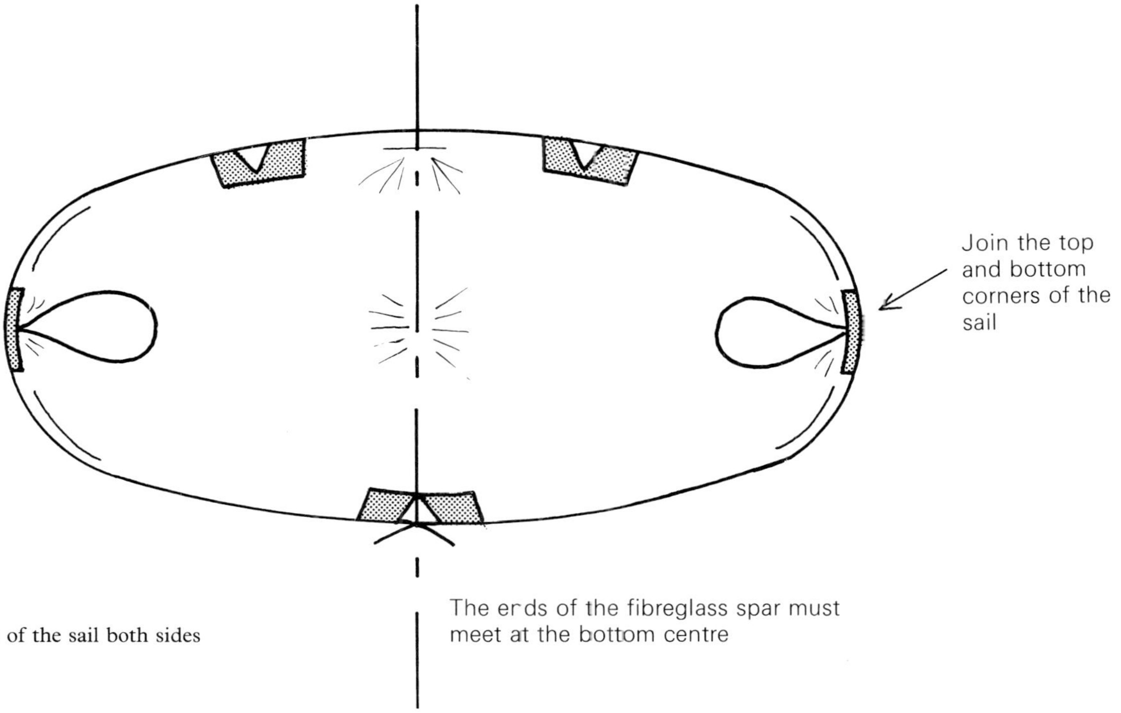

Fig 7.13 Tape the corners of the sail both sides

Unlike previous kites, the Yakko requires not a two, but a three-leg bridle, and this basic construction is also used on kites featured in later sections.

Cut a length of line approximately 105 cm (41½ inches) long and tie the ends to the fibreglass hoop at the two upper notches previously cut. Next tie a small (towing) ring at its centre using the larks-head hitch.

Cut another line 70 cm (27½ inches) long, tie one end to the fibreglass hoop and the bottom centre and thread the other through two holes in a small button. Bring the loose end through the ring, then finally tie it through a third hole in the button. By moving the button, you should be able to alter the length of the lower bridle leg and thereby control the angle of attack for varying wind conditions (Fig 7.14). For average winds, the lower leg should be about 56 cm (22 inches) long.

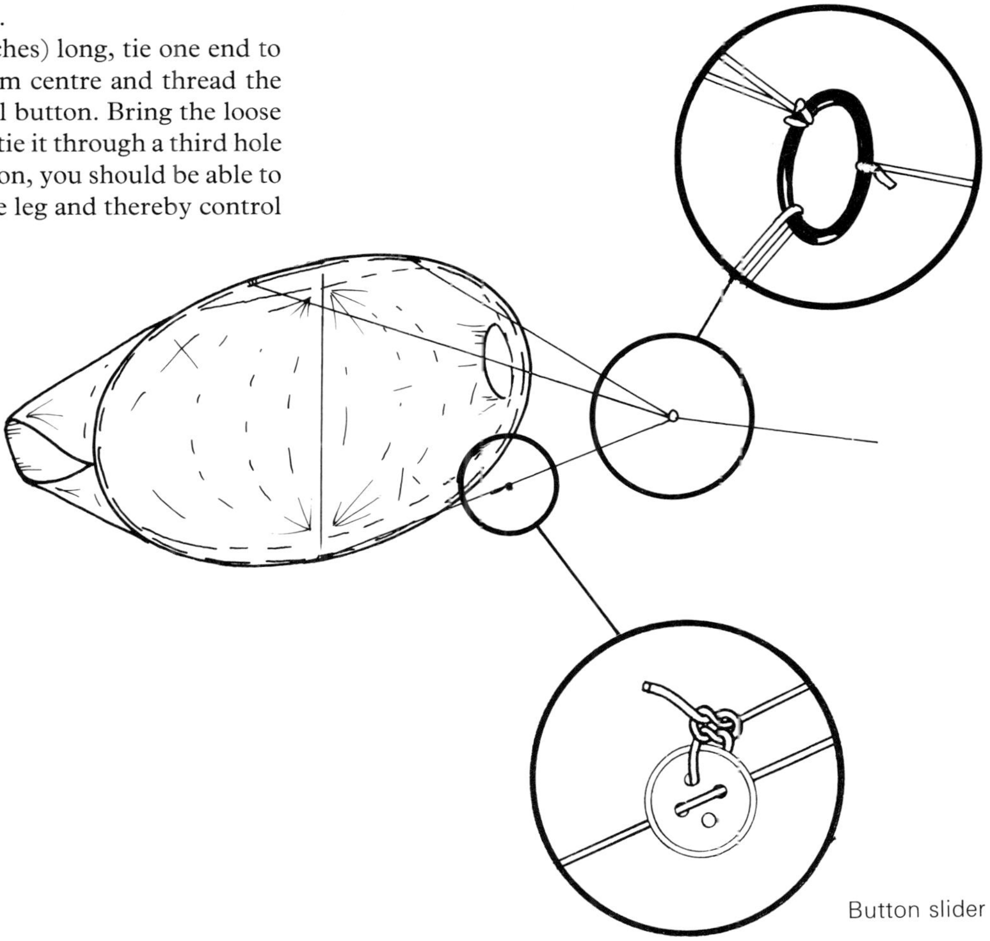

Fig 7.14 Three-leg bridle construction

bowed kites

For Victorian children, there was only one type of kite: a diamond or figure shape with a long flowing tail which danced around in the wind. But towards the end of the nineteenth century, kitemakers began to look more carefully at other Eastern designs, particularly those of countries which now make up Malaysia and Indonesia, in which the cross spar was bowed, allowing the kite to be flown without a tail.

Traditionally on these designs the spars are square, lashed together with twine at their intersection. But this method of construction is not easy, and on modern versions other types of intersection are used. To make a suitable joint, cut a small length of PVC tube 2–3 cm ($\frac{3}{4}$–1 inch) long and punch two sets of closely spaced holes at right angles. Threading the spars through these holes will create a good tight connection (Fig 8.1).

The cross spar is usually bowed by means of an adjustable line called, naturally enough, the 'bow line' or 'string'. Cut a length of line about one and a half times the length of the spar, tie an overhand loop at one end and thread the other through two holes in a small button or aluminium slider. Now bring the other end round, and tie it through a third hole in the button (Fig 8.2). Loop the ends over the notches at each end of the cross spar, and by moving the button you can tension the line to create the desired amount of bow. The degree of bow is usually described as its maximum depth, either as an absolute measure, or as a percentage of the cross spar length (Fig 8.3).

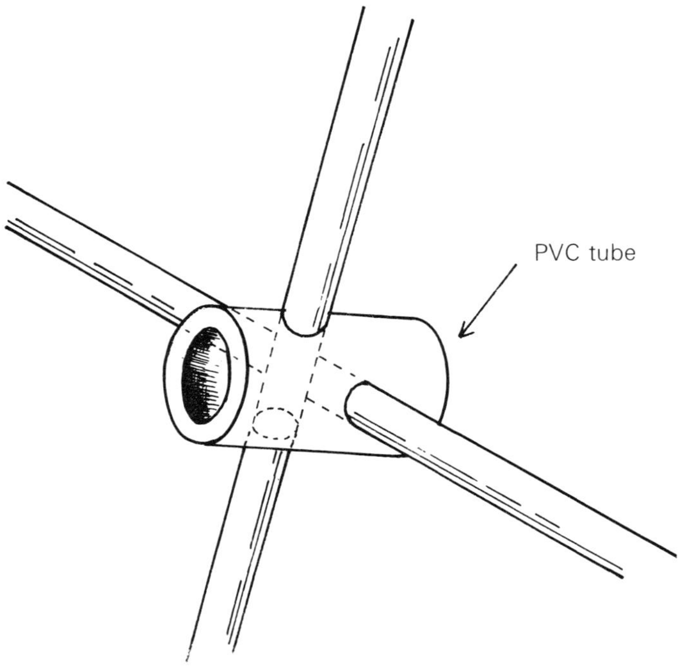

Fig 8.1 Cross spar connection

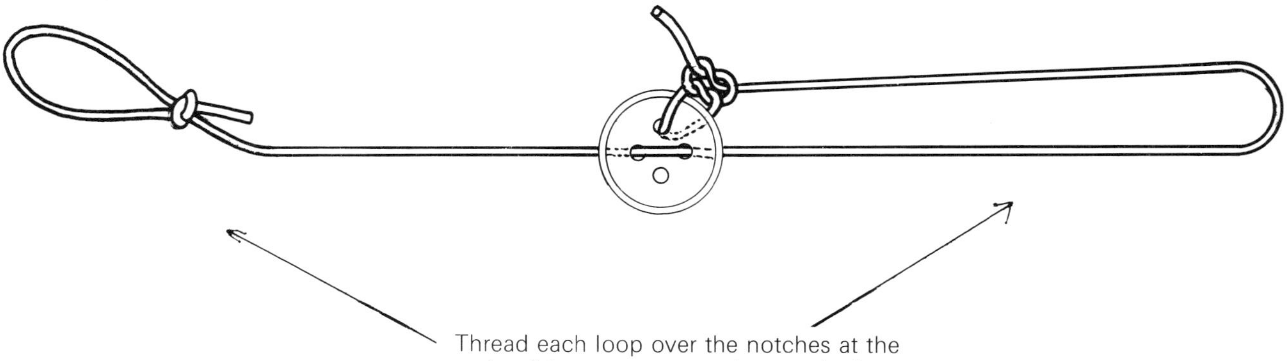

Fig 8.2 Bow string construction

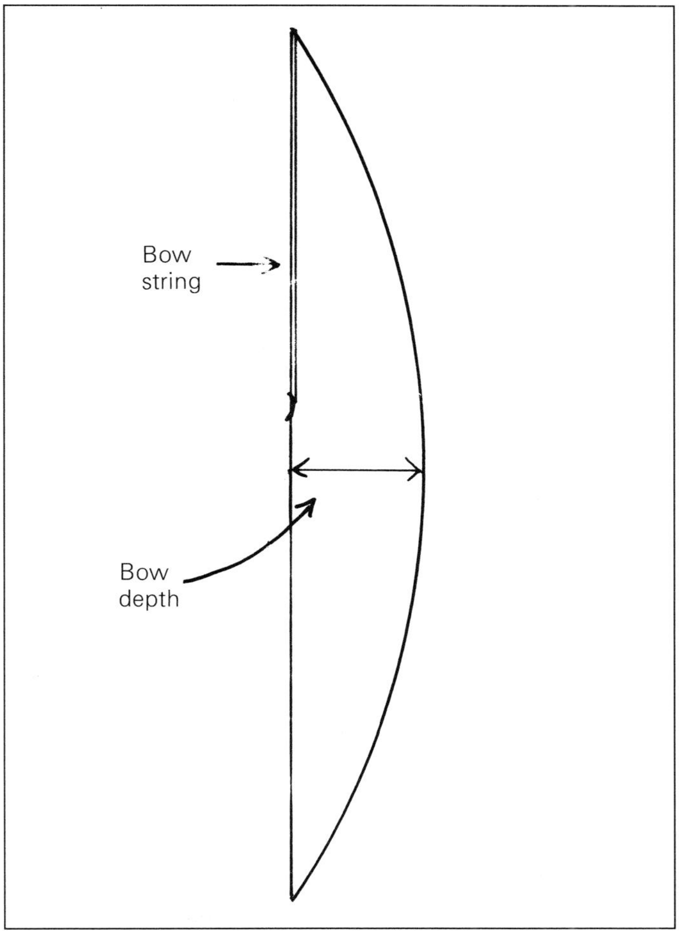

Fig 8.3 Bow depth

EDDY KITE

Sail : Wrapping paper, *Tyvek* 14
Spars : 6.3 mm ($\frac{1}{4}$ inch) *Ramin* dowel; spine 80 cm ($31\frac{1}{2}$ inches) long; spar 82 cm (32 inches) long

Eddy kites are notoriously prone to wobbling, dancing from side to side, particularly in gusts, caused by drag effects as air currents are formed alternately on each side. Some designers have managed to overcome this problem through clever construction techniques, but if you use slightly softer, porous materials, you will find that the wobble almost completely disappears. To soften wrapping paper, for example, crumple it into a ball and straighten it flat, several times.

Roughly cut a triangle of sail material 105 cm (42 inches) base and 85 cm (34 inches) height. As with other designs, fold it in half, crease, then cut out the shape as indicated in Fig 8.4. Although you can reinforce the edges with PVC or strapping tape with *Tyvek* it is just as easy to make a single hem fold approximately 1 cm ($\frac{3}{8}$ inch) wide.

Make the central connection as described above and thread it on the spine.

The spine is best taped to the sail at three or four points along its length, with additional reinforcing strips at the tip and base. The cross spar, on the other hand, is attached to the sail at its ends only. Tie overhand loops in two short lengths of line and tape them, one at each of the wing tips (Fig 8.5). The knots can be neatly hidden under the adhesive tape.

Cut small 'V' notches at the ends of the cross spar and thread it through the central PVC connection. Now thread the loops at the wing tips over the ends of the cross spar and adjust them both so that the cross spar is evenly positioned, but without tensioning the sail too much (Fig 8.6).

To make the bridle, tie one end of the line to the intersection of the two spars and the other to the spine 6 cm ($2\frac{3}{8}$ inches) from the base, such that after tying the loop is 160 cm (63 inches) long. Finally, fit the bow string across the spar ends. For average conditions the upper bridle leg should be around 70 cm ($27\frac{1}{2}$ inches) and the bow depth about 12 cm (5 inches) (Fig 8.7).

Bowed kites have an advantage over other designs, since you can alter the degree of bow as well as the position of the towing point to accommodate different wind conditions. So don't be afraid to do both.

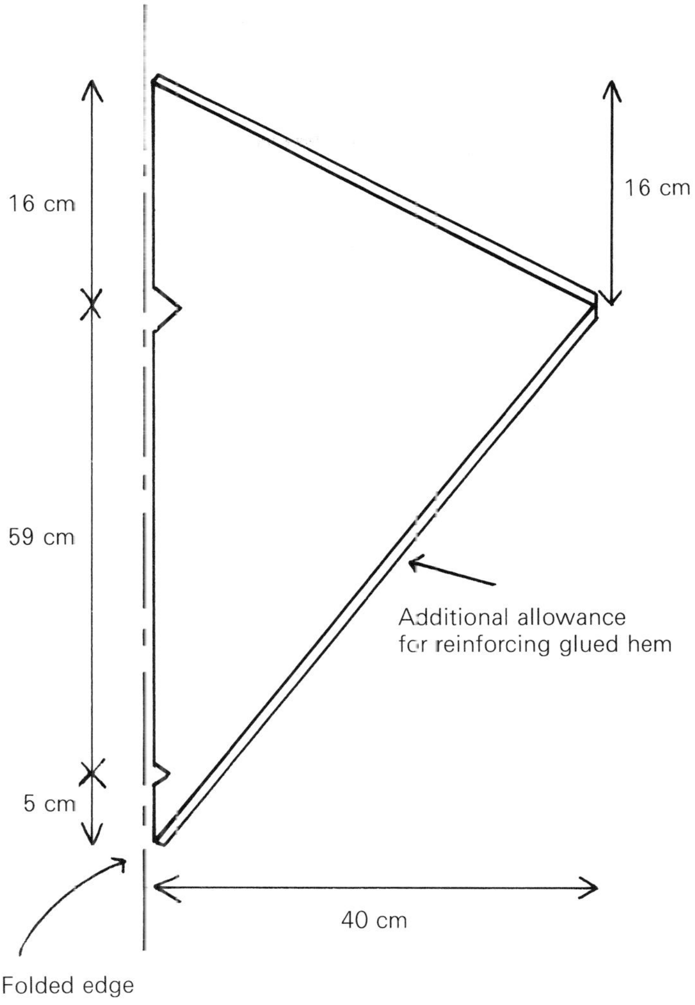

Fig 8.4 Eddy pattern

Fig 8.5 Tape short overhand loops at the wing tips

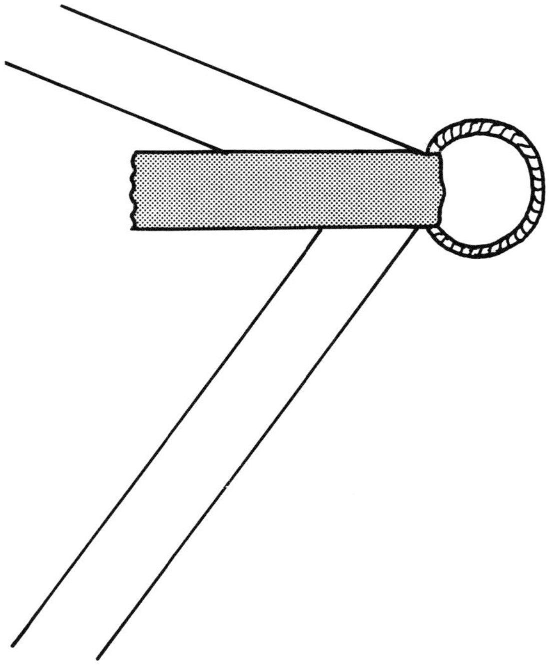

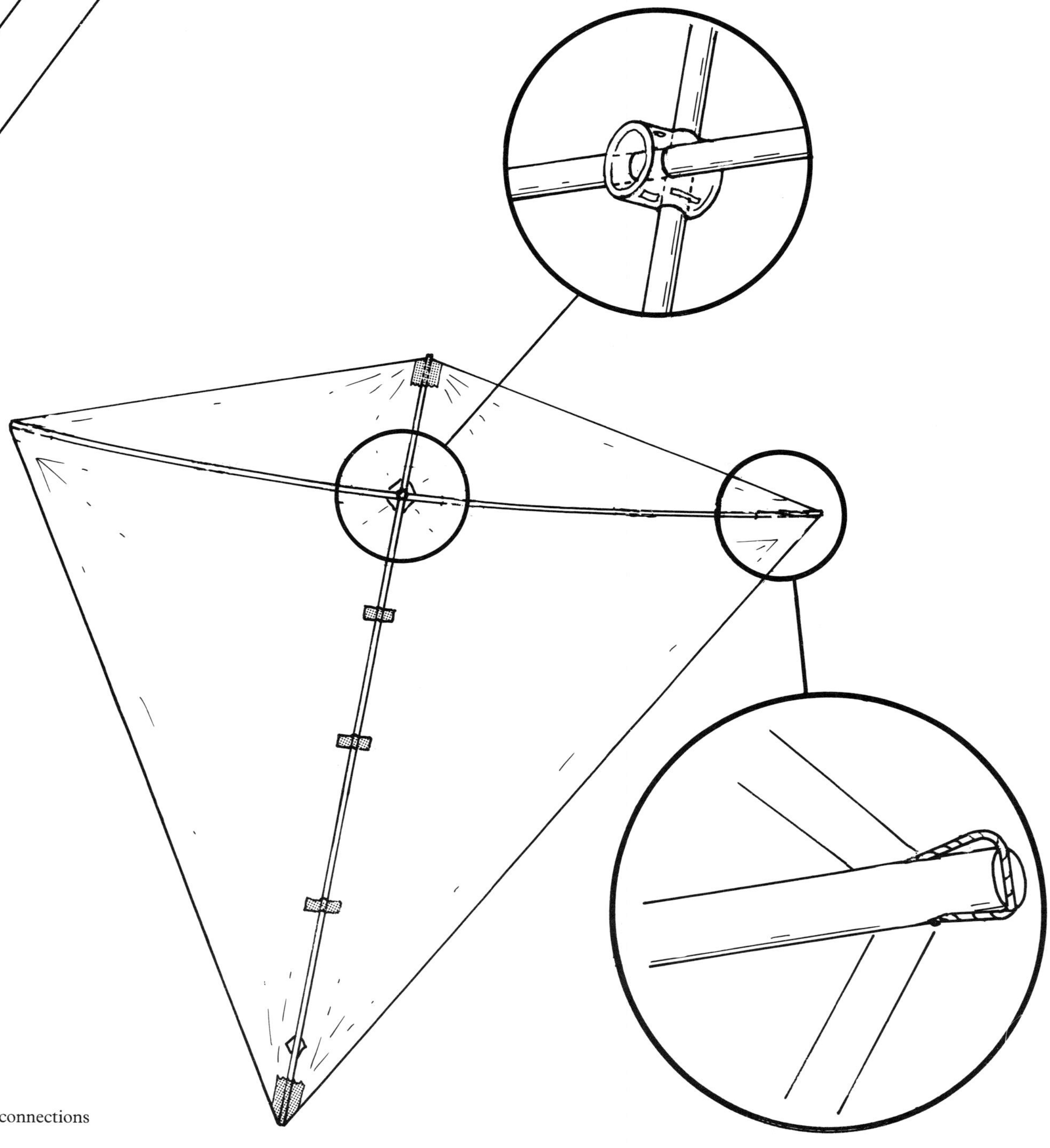

Fig 8.6 Sail connections

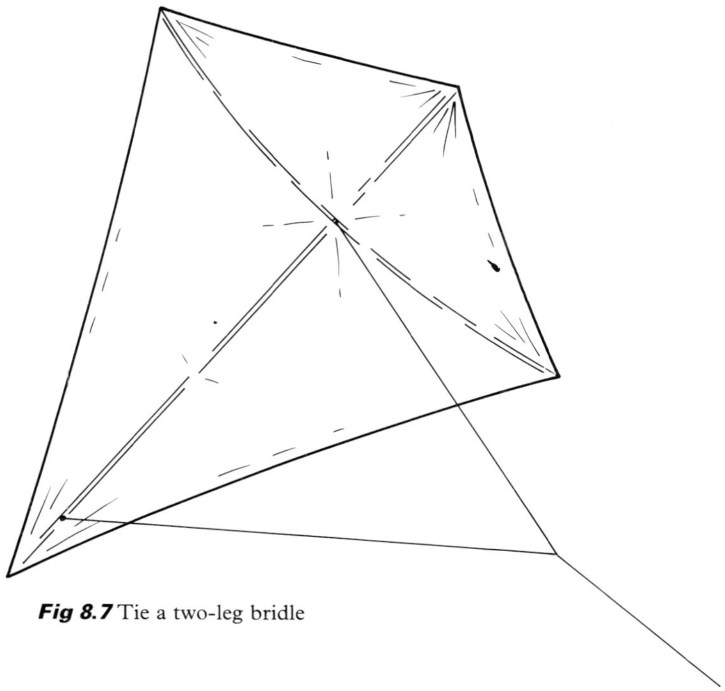

Fig 8.7 Tie a two-leg bridle

JIB SAIL KITE

Sail : Polythene, *Tyvek*, polyester film
Spars : *Ramin* dowel spine 6.3 mm ($\frac{1}{4}$ inch) 77 cm long; spar 5 mm ($\frac{3}{16}$ inch) 90 cm long

As with previous designs, to achieve good symmetry fold the sail material in half and cut out two triangular shapes A and B (Fig 8.8). Cut out the rudder from a single layer of material.

With sail B still folded tape/glue the rudder in place along the centre (fold) line. Reinforce the rudder tip and punch a hole, or fit a small ring to accept the bridle (Fig 8.9).

The cross spar is held not on the surface of the sail but in a tube along the upper edge of sail B. Before making the tube, however, tape small loops (Fig 8.10a) to the wing tips, which will eventually hold the spar ends in position, then fold and glue or tape the tube (Fig 8.10b). Additionally, reinforce the spar tube along the centre fold line and cut a small notch (Fig 8.11).

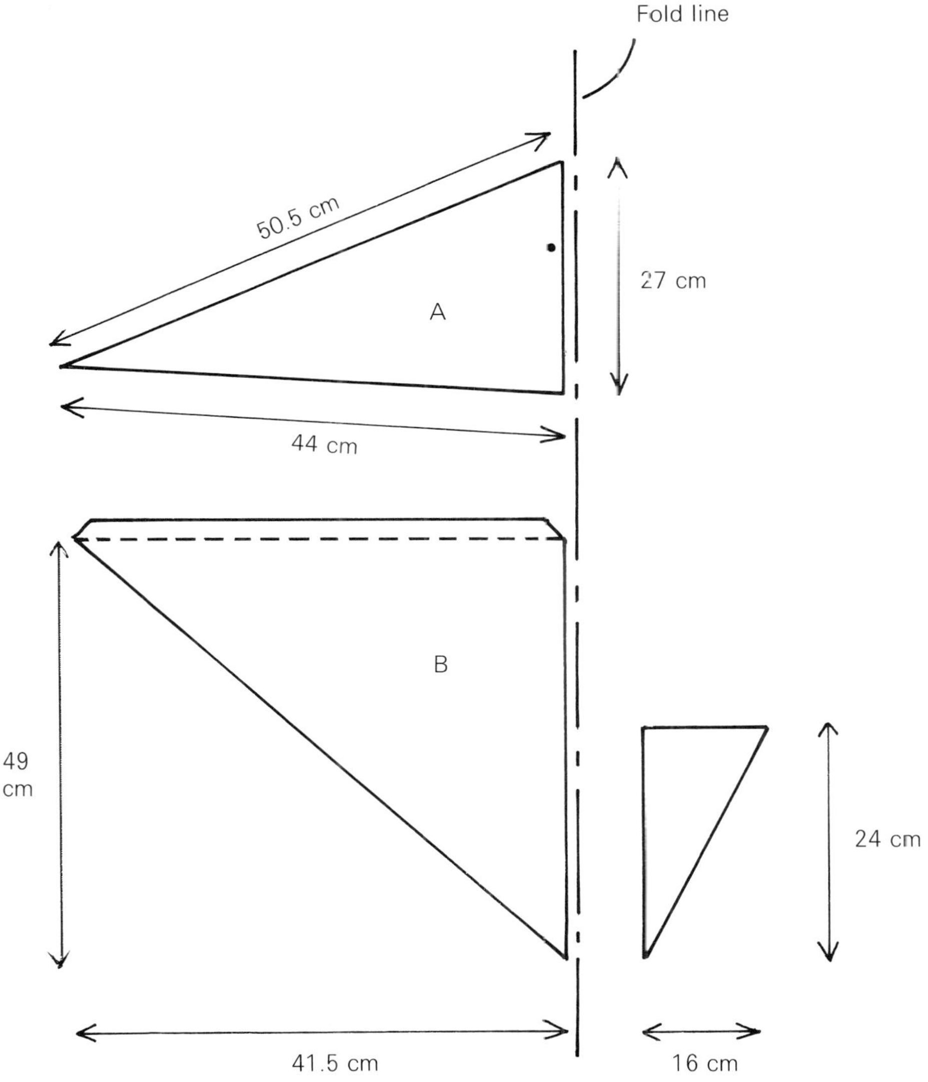

Fig 8.8 Jib sail pattern

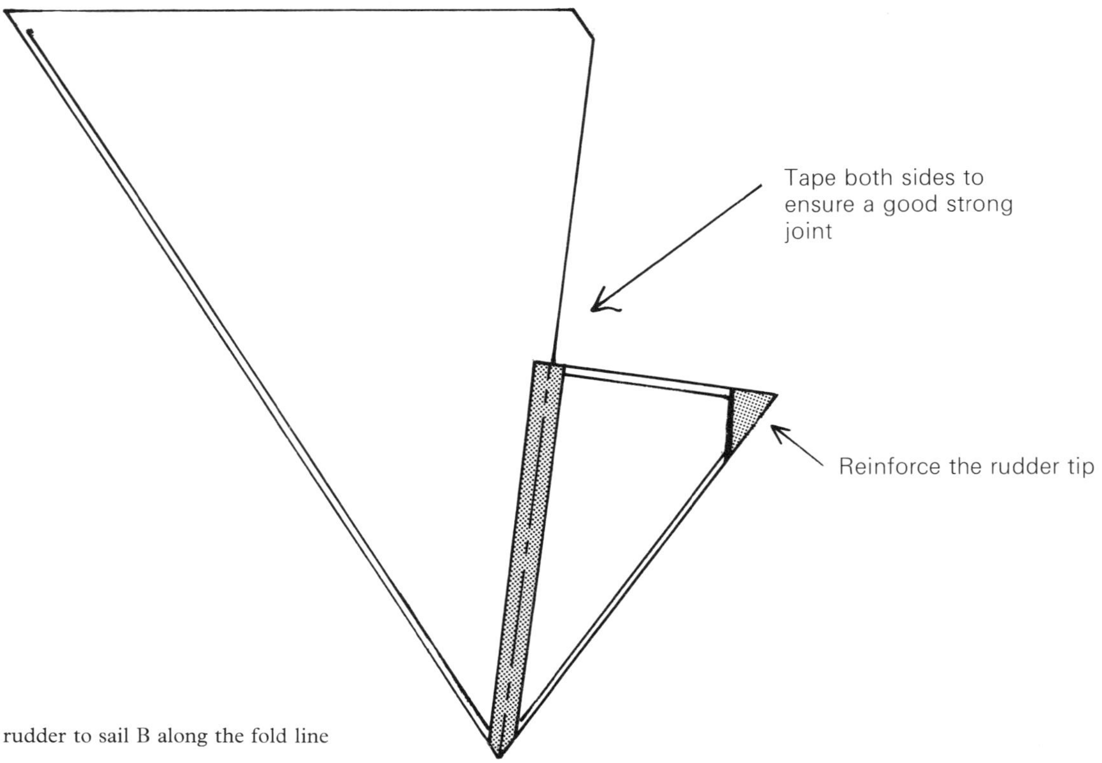

Fig 8.9 Tape the rudder to sail B along the fold line

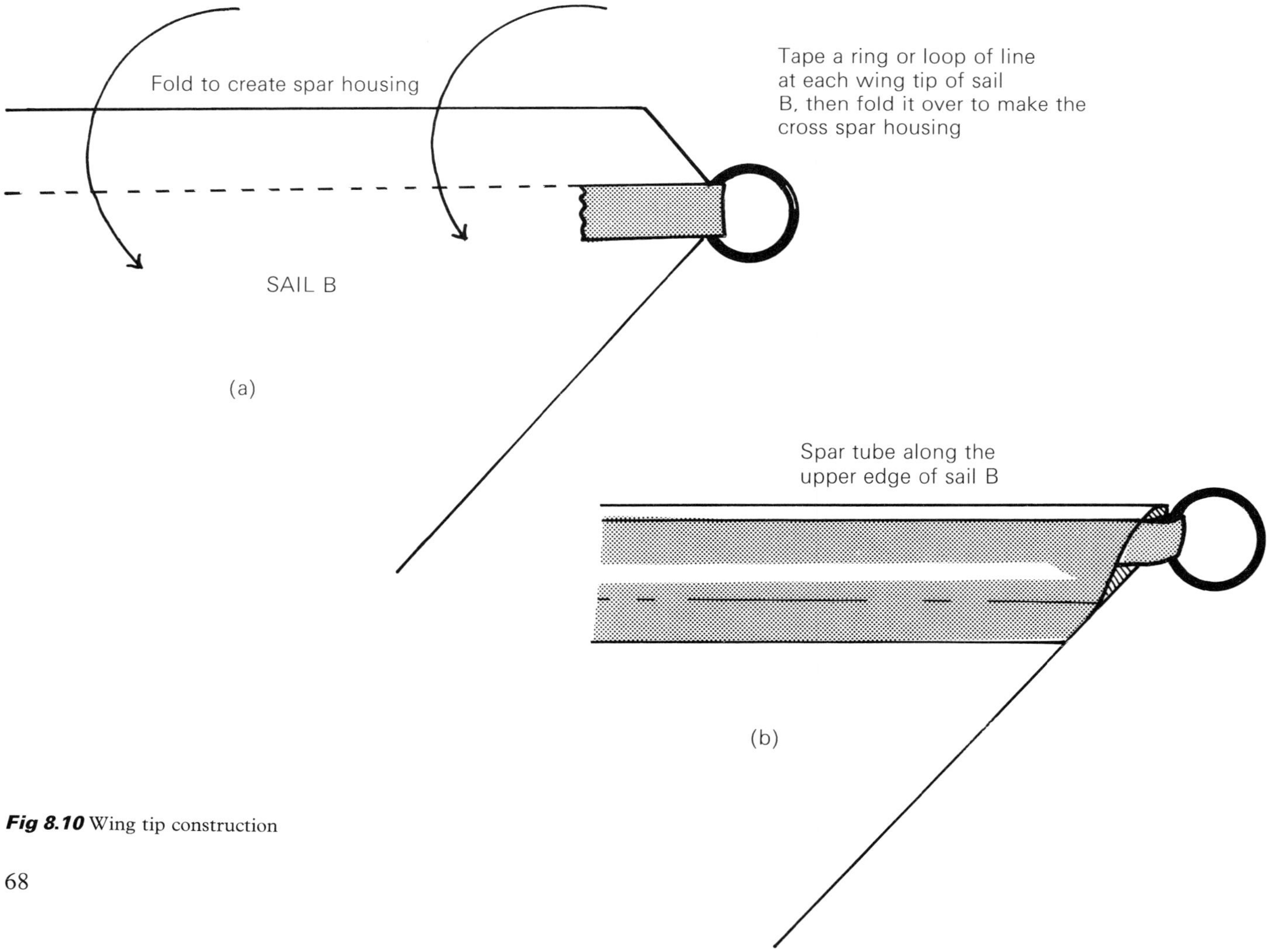

Fig 8.10 Wing tip construction

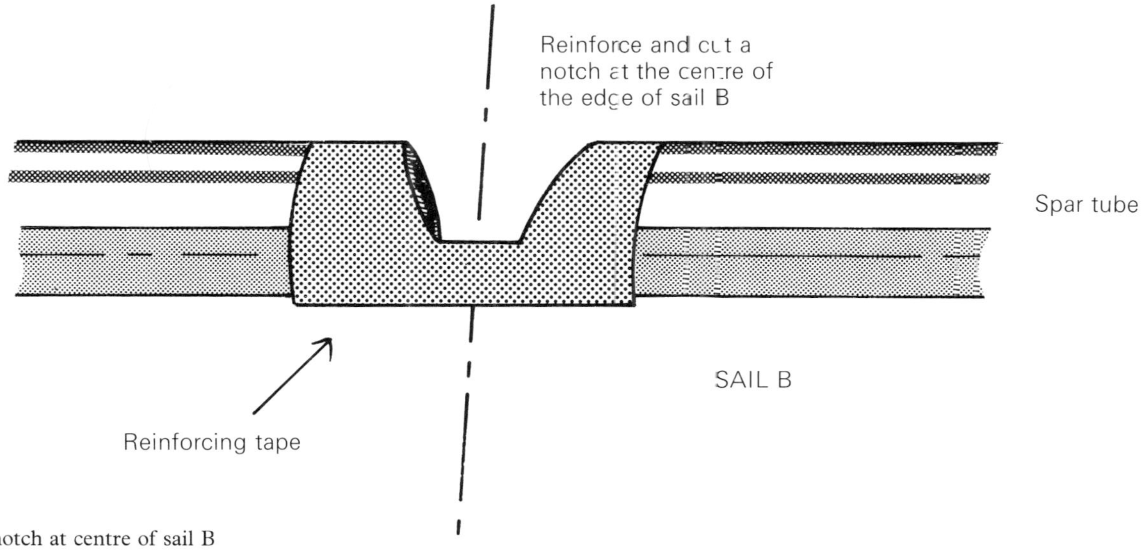

Fig 8.11 Cut a notch at centre of sail B

Similarly, fit small loops of line at the tips of the upper sail (Fig 8.12).

Lay the two sail sections flat, rudder underneath, cut 'V' notches at the ends of the cross spar and thread it through the tube at the edge of the lower sail B, fitting the central PVC connection as you do so. Also position the spine, threaded through the central PVC connection.

Tape the spine to both upper and lower sails at four to six points, including the full length of the rudder, with additional reinforcement at the tip and base (Fig 8.13).

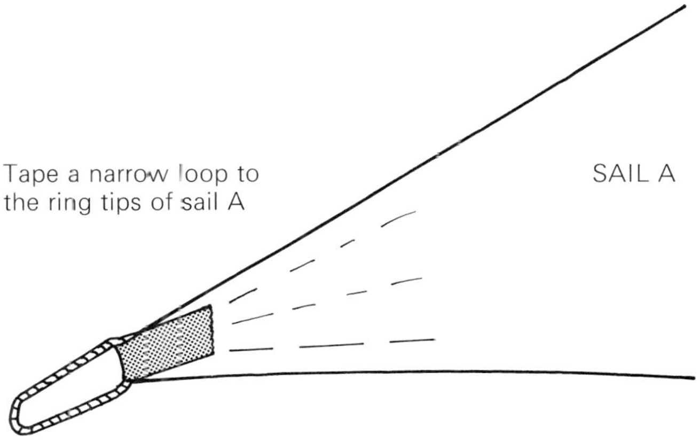

Fig 8.12 Tape short overhand loops to the tips of sail A

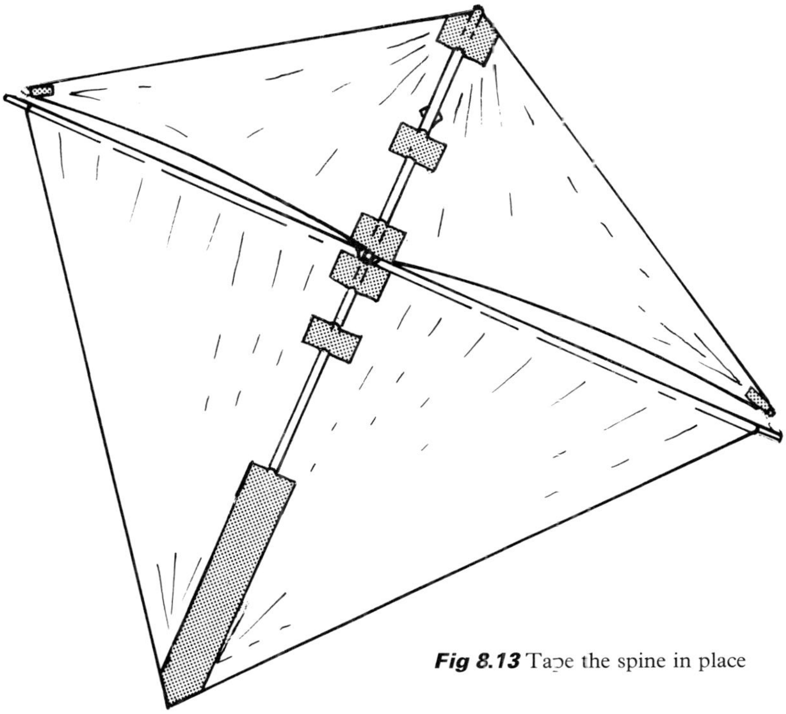

Fig 8.13 Tape the spine in place

Fig 8.14 Thread loops from sails A and B over the ends of the cross spar

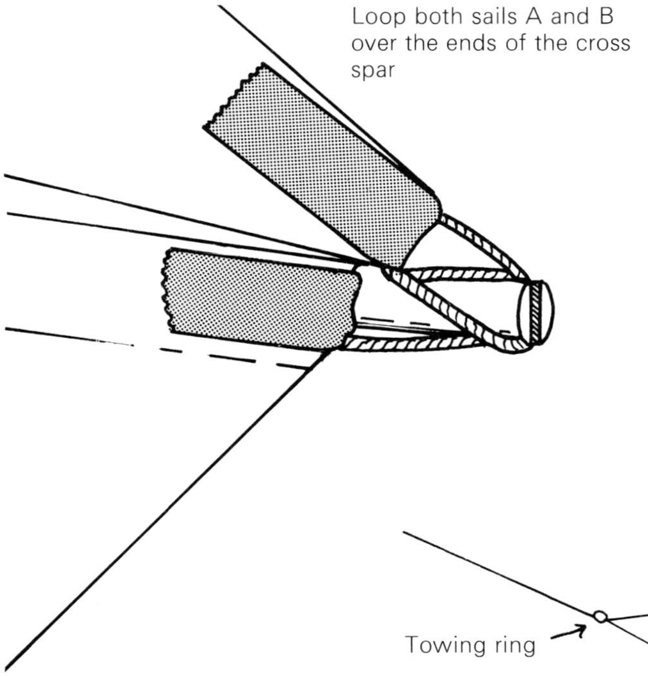

Next, thread the loops from both upper and lower sails over the tips of the cross spar (Fig 8.14). It may be necessary at this stage to trim the cross spar or adjust the loops to provide a slight tension around the perimeter of the sails.

Make and fit the bow string as described above.

Fit a two-leg bridle 148 cm (58 inches) long, tied to the rudder tip and to the spine 14 cm ($5\frac{1}{2}$ inches) from the tip. For average conditions, the upper bridle leg should be around 80 cm ($31\frac{1}{2}$ inches) long, with a bow depth of 10 cm (4 inches) Fig 8.15).

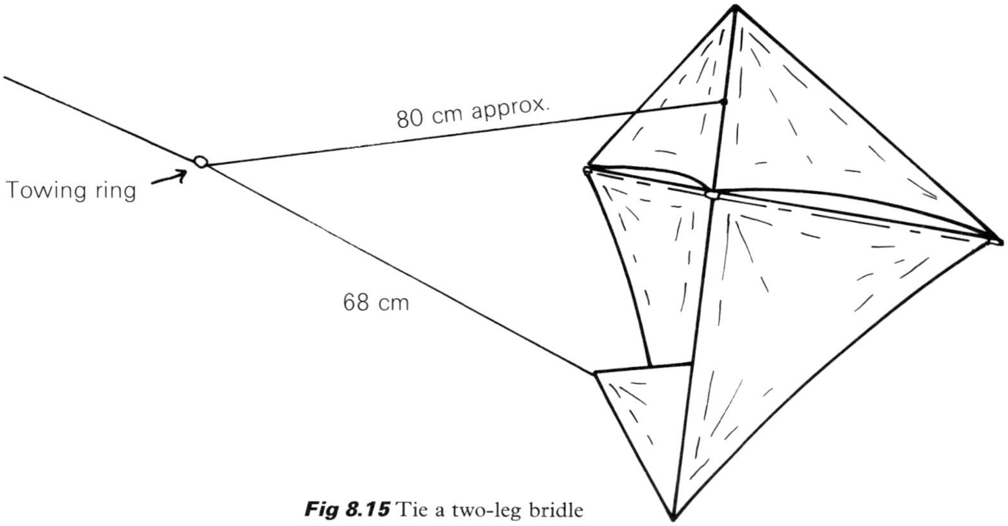

Fig 8.15 Tie a two-leg bridle

ROKAKKU

The Rokakku is a traditional Japanese design, now becoming very popular in Britain as a fighting kite. This version is not designed for fighting, however, but for those fliers looking for a kite with a large flat sail on which to create a masterpiece of decoration.

Sail : *Tyvek*, high density polythene (at least 200 micron)

Spars : 6.3 mm dowel: spine approximately 86 cm (34 inches) long;
spars 2 pieces approximately 72 cm ($28\frac{1}{4}$ inches) long

Start by cutting a rectangular piece of sail material, roughly 85 cm × 75 cm ($33\frac{1}{2}$ inches × $29\frac{1}{2}$ inches) and cut out the pattern Fig 8.16. If you're using *Tyvek* add sufficient to the dimensions shown to allow for a 1 cm glued hem around the perimeter.

Reinforce and cut small holes at the bridle connection points, ABCD.

Thread two PVC connections on to the spine and tape it to the sail with extra reinforcing at the tip and base. Also fit loops of line at the four wing tips, and check that they are all the same size and evenly placed.

The Rokakku has a four-leg bridle, two upper and two lower. To make these, cut out two lengths of line and tie narrow overhand loops at their centres and each end, so that, when tied, one has legs 90 cm ($35\frac{1}{2}$ inches) long, the other 80 cm ($31\frac{1}{2}$ inches) long.

Cut 'V' sections at the ends of the cross spars and fit them through the central PVC connections onto the wing loops, as with the Eddy. As you do so, also push the bridle ends

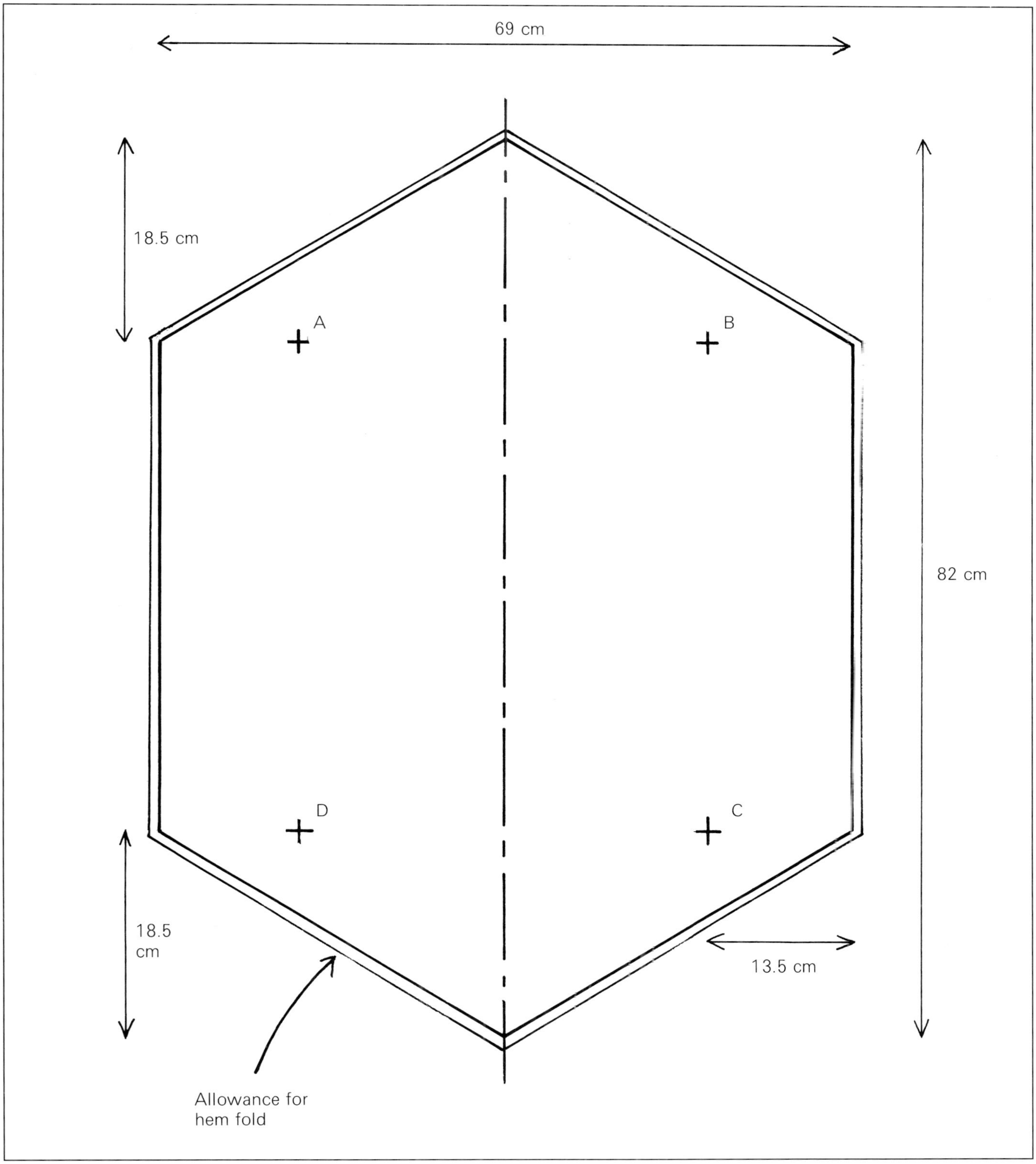

Fig 8.16 Rokakku pattern

through the holes ABCD and thread them on to the spars (Fig 8.17).

Now turn the sail over, to begin adjusting the bridles. Join the centre loops of upper and lower brides with a third length of line about 30 cm long and add a strong towing ring (Fig 8.18). Finally, add the bow strings.

To fly the Rokakku, adjust the bow on the upper spar to a depth of 6–8 cm (2–3 inches) and lower 10–12 cm (3–4 inches). If it is unstable on its maiden flight, adjust the bow on both spars, and/or the position of the towing ring.

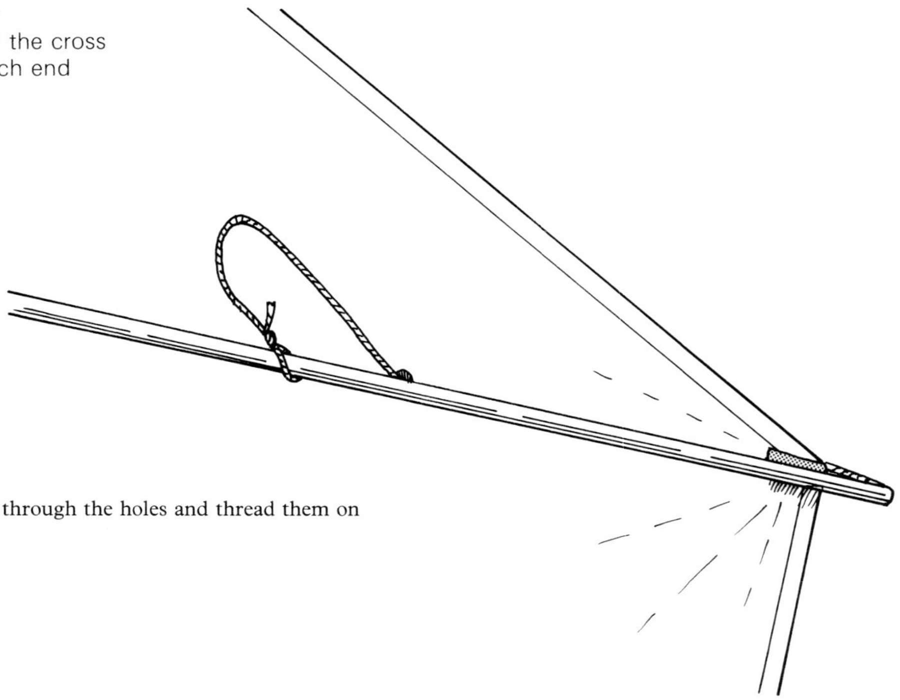

Fig 8.17 Push the bridle loops through the holes and thread them on to the cross spar

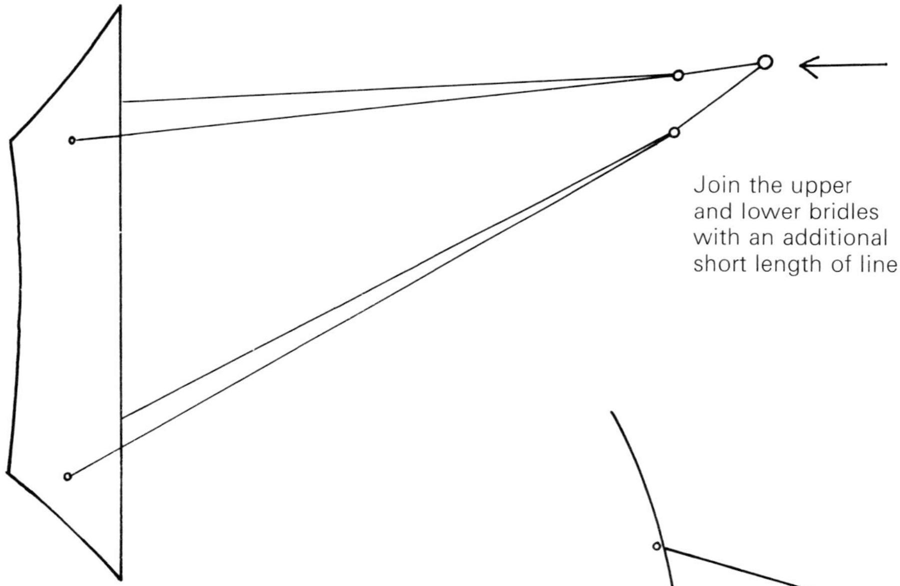

Fig 8.18 Bridles

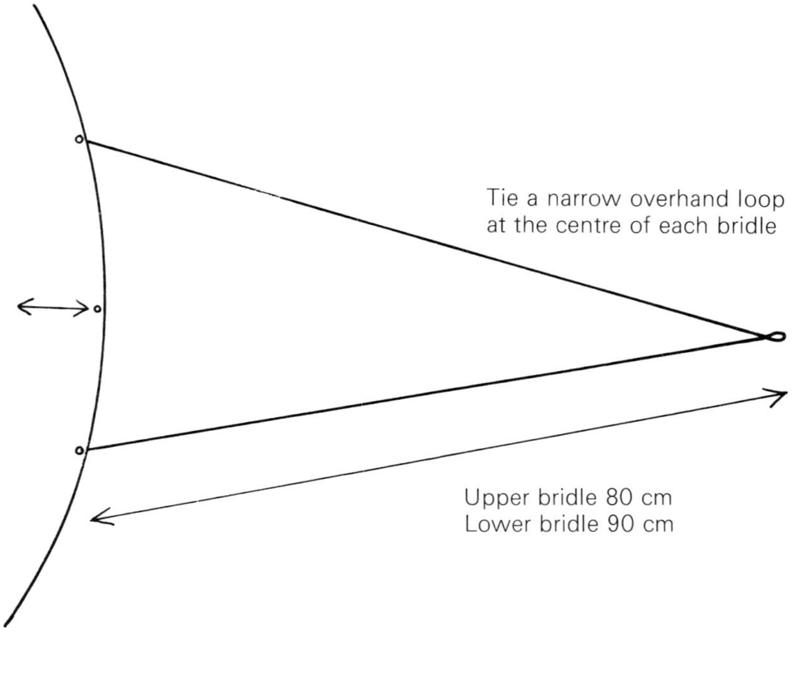

Fig 8.19 Join the two bridles together

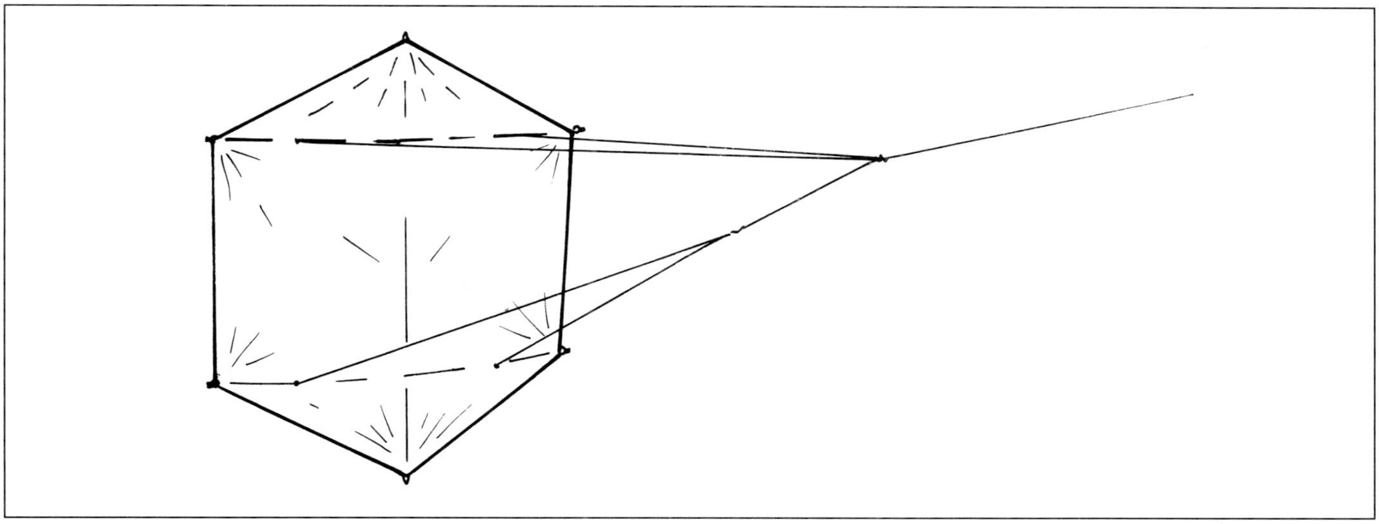

Fig 8.20 Rokakku complete

CHAPTER NINE

box – three-dimensional kites

OXO BOX KITE

This is a good simple workshop box kite, easy to construct and fun to fly.

Sail : Tube made from polythene, paper or *Tyvek*
Spars : 4 pieces 5 mm ($\frac{3}{16}$ inch) dowel approximately 57 cm ($22\frac{1}{2}$ inches) long;
4 pieces approximately 37 cm ($14\frac{1}{2}$ inches) long

The Oxo is best perhaps described as a 'tube' box, since the easiest method of construction requires a whole polythene bag. Ideally, it should be 55 cm ($21\frac{3}{4}$ inches) wide but one or two centimetres more or less will not affect its flying characteristics too much: just alter the spar dimensions accordingly. Alternatively, you can make the 'tube' from a single piece of paper, polythene or *Tyvek*, 110 cm ($43\frac{1}{4}$ inches) by 55 cm ($21\frac{3}{4}$ inches).

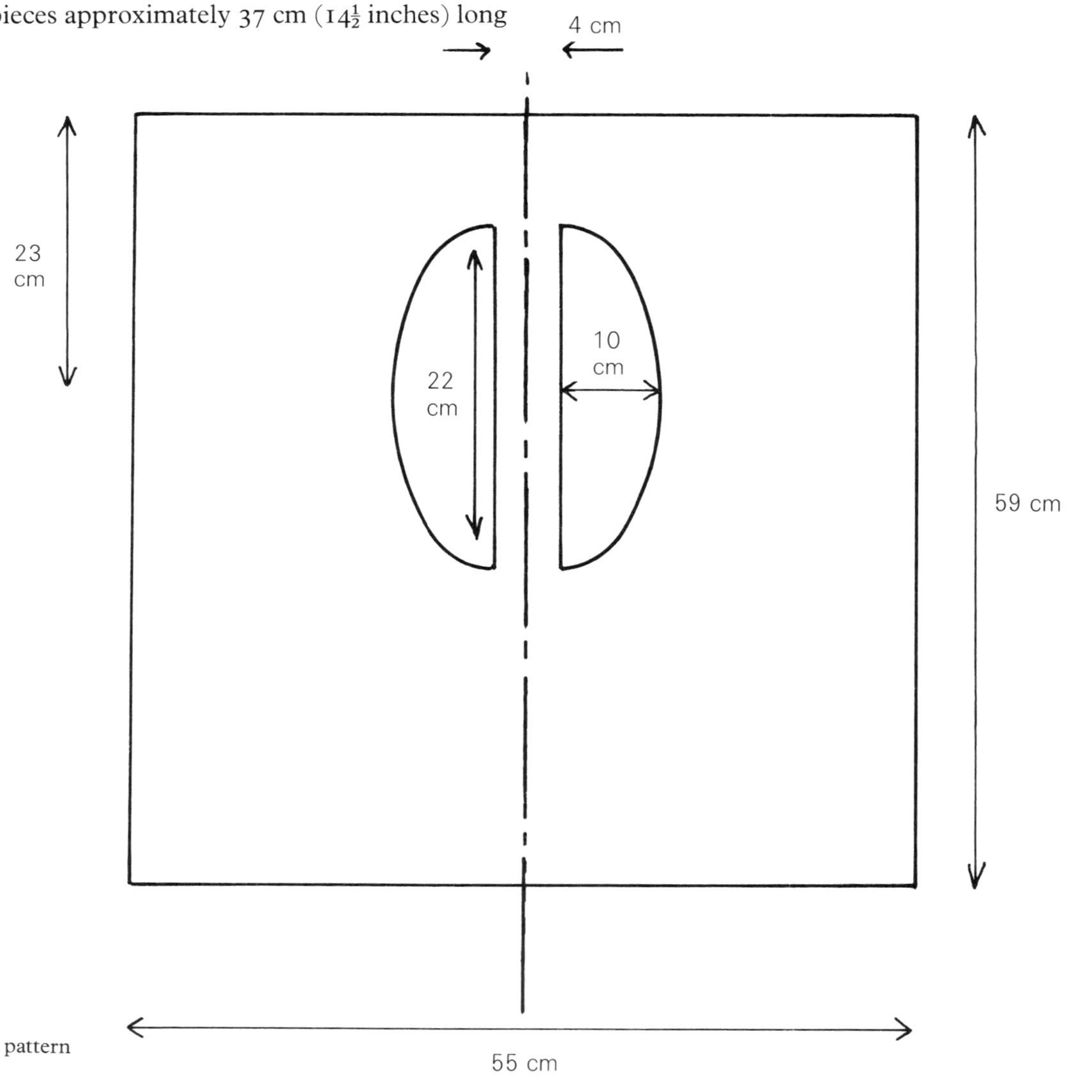

Fig 9.1 Oxo box pattern

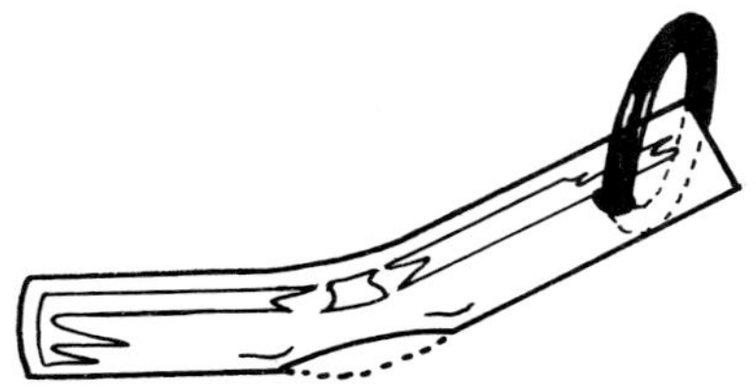

Fig 9.2 Corner connection construction

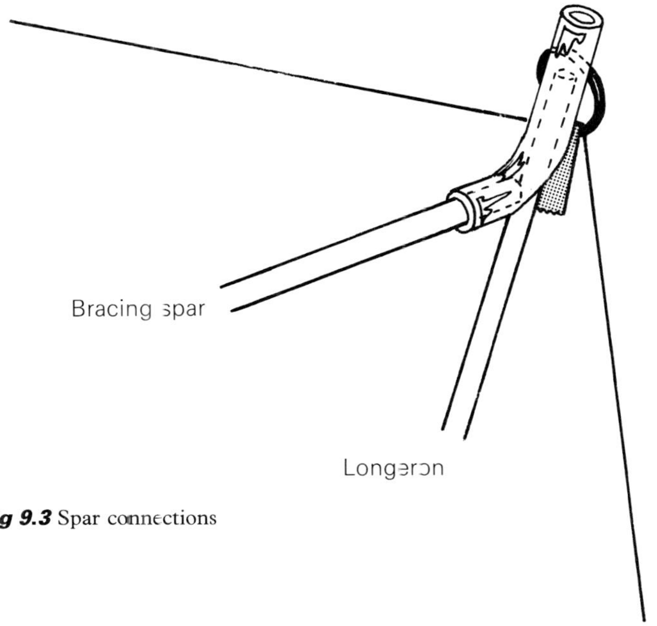

Fig 9.3 Spar connections

Lay the tube flat and crease the edges firmly. Carefully mark the centre line, then mark and cut out the vents as indicated in Fig 9.1. Reinforce the sail along the 'open' edges of the tube if necessary.

Make eight connections (Fig 9.2) and tape them to each of the corners. Fit the longerons (longer spars) into these connections at each of the corners, trimmed so that they are snug, tensioning the sail, but not so tight that they bow. Now fit the bracing spars, again trimmed to slightly tension in the sail (Fig 9.3).

Tie a two-leg bridle to one corner as shown to points 8 cm (3 inches) from the tip and 15 cm (6 inches) from the base of the sail. When tied, the bridle should form a loop 170 cm (67 inches) (Fig 9.4).

The Oxo prefers to fly at quite low angle of attack so, to get sufficient lift, it needs slightly stronger winds to kites in previous sections. For average conditions, the upper bridle leg should be approximately 78 cm (31 inches) long.

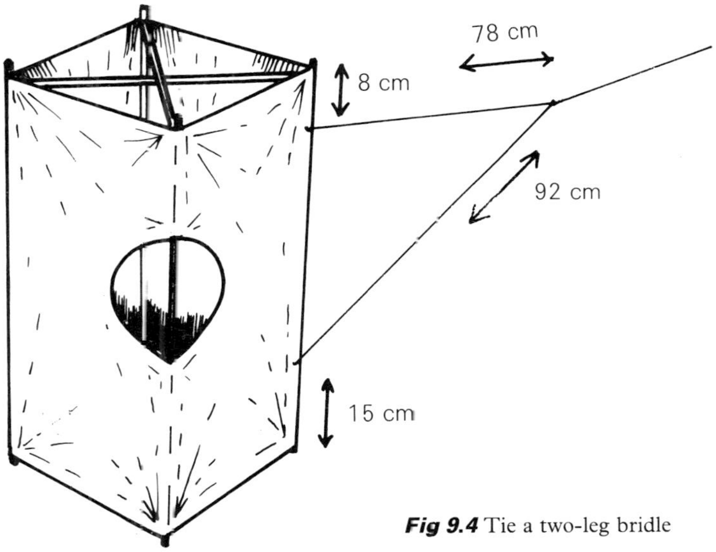

Fig 9.4 Tie a two-leg bridle

FOUR-WING BOX

Sail : *Tyvek* 10, strong paper (manilla)
Spars : Longerons 4 pieces 5 mm dowel 66 cm (30 inches) long; bracing spars 4 pieces 5 mm dowel approx 54 cm ($21\frac{1}{4}$ inches) long

Although many of the earlier designs can be marked out directly on to the sail material, this is one kite where the use of a template is recommended, however many you are going to make (Fig 9.5).

Cut out eight pieces of sail and glue them together as illustrated (Fig 9.6), matching the fold line AB on one section with CD on the next. Glue them together to make

Fig 9.5 Wing box template

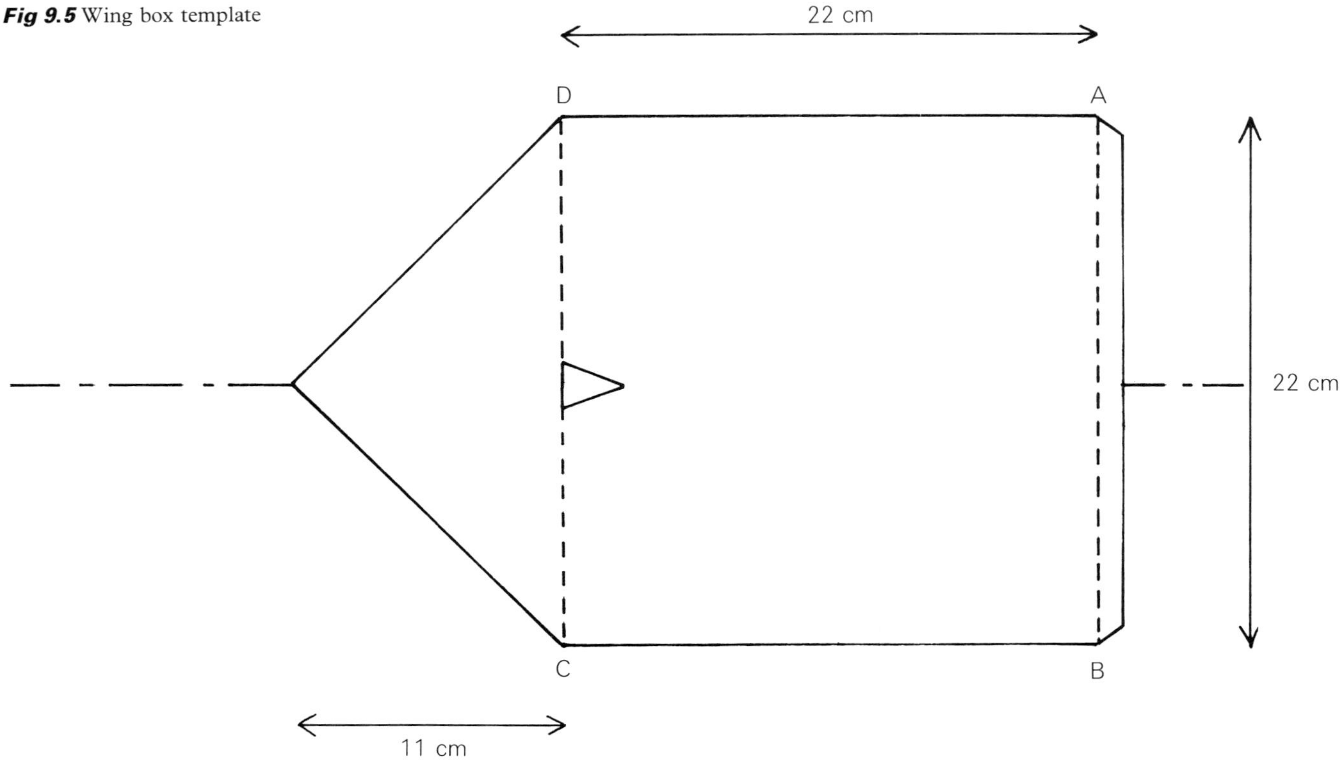

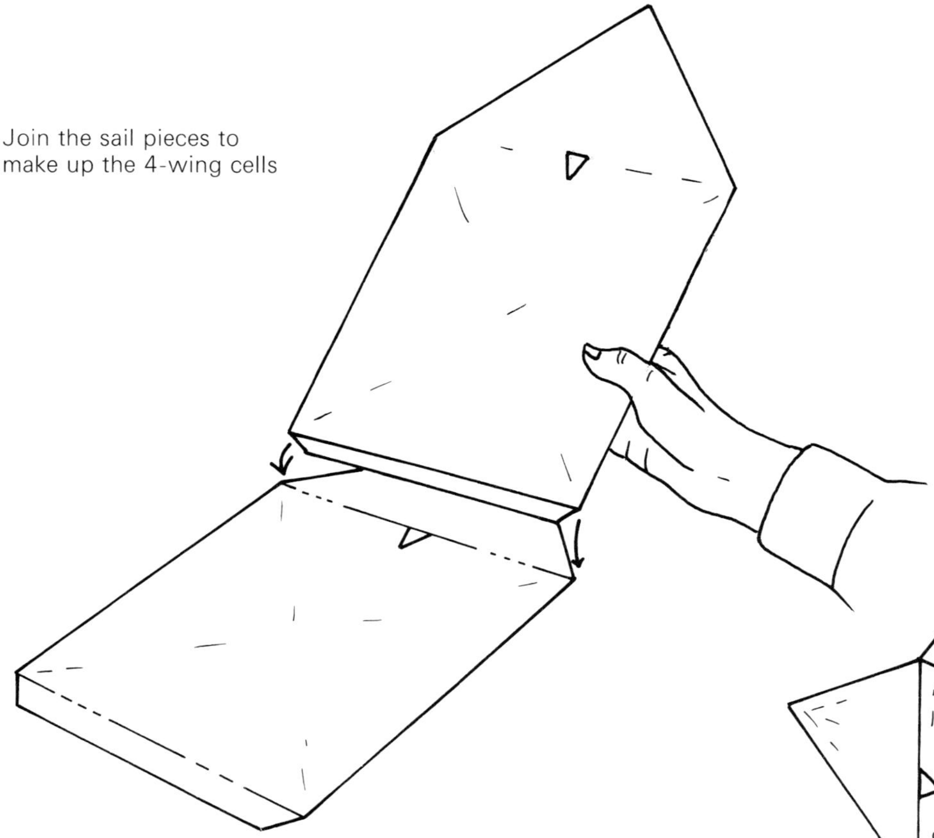

Fig 9.6 Square cell construction

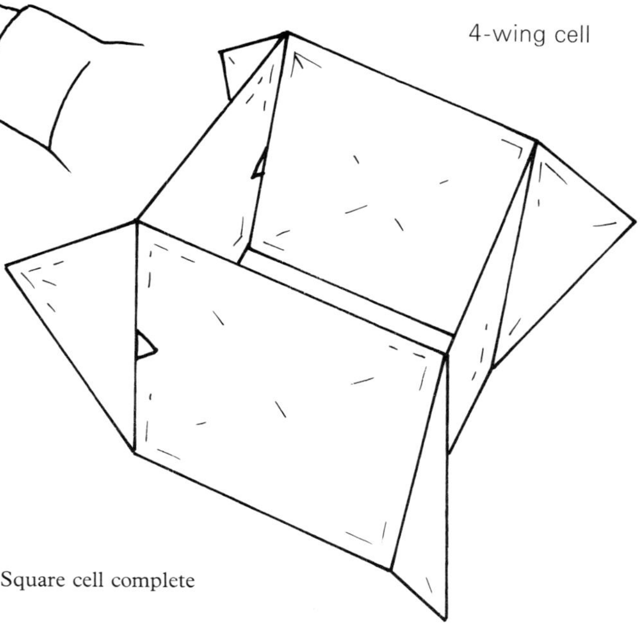

Fig 9.7 Square cell complete

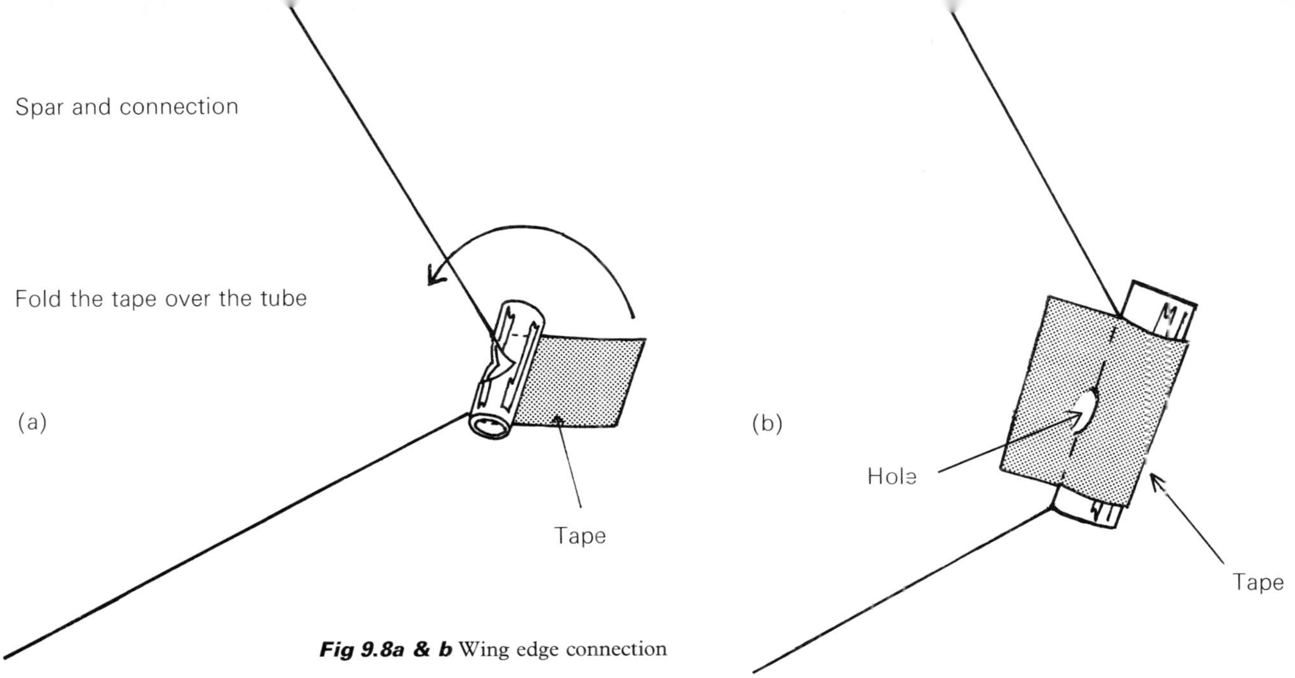

Fig 9.8a & b Wing edge connection

two square cells, four pieces per cell (Fig 9.7). Next make the wing connections (Fig 9.8).

Tape the longerons (long spars) in position at the cell corners (Fig 9.9), then trim and fit the bracing spars into the wing connections to evenly tension the sail.

Attach the bridle to small rings or loops of line taped to the wings as shown in Fig 9.10. After tying, the bride loop should be approx 145 cm (57 inches) long, with, for average conditions, the towing ring 57 cm ($22\frac{1}{2}$ inches) from the upper connection point.

Using the same principles of construction, a six-wing, two-cell version can also be made.

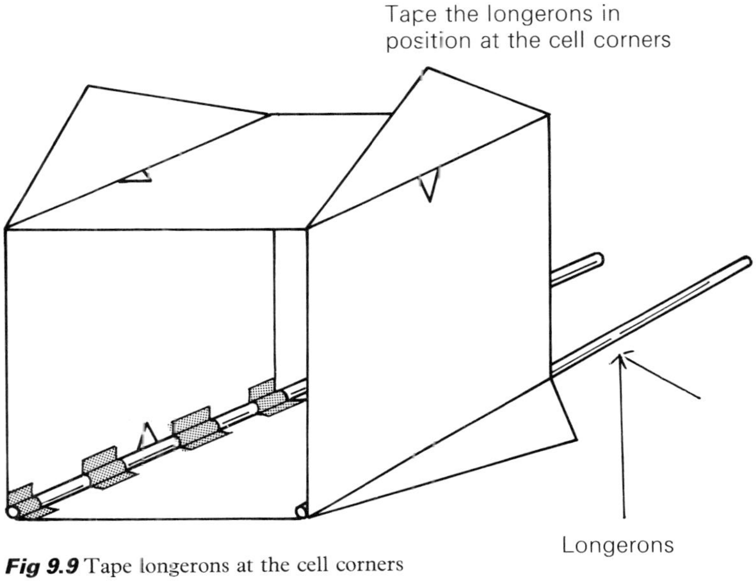

Fig 9.9 Tape longerons at the cell corners

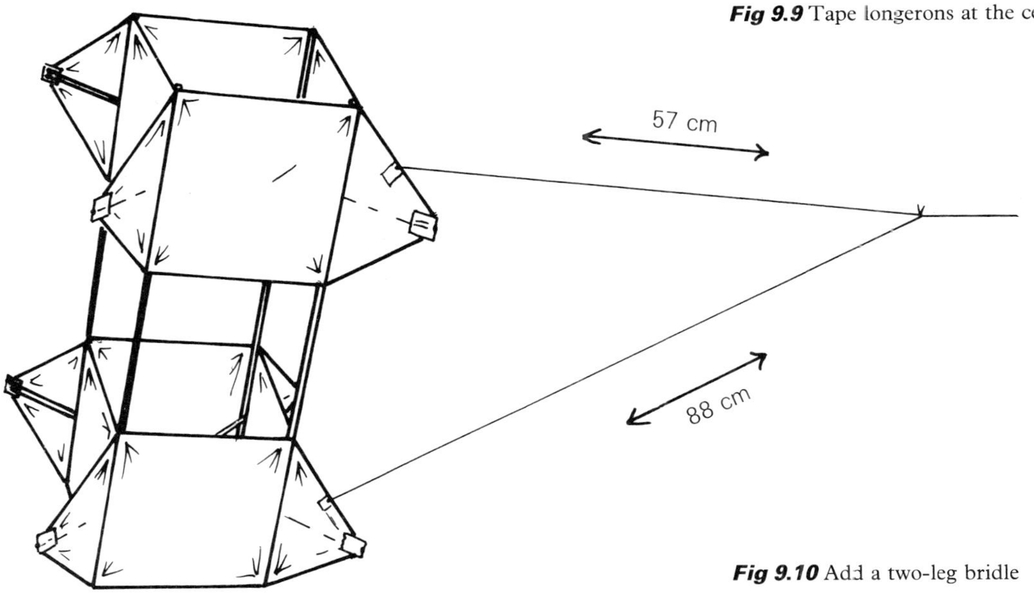

Fig 9.10 Add a two-leg bridle

WINE-RACK KITE

This is a variation on the square-winged box, derived from a kite designed in the late nineteenth century by Joseph Lecornu.

Sail : *Tyvek*
Spars : Longerons 4 pieces 5 mm ($\frac{3}{16}$ inch) dowel 22 cm ($8\frac{1}{2}$ inches) long;
bracing spars 6.3 mm ($\frac{1}{4}$ inch) dowel (or square section), 2 pieces approximately 84 cm (33 inches) long;

As with the Winged Box design, it is probably easier to start by making a template (Fig 9.11a) and use it to cut out four pieces of sail, the wing sections. Additionally you will need two pieces (Fig 9.11b), as the inner sections.

Mark the lines AD and BC on the wing sections and glue them together to make a square cell, similar to the method used with the winged box.

Fold the inner sections along lines 5 mm each side of the centre line, and join them together along the flats this creates (Fig 9.12). Next, glue the inner sections into the box shape (Fig 9.13).

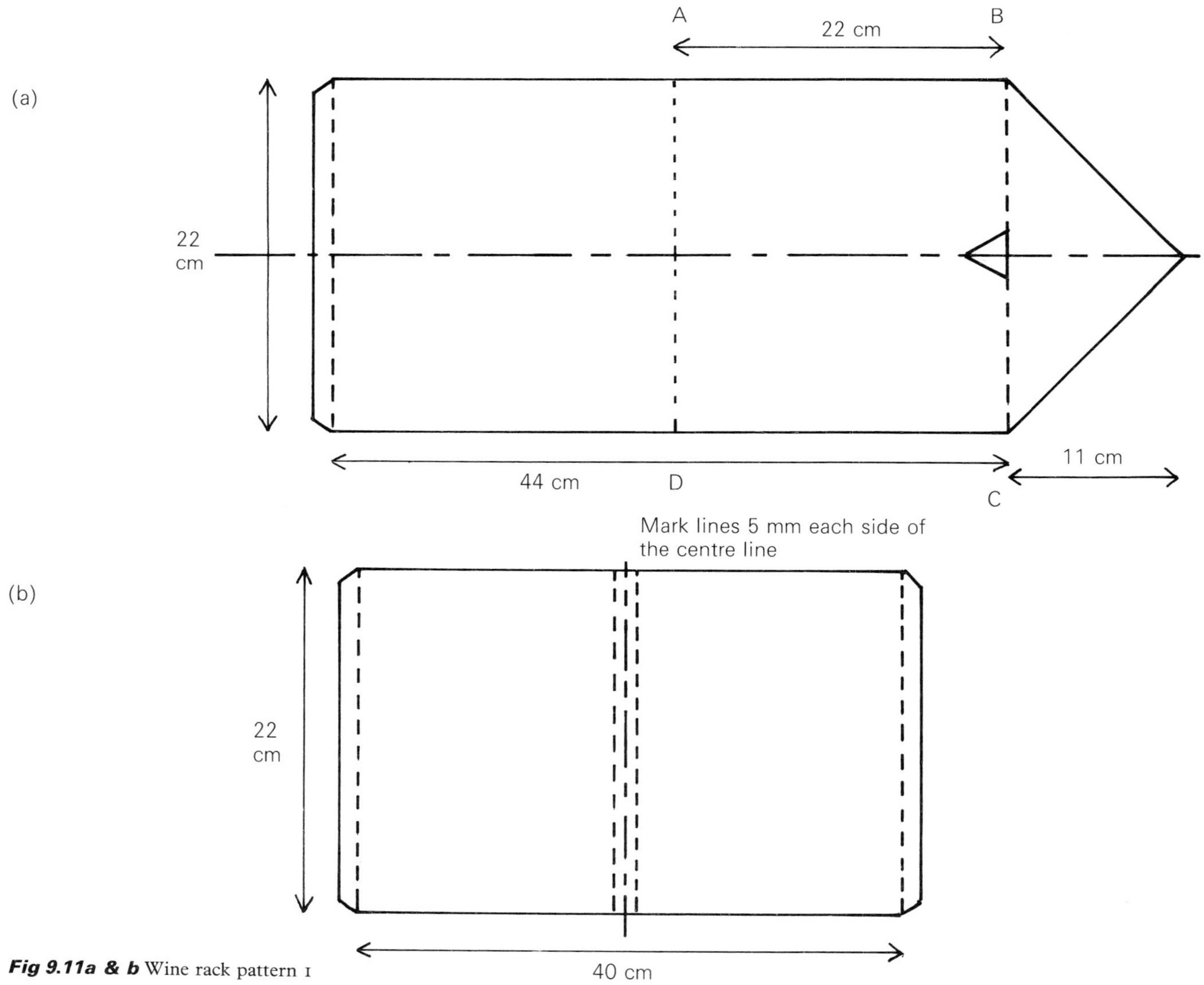

Fig 9.11a & b Wine rack pattern 1

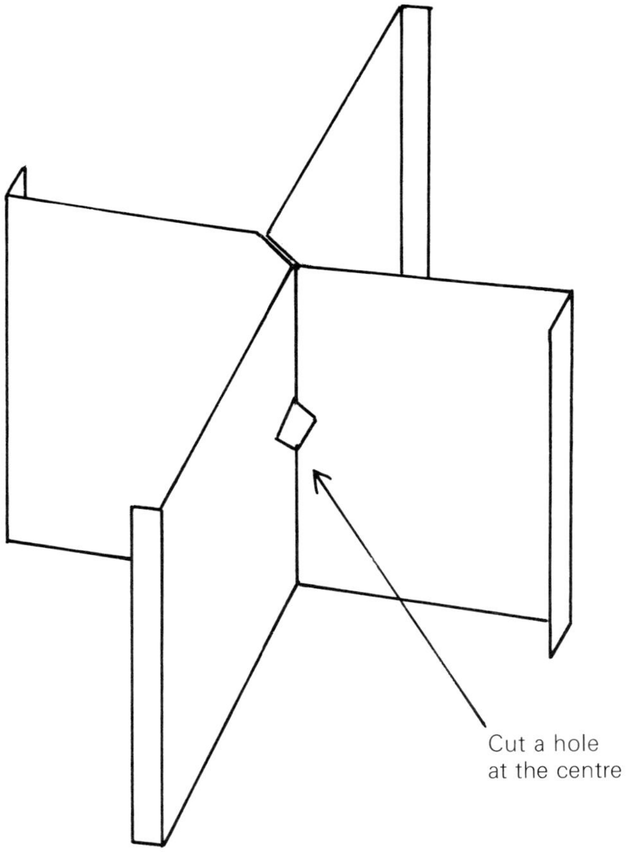

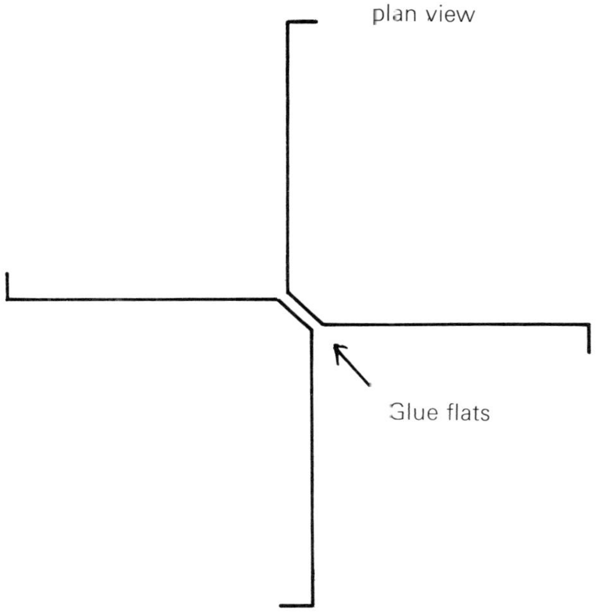

Fig 9.12 Fold and join the inner sections along the central gluing flats

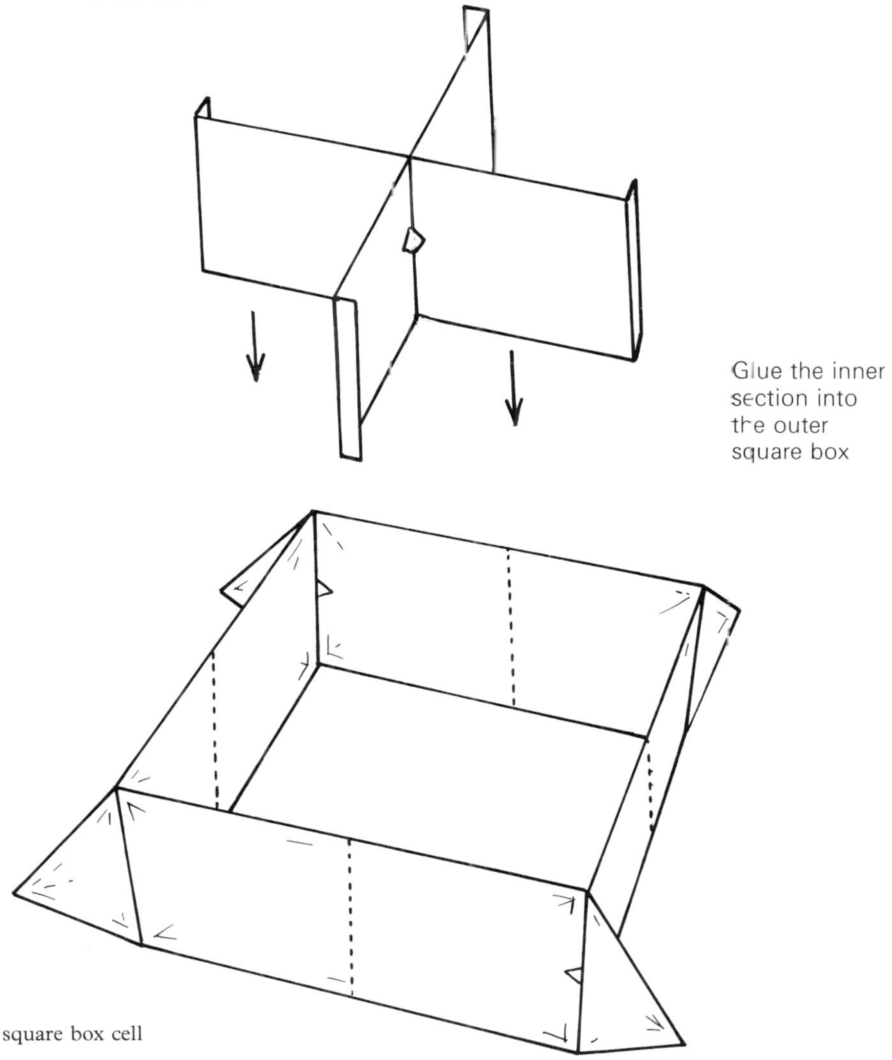

Fig 9.13 Fit the inner sections into the square box cell

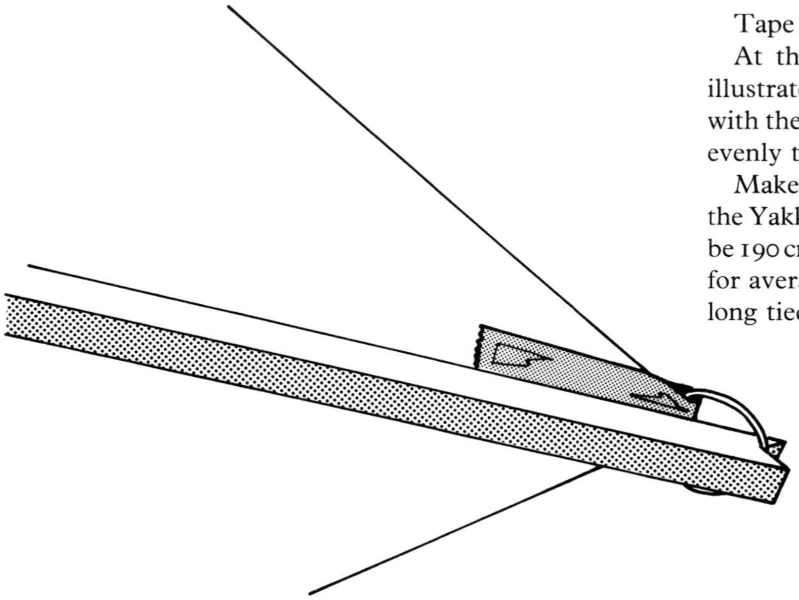

Fig 9.14 Alternative spar end connection

Tape the longerons (shorter spars) in place at the corners.

At the wing tips, you can either use the connection illustrated with the winged box, or one similar to that used with the Eddy (Fig 9.14). Trim and fit the bracing spars to evenly tension the sail.

Make a three-leg bridle as described in instructions for the Yakko (Chapter 7). The bridle 'loop' in this case should be 190 cm (75 inches), tied to the two adjacent corners, with, for average conditions, the third leg 110 cm (43.5 inches) long tied at the central intersection (Fig 9.15).

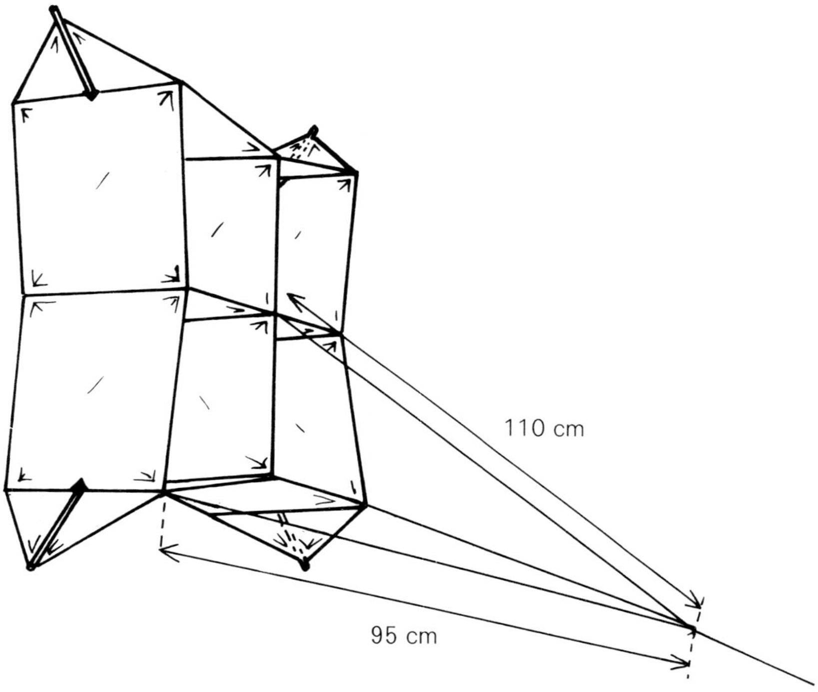

Fig 9.15 Add a three-leg bridle

FOUR-WING CORNER KITE

Sail : *Tyvek*, wrapping paper
Spars : 5 mm ($\frac{3}{16}$ inch) dowel;
spine, 1 piece 63 cm ($24\frac{3}{4}$ inches) long;
bracing spars, 4 pieces approximately 46.5 cm ($18\frac{1}{4}$ inches) long

With this method of construction it is probably better not to have a crease along the diagonal but to cut the sail as two flat squares.

Mark and cut out two square pieces of sail 45 cm ($17\frac{3}{4}$ inches) side (Fig 9.16). Fold them along the two lines AB, CD each side of the diagonal and glue the two sections together along the flats so created (Fig 9.17a,b).

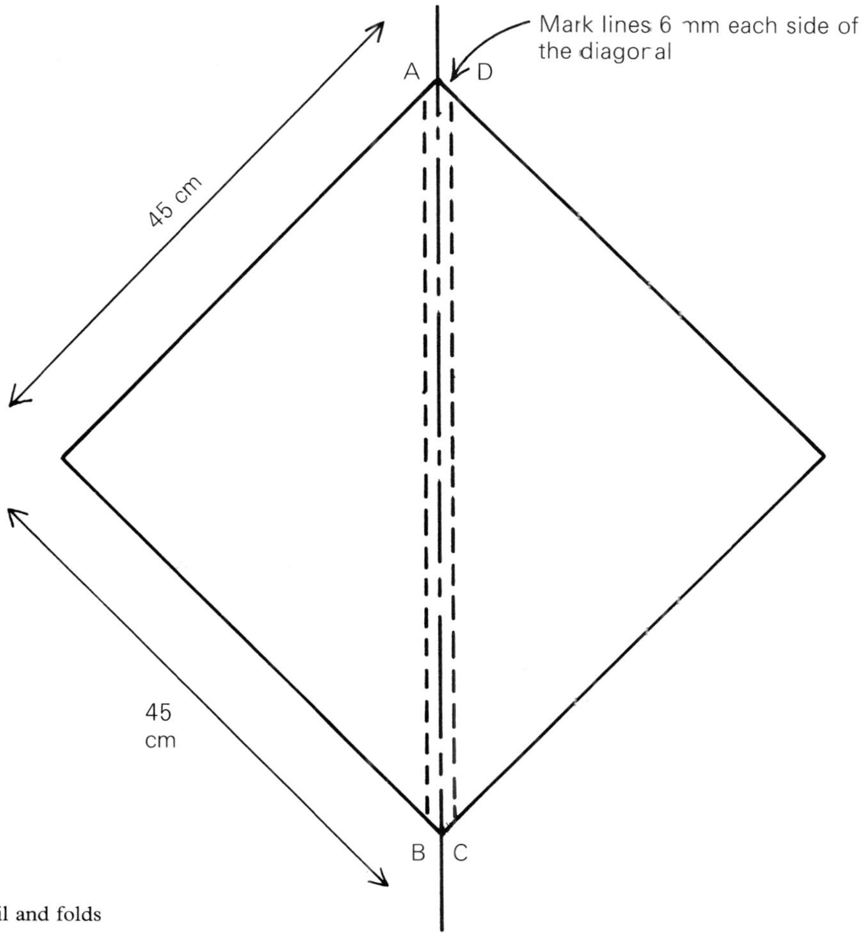

Fig 9.16 Corner kite sail and folds

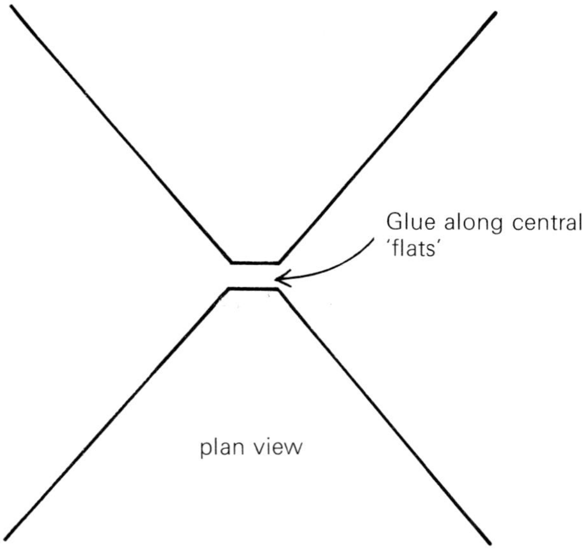

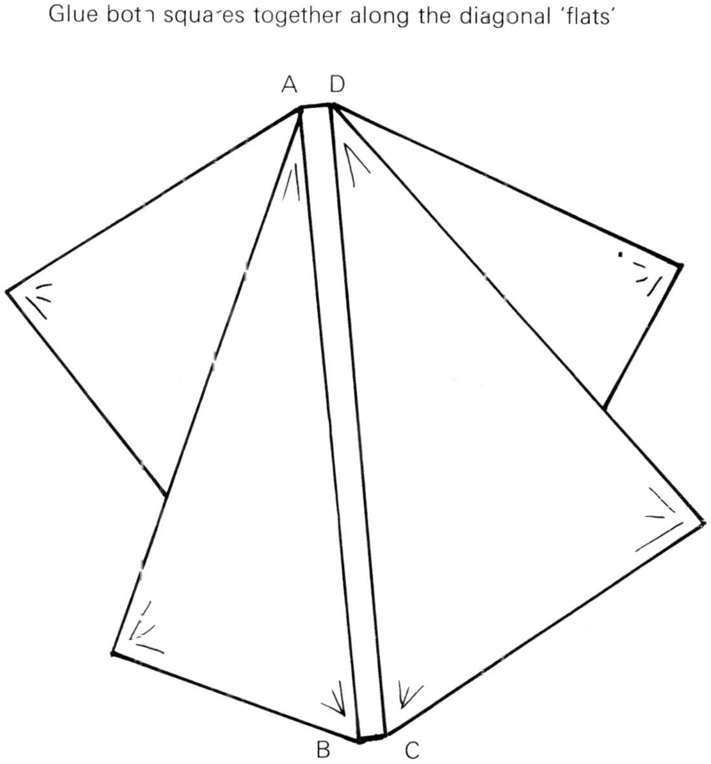

Fig 9.17a & b Glue the two square along the diagonal 'flats'

Make four corner connections by threading a 15 mm split ring through a hole punched at the centre of a short length of 5 mm PVC tube and tape one to each of the wing tips (Fig 9.18).

Tape the spine along the diagonal, with additional reinforcing at the tip and base. Also tape a small ring or loop of line at the spine tip.

Fit the bracing spars into the corner connections to tension the sail, but not so tightly that they bow severely.

The single corner kite can either be flown with a two-leg bridle, taken from one corner and the spine tip, or, more often, a three-leg. When tied, the lower bridle loop should be 150 cm (60 inches) long, with, for average conditions, the upper leg around 65 cm ($23\frac{1}{2}$ inches) long (Fig 9.19).

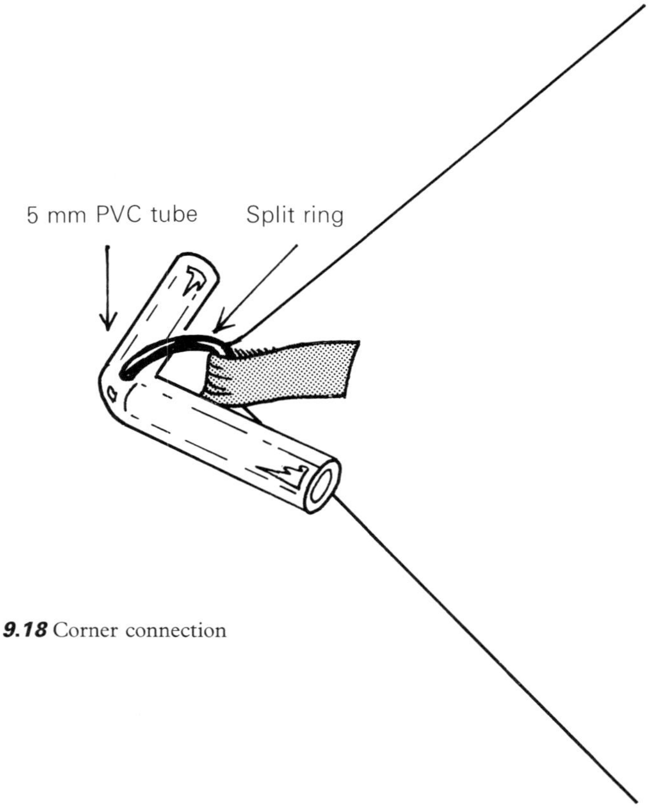

Fig 9.18 Corner connection

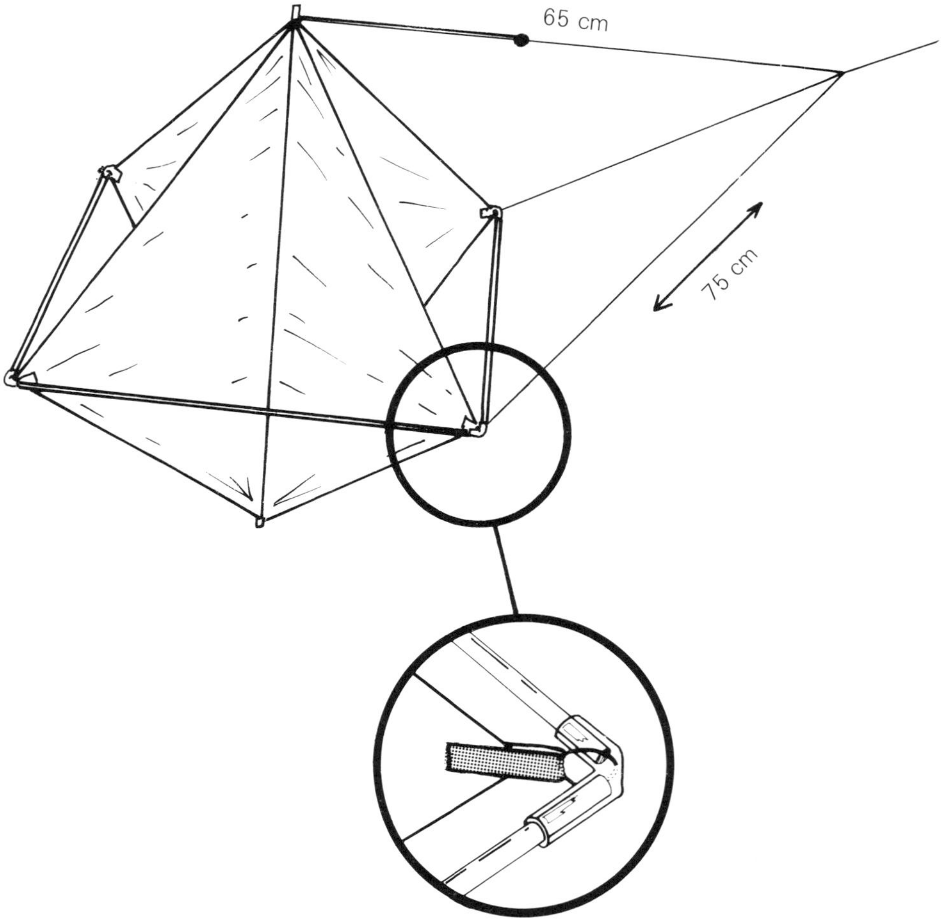

Fig 9.19 Tie a three-leg bridle

SIX-WING CORNER KITE

Sail : *Tyvek*, wrapping paper
Spars : 5 mm ($\frac{3}{16}$ inch) diameter
spine 30 cm (12 inches) long;
spars, 6 pieces 32 cm ($12\frac{1}{2}$ inches) long

Cut out three diamond sail shapes (Fig 9.20). Cut them flat rather than folded along the diagonal. Lightly draw in the short diagonal, then mark and fold along lines 5 mm ($\frac{3}{16}$ inch) either side. Glue the three sail sections along the flats so created (Fig 9.21).

Tape the spine into position along the diagonal, add corner connections and bridle as with the four-wing corner kite (Fig 9.22).

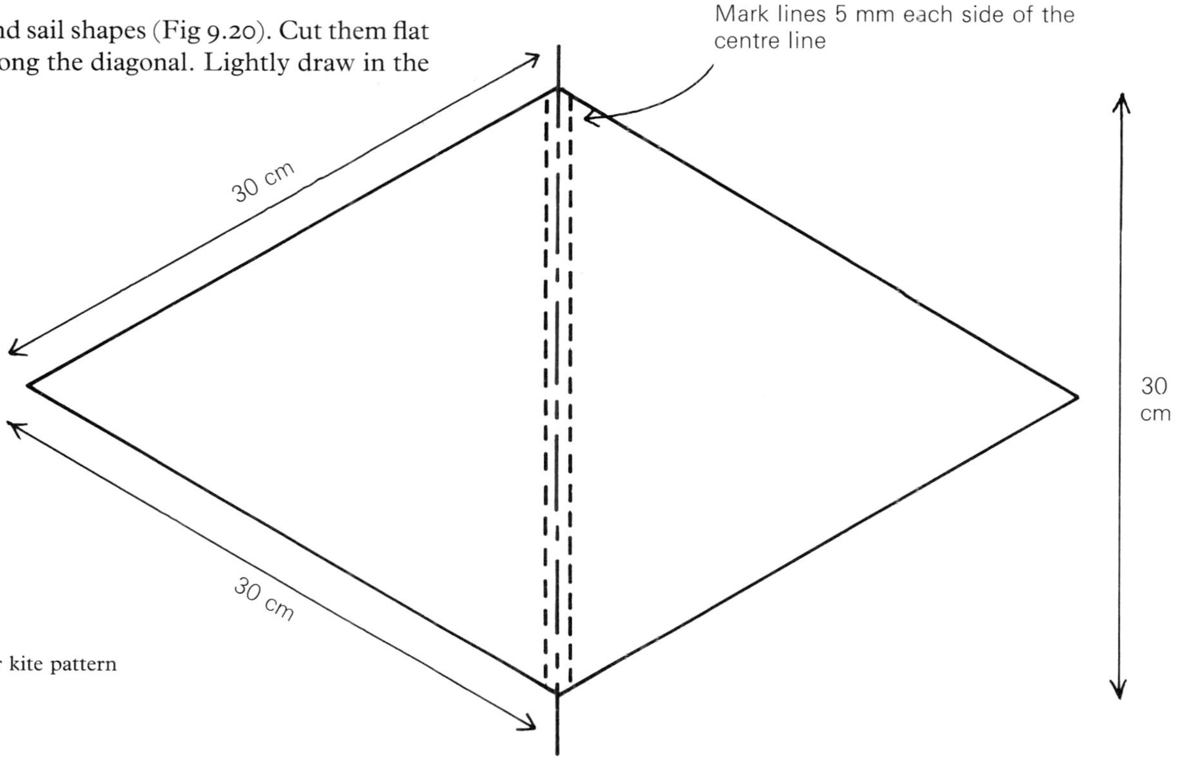

Fig 9.20 Six-wing corner kite pattern

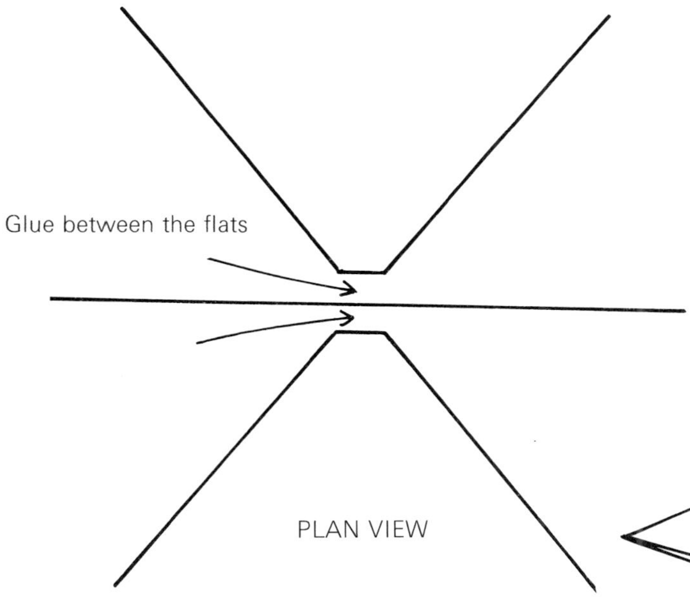

Fig 9.21 Wing construction

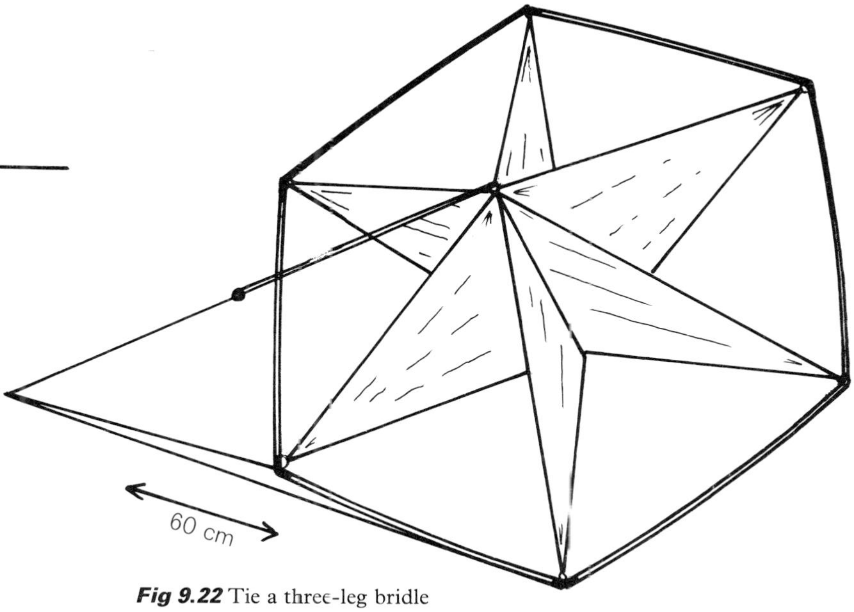

Fig 9.22 Tie a three-leg bridle

FOUR-WING FACET KITE

The Facet is an exciting variation of the corner kite with extra sail sections to make up a sort of snowflake pattern, which, when effectively decorated, can be doubly attractive. But, like the corner kite, it can really only be made from materials which do not stretch appreciably and will accept adhesives.

Sail	:	*Tyvek*
Spars	:	5 mm dowel, spine 70.5 cm ($28\frac{3}{4}$ inches) long; bracing spars, 4 pieces approximately 51 cm (20 inches) long

Cut out two squares of sail 50 cm ($19\frac{1}{2}$ inches) sides and mark them out as indicated (Fig 9.23a). Next join them together as though you were making a corner kite.

Cut out a further eight smaller triangles (Fig 9.23b) with additional narrow gluing flaps, and fix them along the lines AB, two to each wing (Fig 9.24).

Make and fit connections to the four 'main' wing tips as with the corner kites, then tape the inner wings together in pairs, at their tips, enclosing a small ring in between.

Tape the spine along the diagonal, with an additional ring or loop of line at the spine tip. As you fit bracing spars, also thread them through the rings joining the pairs of inner wings.

Bridle as with the corner kites (Fig 9.25).

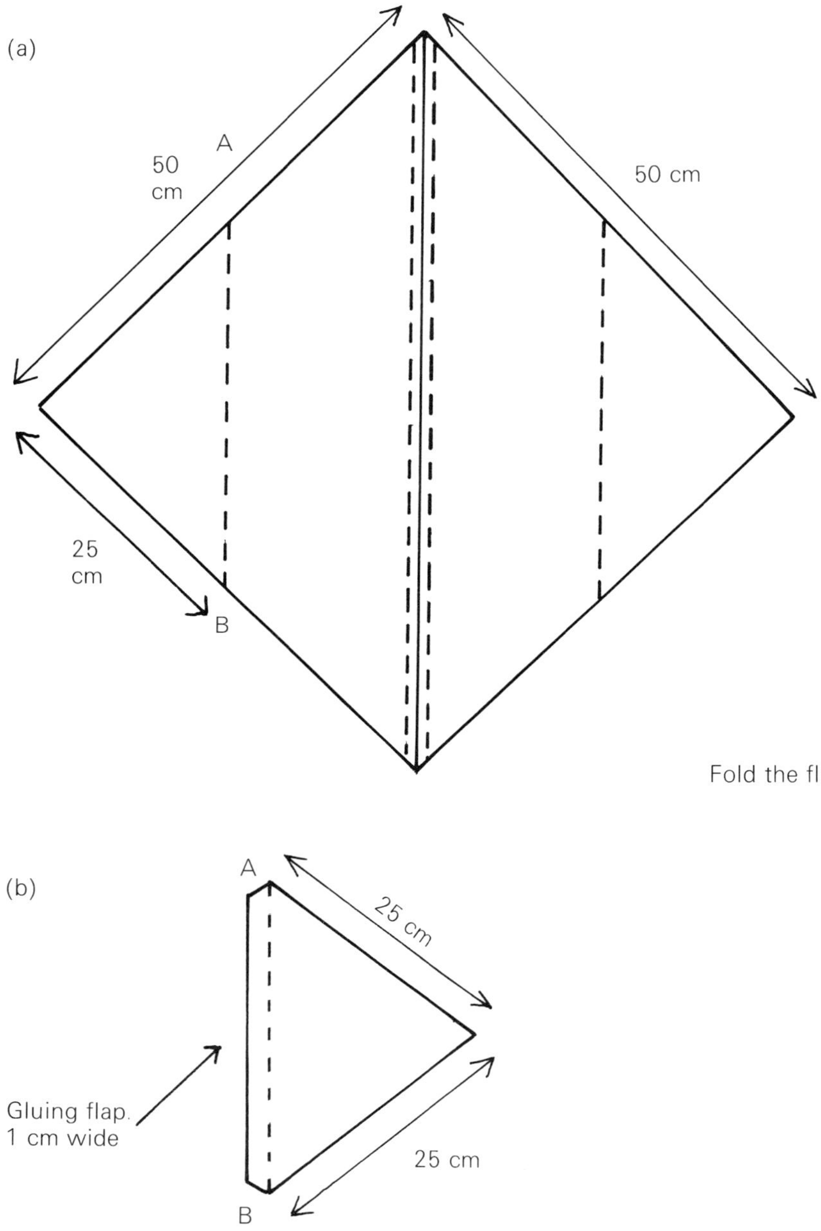

Fig 9.23a & b Facet template patterns

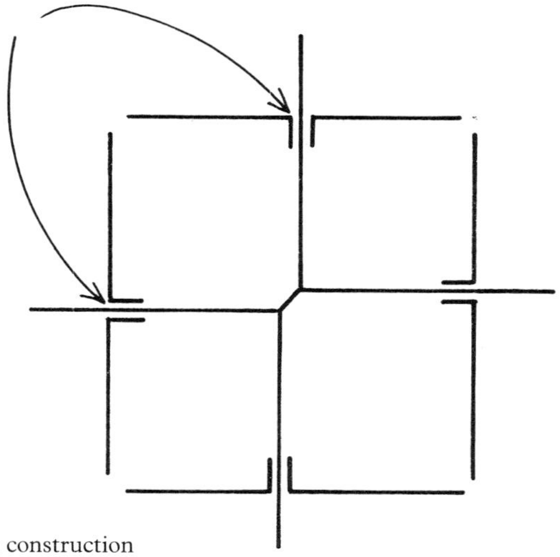

Fig 9.24 Wing construction

Fig 9.25 Join the wings, add the spars and tie a three-leg bridle

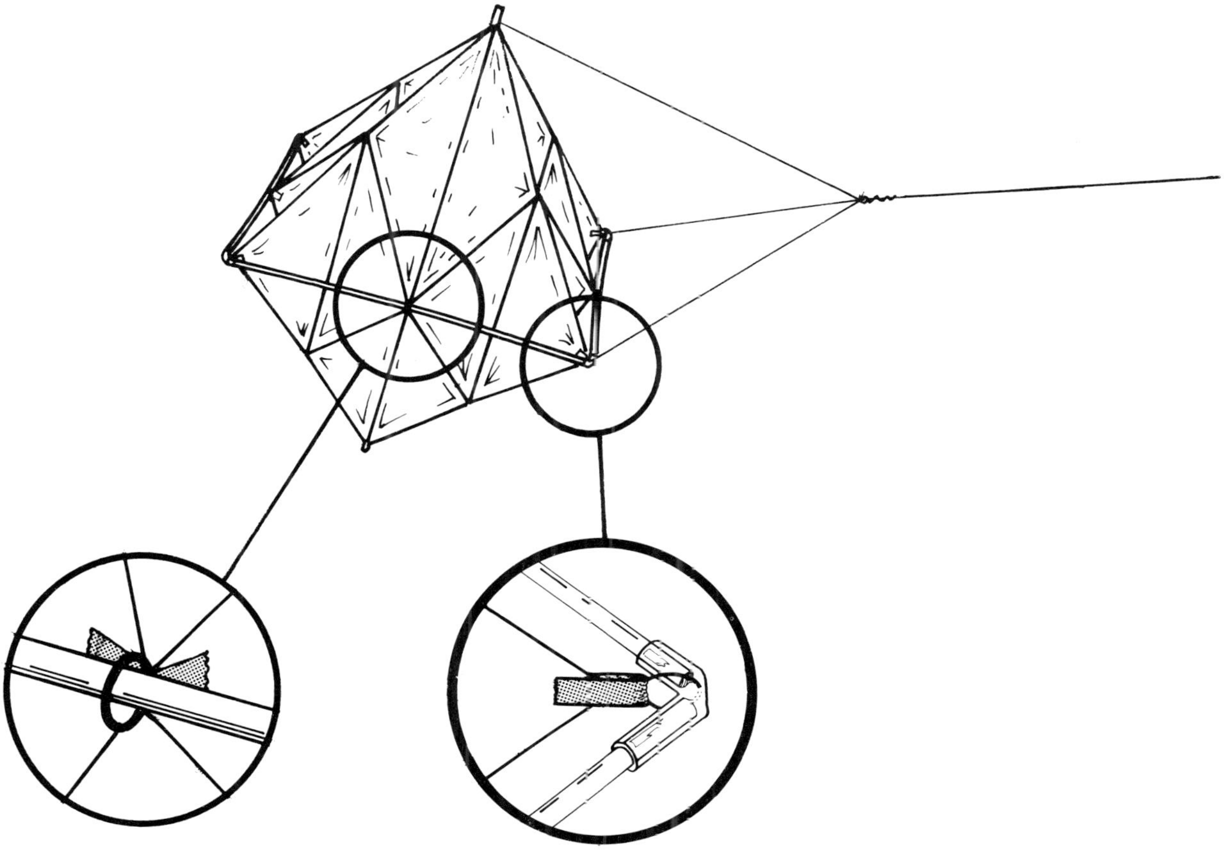

CHAPTER TEN

stunter kites

Stunter kites are those with two lines, one connected to each side. Pull on the left line and the kite turns in an arc to the left; pull on the right line and it turns in an arc to the right; pull on both lines evenly and the kite will start to lift upwards. Through controlled line tension, it is possible to make the kite perform a variety of manoeuvres under control of the flier.

A simple stunter is a bit of a contradiction, however: stunters are neither easy to make nor easy to fly. The designs featured below are not overtly difficult, but should only be attempted after you have successfully made a number of the kites from earlier sections.

One of the secrets with stunters is to keep the flying lines exactly the same length and relatively short; around 40 metres (125 feet) is plenty long enough.

SKY BUSTER

Sail : Polythene, *Tyvek*
Spars : Fibreglass,
spine 4 mm ($\frac{5}{32}$ inch), 83 cm ($32\frac{1}{2}$ inches) long;
spar 3 mm ($\frac{1}{8}$ inch), 82 cm long

Fold the sail material and cut out the shape Fig 10.1, again shown as a half.

Cut two pieces of 3 mm ($\frac{1}{8}$ inch) PVC tube, approximately 5 cm (2 inches) long and tape them to the wing tips to create firm connections for the cross spar (Fig 10.2). Next fold and tape or glue the flaps along the wing edges.

The spine connections are similar to those with the winged box kites. Make a 'V' shaped notch at the centre of two short lengths of PVC tube and tape them to the tip and base of the kite. Then, with a knife or the end of the scissors blade, just nick the tape over the position of the hole.

Fit the spine into these connections, trimmed just tight without putting too much tension on the sail, then fit the cross spar into the tubes at the wing tips, again giving the sail a slight tension (Fig 10.3).

Measure the upper bridle connection points 23 cm (9 inches) from the tip of the spine to the cross spar. Reinforce the sail and make a hole at these points, which should also be checked for symmetry. Similarly, reinforce and cut the lower bridle point 13 cm ($5\frac{1}{8}$ inches) from the base (Fig 10.4).

The two bridles are made as a single line. Cut a line 235 cm ($92\frac{1}{2}$ inches) long and tie a short overhand loop at the centre. From the front, push the centre loop through the bottom bridle point and thread it on to the spine. Make loops at the two other ends so that each half is 110 cm ($43\frac{1}{2}$ inches) long and thread them through the upper bridle holes and on to the cross spar.

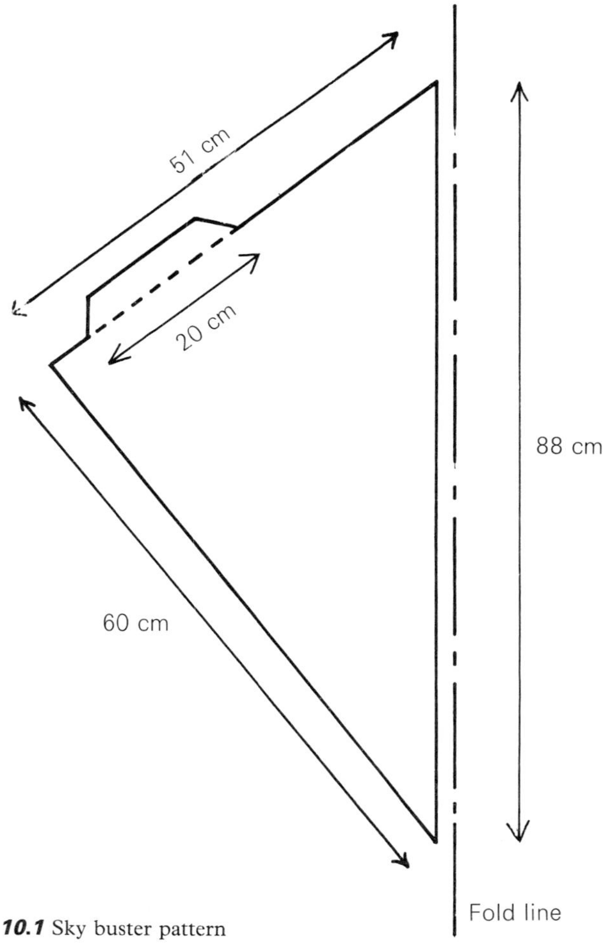

Fig 10.1 Sky buster pattern

Fit a long ribbon tail about 9 metres (30 feet) to the bottom point. Finally, fit towing rings to each bridle approximately 53 cm (21 inches) from the upper bridle connection point (Fig 10.5).

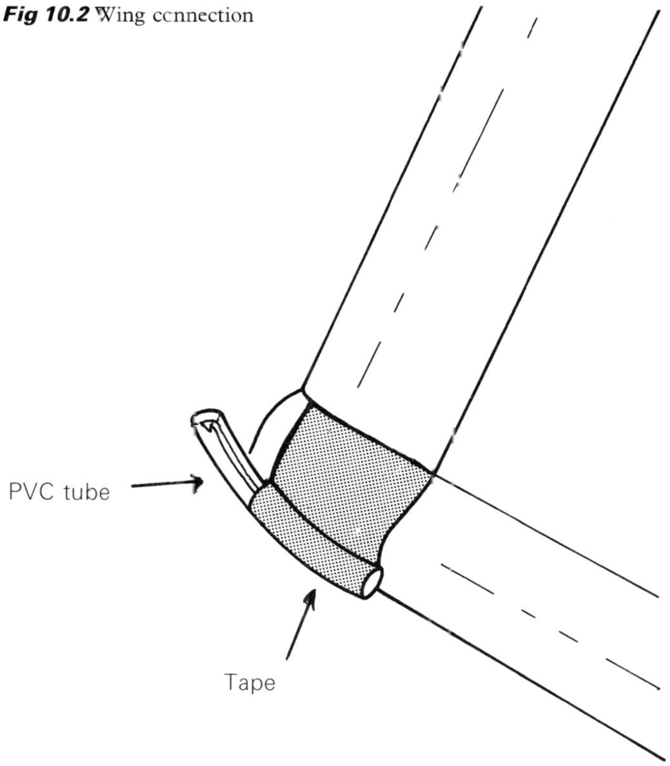

Fig 10.2 Wing connection

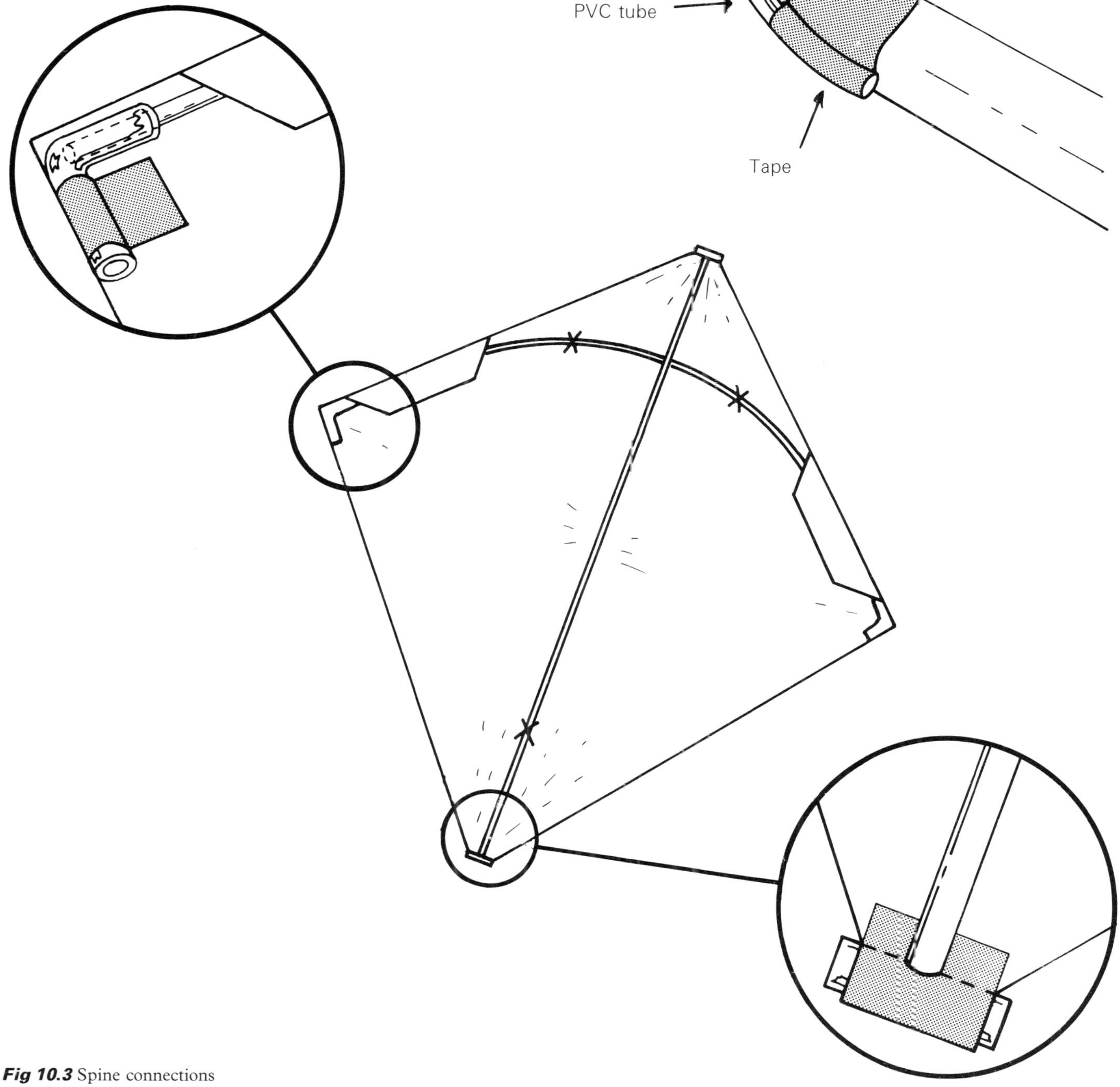
Fig 10.3 Spine connections

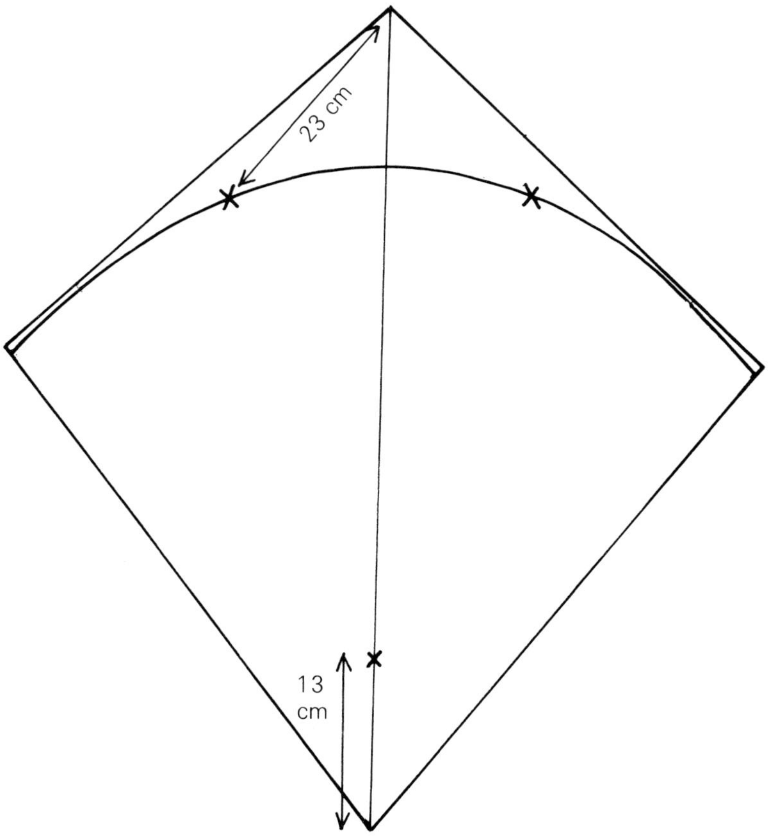

Fig 10.4 Bridle connections

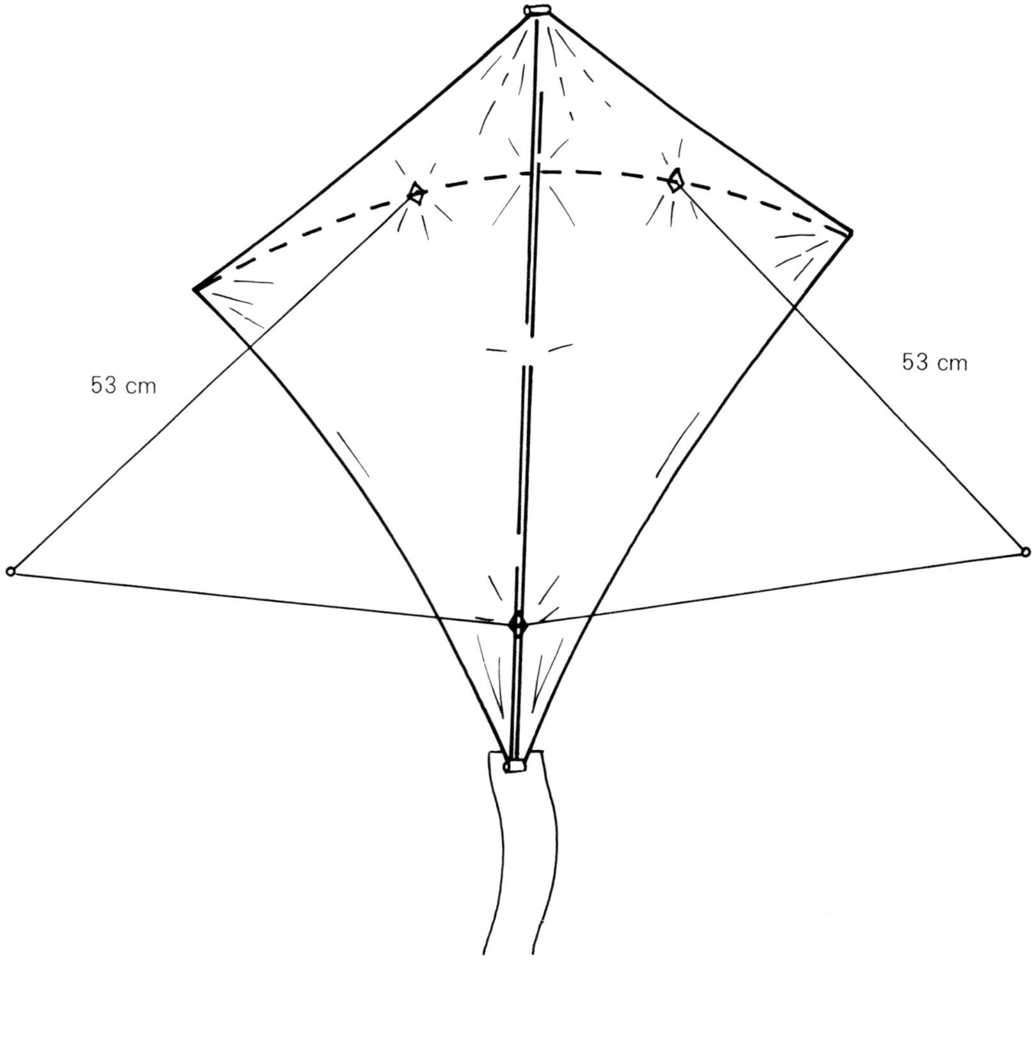

Fig 10.5 Bridles

CRUSADER

Those fliers familiar with the range of kites coming from America will of course recognise the 'A' frame form of this design immediately. Surprisingly, the rigid framework offers the flier increased control over conventional, flexible designs, allowing the performance of more precise manoeuvres. On the other hand, the Crusader is less tolerant of mistakes and demands much greater skill to fly. Also, beware that it will pull *very* hard, even in what you might think is a light wind!

Sail	:	Polythene, *Tyvek*
Spars	:	8 mm ($\frac{5}{16}$ inch) dowel, spine 60 cm (21½ inches) long; wing spars 2 pieces 125 cm (50 inches) long; spreader 100 cm (39¼ inches) long

As with previous designs, to achieve good symmetry, fold the material in half and cut out the shape indicated in Fig 10.6.

Firstly, tie overhand loops in short lengths of line and tape them at the wing tips, then fold and tape or glue the flaps at the wing edges to create spar tubes as described in the chapter on delta kites (Fig 10.7). Additionally, cut and reinforce two sets of notches in the tubes, 33 cm and 80 cm (13 inches and 31½ inches) from the spine tip.

The 'T' connections at the spine tip and base are made by threading a short length of 8 mm ($\frac{5}{16}$ inch) diameter PVC tube through a hole towards one end of the other (Fig 10.8). The joint should be further reinforced with a vinyl glue. The spreader bar connections are similarly made from short (5 cm, 2 inch) lengths of 8 mm PVC tube, with holes cut towards one end. Note that holes are slightly offset from one another (Fig 10.9).

To make the bridles, cut a length of line about 155 cm (61 inches) long and tie a narrow overhand loop at the approximate centre point. Tie overhand loops at the other ends, so that the 'legs' are 73 cm and 67 cm (28¾ inches and 26¼ inches) long respectively. Make two such (wing) bridles. Similarly, cut a third length of line 165 cm (65 inches) long and tie a broad loop at the centre, with narrower loops at the ends, making each 'leg' 73 cm (28¾ inches) long.

Tape the spine along the centre line at three or four points along its length and fit the 'T' connections (Fig 10.10a) at the tip and at the base (Fig 10.10b).

Cut a 'v' section at one end of the spars and fit them into the tubes along the wing edges. As you do so, also thread the spreader connections in position at the lower notches and the wing bridles, the 73 cm leg at the upper notch, and 67 cm leg at the lower notch. Next, thread the centre loop of the third bridle around the 'T' connection at the lower end of the spine (Fig 10.11).

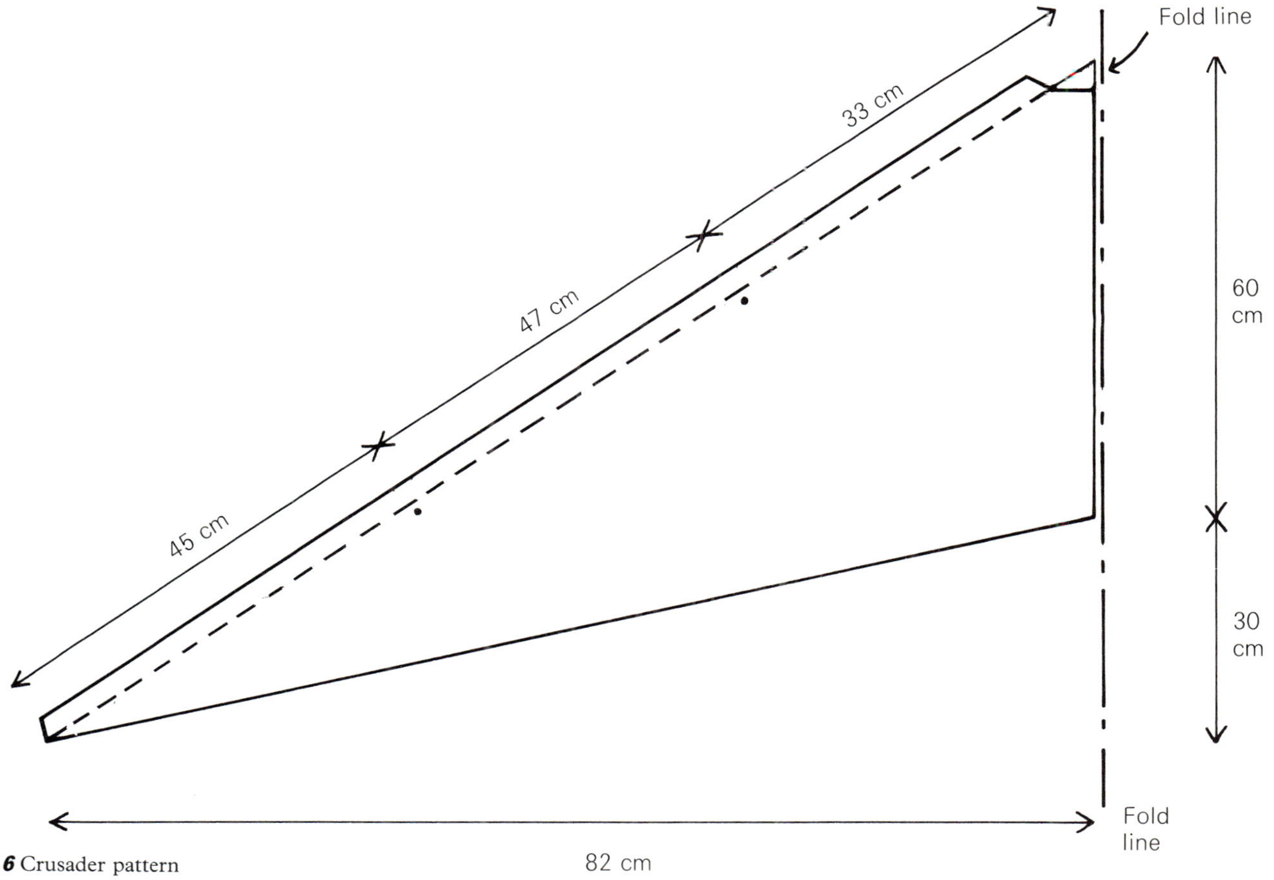

Fig 10.6 Crusader pattern

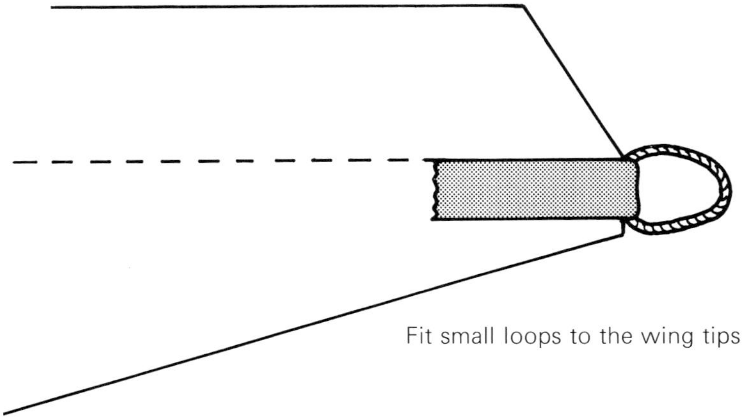

Fig 10.7 Tape short overhand loops at the wing tips

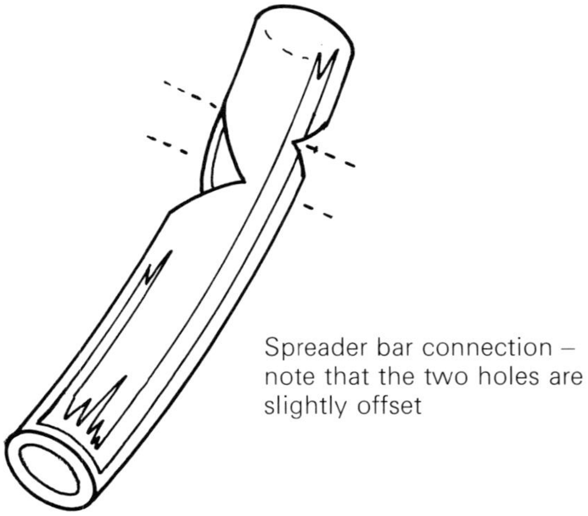

Fig 10.8 Spreader bar connections

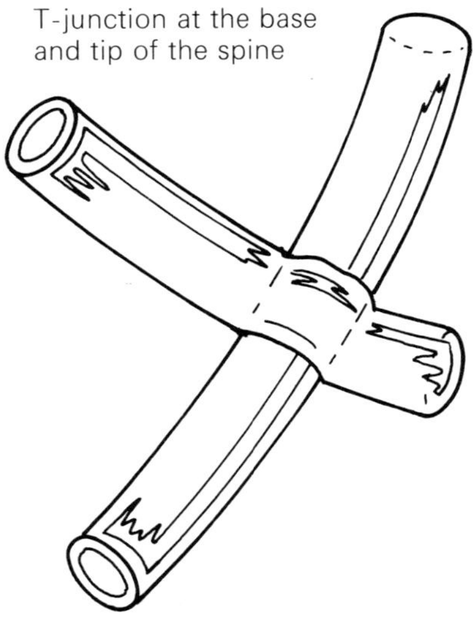

Fig 10.9 Spine 'T' connections

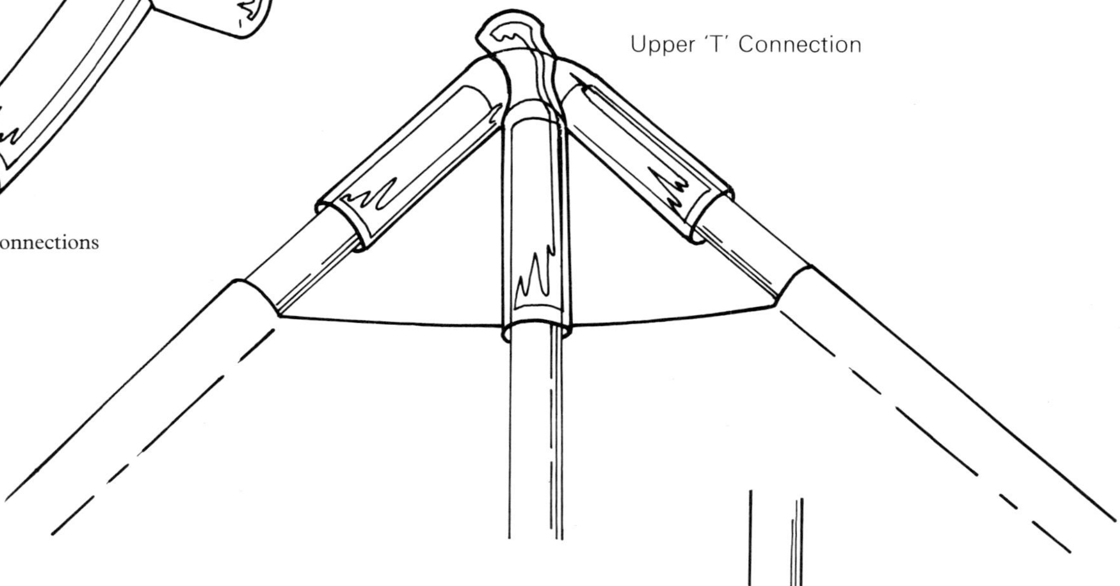

Fig 10.10a Upper 'T' connection

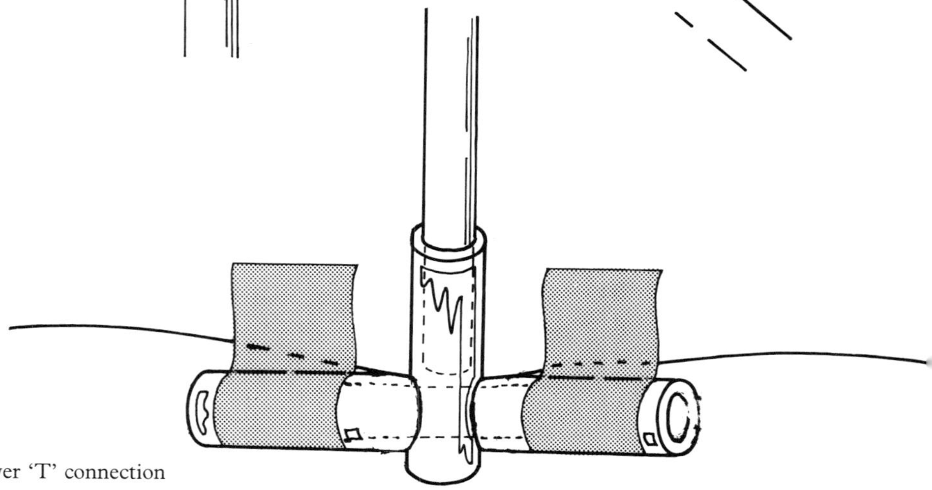

Fig 10.10b Lower 'T' connection

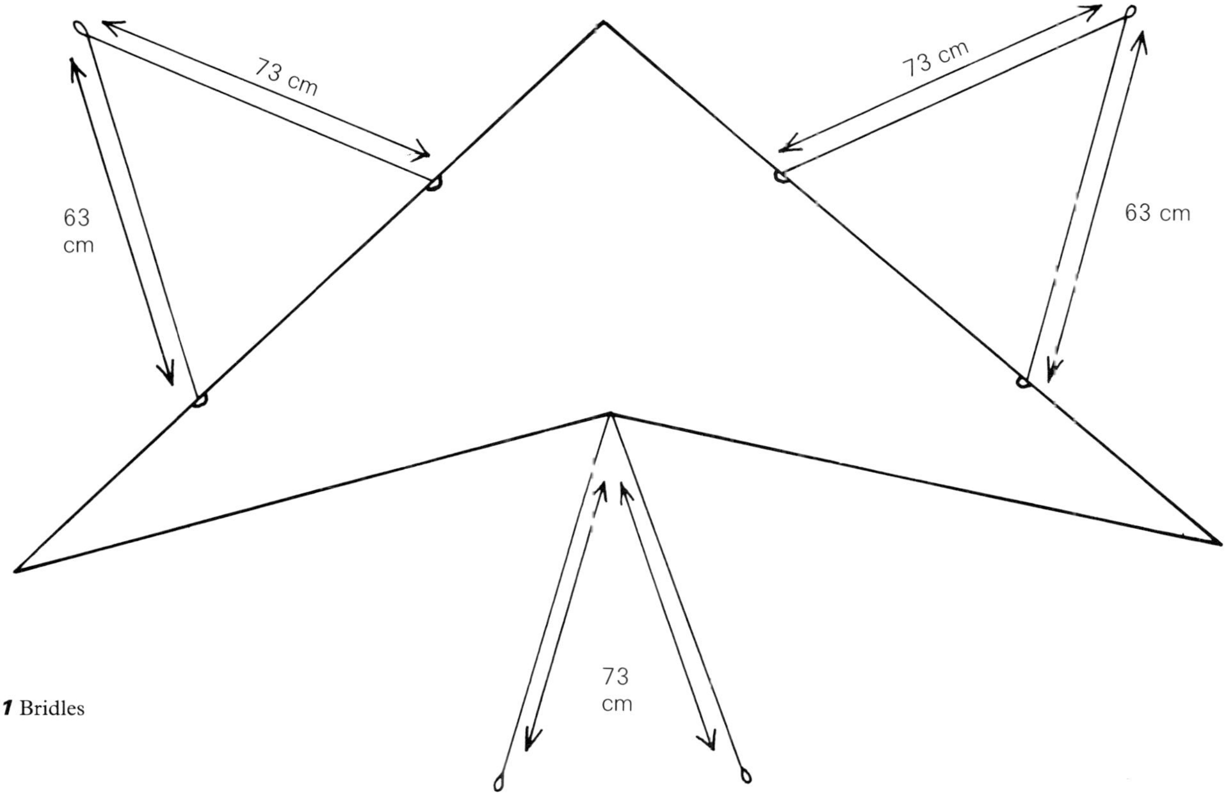

Fig 10.11 Bridles

Thread the short loops of line at the wing tips over the spar end to hold the sail tight in position (Fig 10.12).

Mark the centre of the spreader bar and thread it through the central 'T' at the base of the spine, into the wing connections. Adjust the position of the 'T' so that it sits at the centre of the spreader bar.

To complete the 'three-leg' bridles, join the loops as indicated in Fig 10.13.

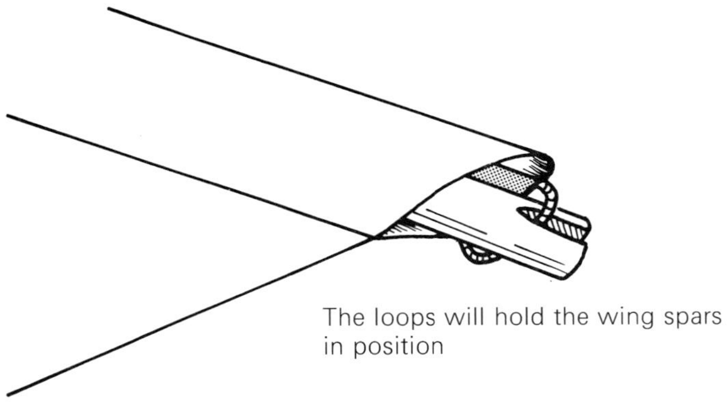

Fig 10.12 Thread the loops at the wing tips around the end of the spars

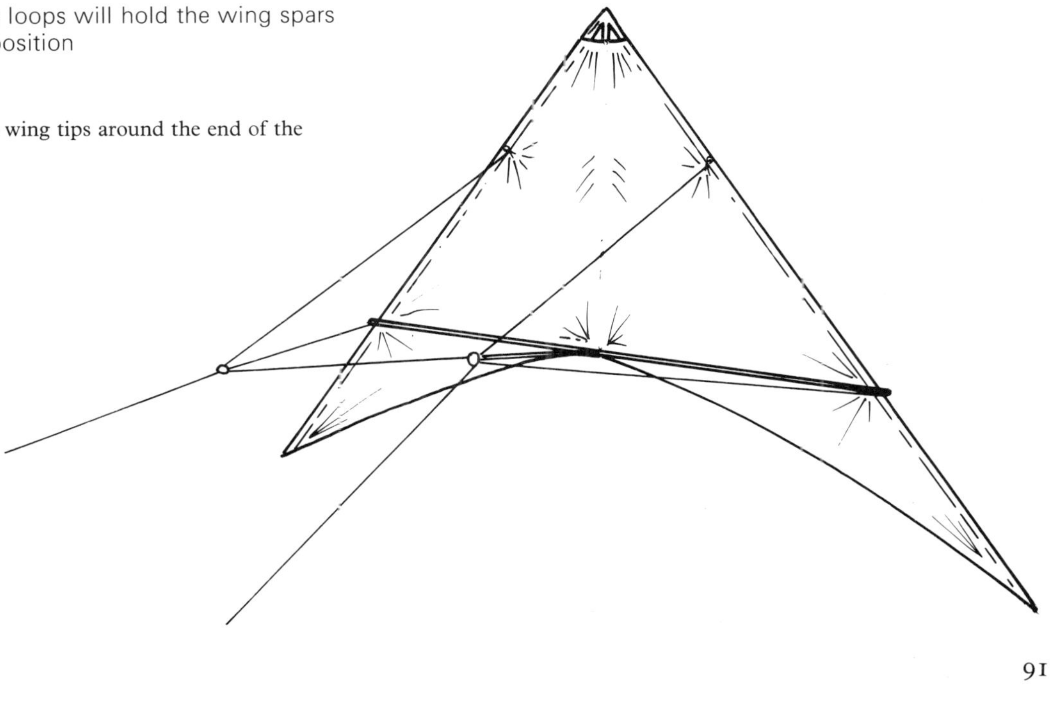

Fig 10.13 Crusader complete

DELTA DART

Sail : *Tyvek*, Polythene
Spars : 5 mm ($\frac{3}{16}$ inch) dowel;
spine 44 cm (17$\frac{1}{4}$ inches) long;
wing spars 62 cm (26 inches) long;
spreader 34 cm (13$\frac{1}{2}$ inches) long

As with previous designs, fold the sail material in half and cut out the pattern (Fig 10.14). Next fold and glue/tape the wing edges to create spar tubes as with the deltas.

Reinforce and cut small notches in the wing tubes at points 25 cm and 50 cm (10 inches and 20 inches) from the spine tip. Similarly, reinforce the sail and cut small holes along the centre line at 8 cm and 32 cm (3$\frac{1}{2}$ inches and 12$\frac{1}{2}$ inches) from the tip.

Make two spreader connections by slicing a section from the centre of a short length of 5 mm PVC tube (Fig 10.15).

As with the Crusader, the bridles and spars must be made and fitted at the same time. You will need four lengths of line, each approximately 110 cm (44 inches) long. Tie a narrow overhand loop at the centres of each of them, then tie loops at the ends so that you have two lines with legs 36 cm and 38 cm long (14 inches and 14$\frac{3}{4}$ inches); and two with legs 50 cm and 32 cm (19$\frac{1}{2}$ inches and 12$\frac{1}{2}$ inches) long.

Fit the spars along the wing edges and the spine along the centre line, fitting both the spreader connection (Fig 10.16) and the bridles as you do so (Fig 10.17).

Reinforce the spine tip, and tape or staple the wings spars in position to prevent them moving.

To complete the bridles join the two sets of loops, left-hand upper to right-hand lower, and vice versa (B – B[1] and A – A[1] as in Fig 10.18).

With the bridles as indicated, you will find that the Dart can be flown quite fast with very light control, but don't be tempted to alter the bridle lengths, since changing one changes them all!

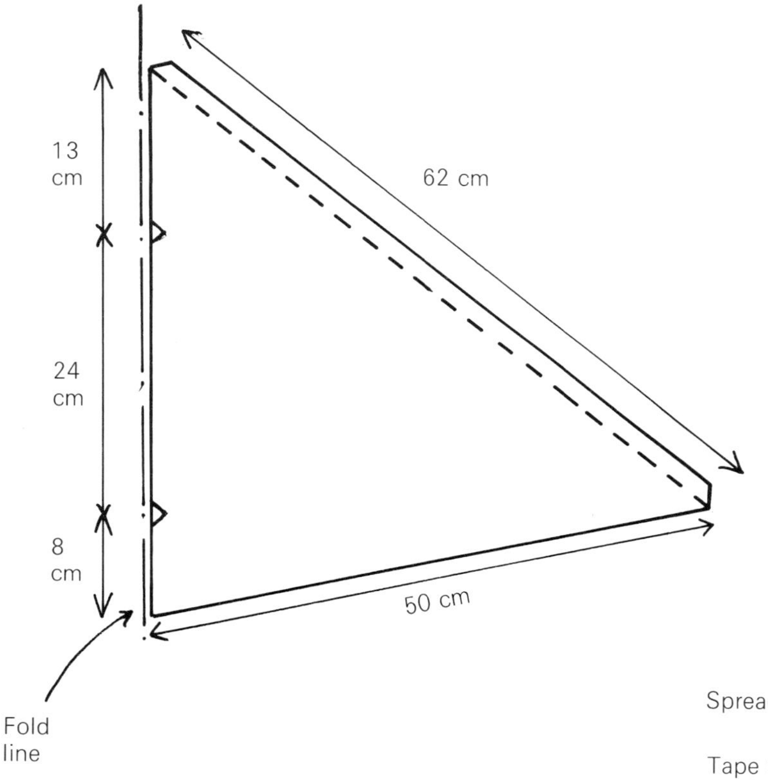

Fig 10.14 Delta Dart pattern

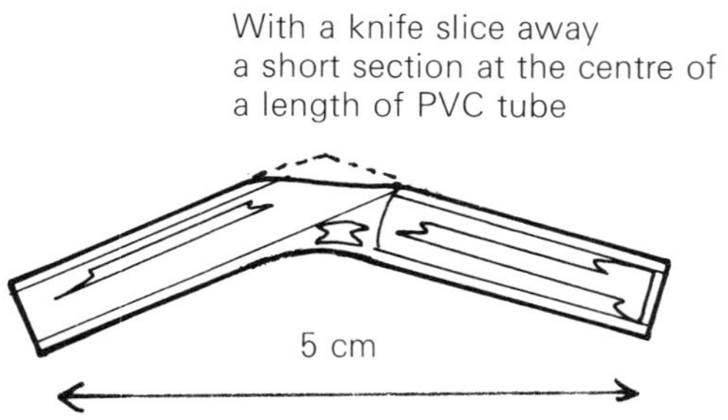

Fig 10.15 PVC connection

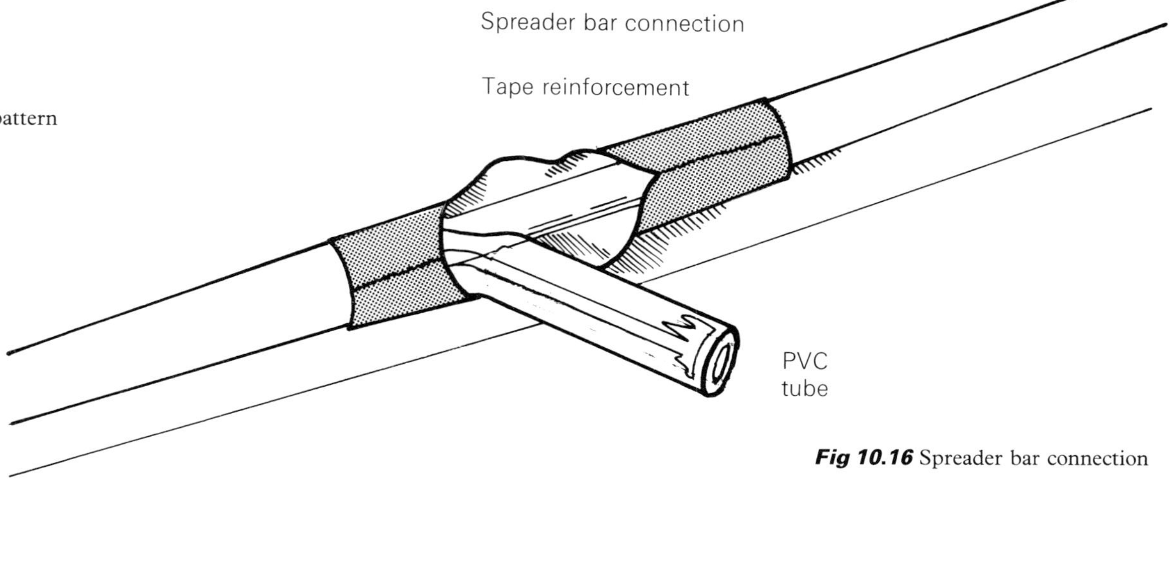

Fig 10.16 Spreader bar connection

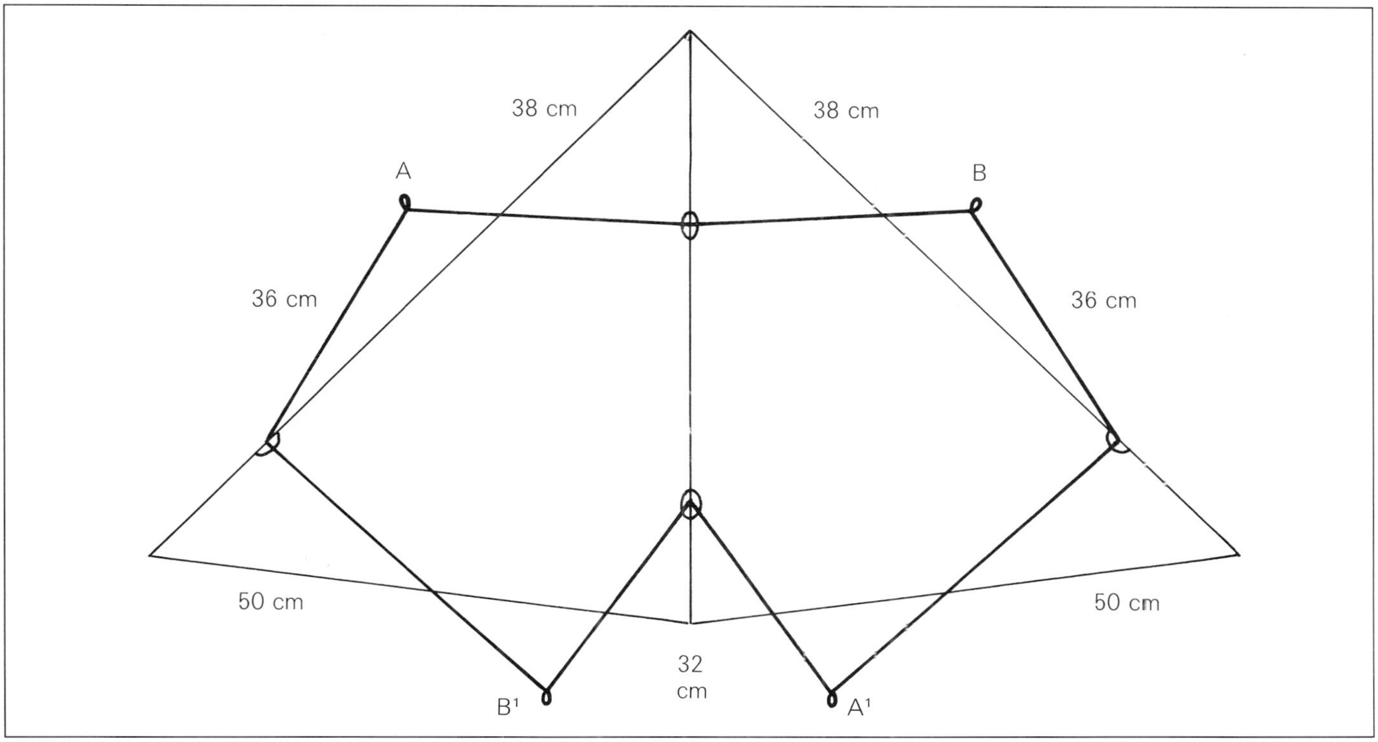

Fig 10.17 Bridles

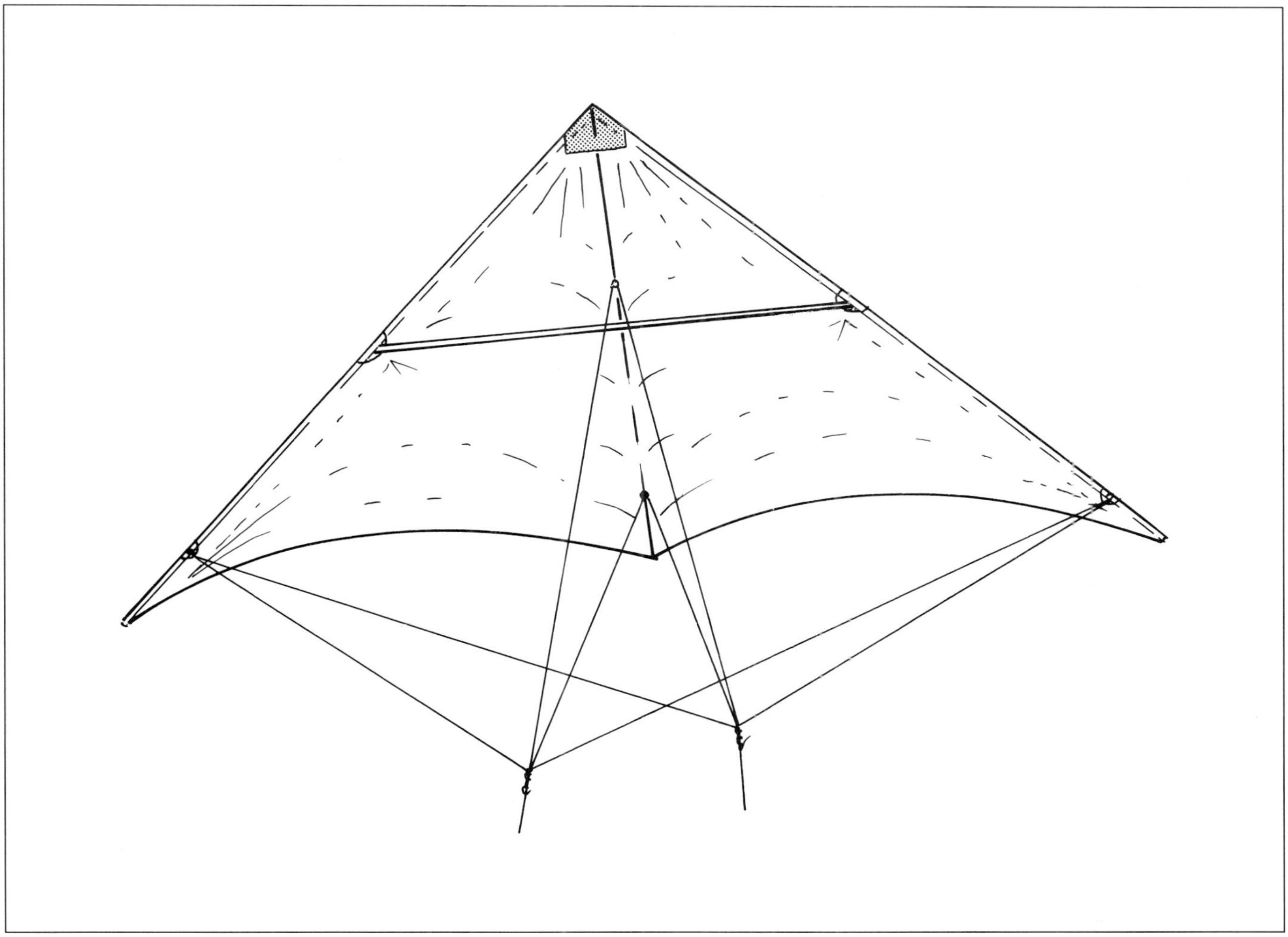

Fig 10.18 Delta Dart complete

further reading

This is a fairly comprehensive list of books on kites and other flyable objects made from paper. Most, unfortunately, are out of print, but may be obtained through the public library service.

Highly recommended books are marked *

Badahur, D., *Kite building and kiteflying handbook*, TAB, 1984
Barwell, E., *Making kites*, Studio Vista, 1976
Bridgewater, A., *Easy to make decorative kites*, Constable, 1985
*Botermans, J. & Weve, A., *Kite flight*, David & Charles, 1986
Botermans, Jack & Weve, A., *Kite flight: 40 models ready for takeoff*, Henry Holt & Co., 1986
Burkhardt, T., *Kitefolio*, Wildwood House, 1974
Carpentier, D., *Kites*, E.P. Publishing, 1981
Deiches, I.W., *The greatest puzzle: aeronautics 2500 – 1350* BC, Time Energy Information, 1983
Dunford, D., *Kite Cookery*, 1978 (Available from kite shops only)
Dyson, J., *Fun with kites: how to make 18 beautiful kites*, Dyson, John & Dyson, Kate, *Fun with Kites*, Salem House Publishers, 1987
Angus & Robertson, 1976 (Republished 1987)
Flood, J., *Kitemaking and flying*, EARO, 1980
Folon, J., *Kites*, Barrons Educational Services, 1981
Gallot, P., *Making and flying fighter kites*, B.T. Batsford, 1989
*Greger, M., *Kites for everyone*, 1983 (Available only as an import from specialist kite shops)
Gribble, D. & McPhee, H., *Kites*, Kestrel, 1977
*Hart, C., *Kites: an historical survey*, Faber, 1967
Hart, C., *Your book of kites*, Faber, 1964
*Hiroi, T., *Kites: sculpting the sky*, Elm Tree Books, 1978
*Hunt, L., *Twenty-five kites that fly*, Dover, 1971
*Ito, T., *Kites; the science and wonder*, International Book Distributers, 1983
Johnson, Michael, *Fantastic paper gliders*, St. Martin's Press, 1987
Johnson, Michael & Austin, Alan, *Classic paper planes*, St. Martin's Press, 1989
Jordan, John W., *Make your own kite*, Houston, TX: D. Armstrong, 1981
*Jue, D., *Chinese kites and how to make them*, C.E. Tuttle, 1967
Kettlekamp, L., *Kites*, Wheaton, 1961
Kine, J., *Making and flying kites*, Model and Allied Publications, 1978
*Lloyd, A., *Kites and kite flying*, Hamlyn, 1978
*Lloyd, A., *Making and flying kites*, Beaver Books, 1977
McPhun, M., *Kites*, MacDonald Educational, 1979
Mitton, B.H., *Kites, kites, kites, the ups and downs of making and flying them*, Oak Tree Press, 1980
Moran, T., *Kite flying is for me*, Lerner Publications Co., 1984
*Moulton, R., *Kites*, Pelham, 1978
Mouvier, J.P., *Kites*, Collins, 1974
Newham, J., *Kites to make and Fly*, Kestrel, 1976
Newman, L.S., *Kitecraft: the history and processes of kitemaking throughout the world*, Allen & Unwin, 1974
*Pelham, D., *Penguin book of kites*, Penguin, 1977
*Pelham D., *Kites to make and fly*, Pan, 1981
Ridgeway, H., *Kite making and flying*, Mayflower, 1969 (First published by ARCO 1962)
*Rowlands, J., *Making and flying modern kites*, Dryad Press, 1988 (published in USA as *The big book of kites*, St. Martin's Press, 1988)
Rutland, J., *Kites and gliders*, F. Watts, 1977
*Schimmelpfennig, W., *Making and flying kites*, Hamlyn, 1988
Schmitz, Dorothy C., *Kite flying*, Crestwood House, 1978
Streeter, T., *The art of the Japanese kite*, J. Weatherhill, 1974
Theibault, A., *Kites and other wind machines*, Blandford, 1982
Weiss, Stephen, *Wings and Things*, St. Martin's Press, 1984
White, B., *Kites*, Scimitar, 1977
Wiley, J. *The kite building and flying handbook*, Foulsham, 1984 (2nd edition 1988)
Wiley, Jack & Cheatle, Suzanne L., *Dynamite kites: thirty plans to build and fly* (2nd edition), TAB Books, 1988
Wood, C., *Making simple kites*, Studio Vista, 1977
*Yolen, W. *The young sportsman's guide to kite flying*, Nelson, 1963

Index